Hole 1 — Par 4
Yards 418 — Bohereen Road

Hole 2 — Par 4
Yards 413 — The Tunnel

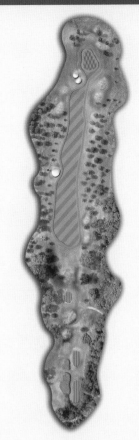

Hole 3 — Par 3
Yards 170 — The Island Beach

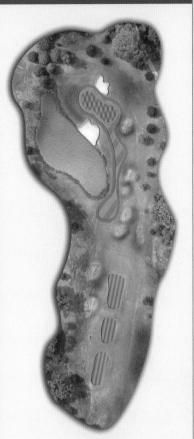

Though this looks to be a simple challenge, the most productive line is down the right side of the fairway, which means taking on the trees. This also happens to be the faster side of the fairway, while it takes a dangerous bunker out of play. Anything favouring the right, will deliver the reward of an open shot to the green whereas going down the left will leave a second shot blocked by the mound protecting the left, front of the target, so posing a visual problem for the player.

But all is not plain-sailing down the right. On Woosie's advice, three additional, large trees have been put in on the corner and through their familiarity with the angles and the wind, I would expect the European players to be better equipped to handle this new challenge. With the banks of the greens shaved, anything coming in there at speed is likely to filter off, possibly into a bunker.

A long par four which climbs gently uphill along a secluded valley and where subtlety of design makes it a lot more difficult than it looks. Problems are presented by a bunker on the left and trees up the right. Anything heading up the left is almost certain to have an unpleasant outcome, either by finding the bunker or heavy rough. So it is advisable to follow the tree-line up the right and allow the natural contour of the ground to kick the ball left.

There's a big, new bunker to the front-left of the green so as to give it more depth and another pin position, and anything hit to the left half of the green will move further left into varying degrees of trouble. The uphill nature of the second shot heightens the elusiveness of a green which is narrow, especially towards the rear and where club selection can be confused by a hidden dip before the putting surface.

This wide but shallow, angled green, is a lot like the 12th at Augusta National in the difficulty it presents for club selection. Seriously susceptible to crosswinds, its shaved banks will mean that anything coming up short will finish either in the water or in sand. There will be no escape. The challenge is to land the tee-shot on the correct side of the ridge in the middle of the green.

Though it's a relatively short par-three, picking the correct club can be a problem, especially when attempting to access the more favoured pin position on the left. Too little and the water beckons; too much and you face a tricky recovery from sand. The safe line is unquestionably to the right, but with the pin left, this is unlikely to be an option in matchplay.

Note: The order and routing of the course for the Ryder Cup is different to that enjoyed by members and visitors to The K Club. This hole-by-hole guide is based on how the course will be played during the Ryder Cup.

Hole 4 — Par 5
Yards 568 — Arnold's Pick

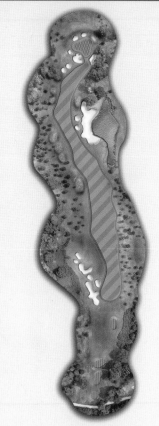

Hole 5 — Par 4
Yards 440 — Square Meadow

Hole 6 — Par 4
Yards 478 — The Liffey Stream

I can well understand why Arnold Palmer chose this hole as his favourite. In my view, it's the most spectacular-looking hole on the course and Woosie has had some fun with it. With the natural fall of the land from left to right, he has tightened up the fairway on the right so as to encourage a drawn shot off the tee. By taking players down the left-hand side over a nest of bunkers, they have the option of going around the trees guarding the green, or going over them.

Most players will have the length to get home here in two. The key question will be whether players are in the correct position off the tee to access the green properly. From the right-hand side, the trees are deeper and higher than a lot of people imagine. I expect the left-hand bunkers to find plenty of action, because of the way this particular area opens up the target.

Sweeping uphill and severely testing into the wind, the ideal line here is the right-half of the fairway from where the ball will feed left, as on the second. Another advantage of being on the right is that it will provide a better view of the green, which is difficult to locate. With a mound to negotiate, the main difficulty is in being aware of the precise boundaries of the putting surface which the player cannot see in its entirety. As it happens, it is far more generous on the left than it appears to be.

Conversely, there is far less room on the right-hand side of the green than the player imagines. Everything going right will feed into a swale. This is where local knowledge is going to help the Europeans and, significantly, Woosie hasn't considered it necessary to make any significant changes.

With the terrain falling away dramatically from the tee, the more productive line here is down the left, and by way of emphasising this, we have put in a few additional trees on the right. Anyone who pushes his drive while gambling on this side as a fast route, will have to hit a low shot beneath overhanging branches and over water, to reach the green. Even down the left, the player is likely to face a hanging or at best, uneven lie, which will promote a lower approach shot with more top-spin. There is the additional awareness of swirling winds in this area of the course.

A hanging lie with the pin at the back of the green will pose no problem, though there is a "Valley of Sin" on the right-hand side. So, anything up the left side is easier. As a general observation, this hole is a lot less difficult for elite players than for club golfers, largely because of the shortness of the approach shots.

Hole 7   Par 4
Yards 395   Michael's Favourite

I must plead guilty to having had an input into re-shaping this hole. In mitigation, however, I should point out that trees up the left-hand side, which were once a major factor in the tee-shot here, were lost in a storm. The result was that it became possible to hit one-iron and wedge to what used to be a formidable hole. By bringing the tee back 30 yards, it remains a very manageable par four, but the new tee brings trees on the left into play while forcing the player to aim for the water on the right.

As a consequence, the drive must be shaped right to left. And if you happen to choose a one iron, you'll now be hitting a four or five iron second shot, whereas a driver will leave a seven or eight-iron approach. Come off the drive and you're in the water on the right; protect yourself too much and you're in the trees on the left.

Hole 8   Par 3
Yards 173   Mayfly Corner

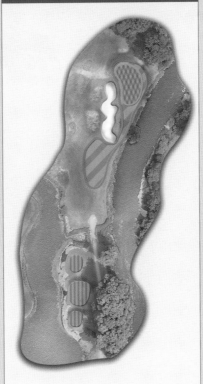

This is a pretty straightforward hole with the Liffey on the right and an absolutely stunning backdrop of mature trees behind the green. A large bunker runs diagonally across the entrance to the green, but players will still favour the left side because of the manner in which the putting surface feeds towards the water. There's a knuckle up in the top left-hand corner where a pin is going to be positioned and the hole plays longer than it looks.

Over the back left, a swale has been cut down on Woosie's instructions so that anything going long will finish up even further from the target. The hole could become really exciting if the wind gets up and the pin is on the top right-hand corner, inviting players to take on the Liffey. But typically, I would expect competitors to play it safe and leave themselves a 10 or 15-foot putt for birdie.

Hole 9   Par 4
Yards 461   Eye Of The Needle

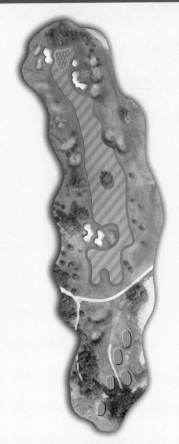

This has become a decidedly tricky prospect off the back tee, justifying its name as the Eye of the Needle. But by way of compensation, it is intended to raise the limbs of the main tree towards the middle of the fairway. Only the biggest hitters could fly the tree and even then, it will depend on the wind. Otherwise, you're going to have to go right or left. For the Ryder Cup, however, raised limbs will permit players the scope to hit more of a full approach – though the ball will still have to be kept low.

At 285 yards from the tee, this charming chestnut is critical to the play of the hole. Expect up to 60 per cent of competitors to hit it. Ultimately, they will have to negotiate a tricky green where the right side is protected pretty well by bunkers while anything going low and hard onto the front, will find sand on the left.

The view back down the fairway from the 6th green. The hole can feature swirling winds but is regarded as one of the more benign holes for elite golfers.

The Palmer Course Hole By Hole

With John McHenry

Director of Golf and Head Professional at The K Club

Right: The magnificent sweep down to the 4th green. This par 5 is Arnold Palmer's favourite hole.

Far right: The 8th green with the hotel in the distance and the River Liffey to the right.

Below: A view down the 7th fairway with the green to the right. The tee has been placed a further 30 yards back forcing players to use driver or face the prospect of a long second over the water.

The K Club

I

◆

Above: Side view of the 11th, Liffey Pond.

Far left: The par 3 12th has seen the green enlarged to the left thus bringing the water hazard more into play. There is a small spine on the green which moves balls hit left of the flag towards the hazard.

Left: A view from behind the 17th looking back down the fairway with the River Liffey on the right – a likely make or break hole as matches reach their climax.

Hole 10 — Par 5
Yards 584 — Mick Holly

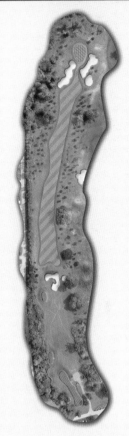

Hole 11 — Par 4
Yards 415 — Liffey Pond

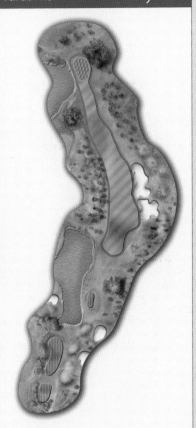

Hole 12 — Par 3
Yards 173 — The Domain

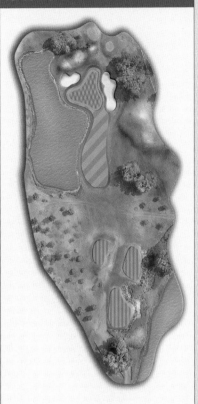

On one of his private visits, Tiger Woods reached the green here with a drive and four iron. But the ball has to be flown all the way into the green and the fairway is going to be narrowed at between 90 and 120 yards of the target. Any player finding rough off the tee will have the option of laying up or flying over that bottleneck. It's very much a big-hitter's hole where the tee has the backdrop of tall pines in which crows tend to congregate.

The bunkers directly in front of the tee are more cosmetic than strategic, but I like to aim my drive off the left-hand side of the middle one. By aiming down the left, you have to be conscious of the out of bounds, but a well-placed drive into that area opens up the entire left-hand side of the green where, incidentally, we've deepened the bunker which will give greater definition to the entrance to the putting surface.

Water threatens here, both off the drive and the approach and with a view to tightening the tee-shot even more, we've put in some new trees down the left-hand side, on Woosie's advice. The objective is that if big hitters such as Woods decide to cut the dog-leg with the driver, they will face a daunting carry. If they happen to pull it left, they'll be in trees and if they push it slightly, they'll be blocked out by trees further down the right-hand side.

So, what we're really encouraging people to do is to chase a three-wood up the fairway, leaving a slightly longer shot to the green. The difficulty with the green here is that the left side will be shaved going down to the water. So any approach shot, which is not controlled, especially from the rough, will almost certainly be destined for a watery grave.

There's been a big change to this hole, where we've brought the water into the green, while creating a little spine up the middle whereby anything bouncing to the left of it will move further left towards the hazard. And we've brought in a number of new pin positions. I expect this to be an especially inter-esting hole for the fact that matches could be reaching a pivotal point by the time they arrive here.

In the most basic terms, a good shot will win the hole and a bad shot will lose it — which could be the difference between going from one to two up or two to three ahead. The Europeans are going to have a huge advantage here because even though the green has changed, the distance has remained the same. Either way, I think they control the ball a lot better than the Americans.

Hole 13 — Par 4
Yards 423 — Laurel Heaven

There are no additional trees here, but we've brought the teeing area back about 30 yards. This means that the trees on the left can still be carried, but it will be an all or nothing shot. The more prudent drive would be with a three-wood down the right-hand side, drawing it around the trees. Take the driver here and you're bringing water on the far side of the fairway into play. We've put in a new bunker on the front left of this green, to enhance definition and for an additional pin placement.

This green is quite raised and again, the edges will be shaved so that anything falling off the right is going to go into the water. Though the player may have no more than an eight or nine iron in his hand for the second shot, I think it's a particularly difficult hole, especially in a swirling wind and with the pin in the front, right-hand corner. Anything big is going to bounce out the back end.

Hole 14 — Par 3
Yards 213 — Churchfields

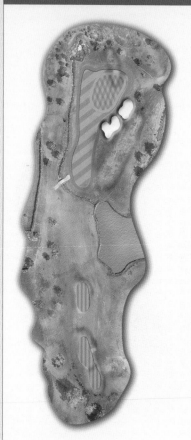

This is a good hole which has been greatly enhanced by the water feature on the left. The principal slope on a fairly generous green is from front to back on the right side, beyond the bunker, which represents the main carry. But ideally, the shot should be taken down the left side of the green because everything will filter right.

However, anything tugged too far left, for a left-side pin position, will move further left towards the water. Woosie considered it to be a very strong par three, yet if the pin happened to be on the right, I would consider it a birdie opportunity. It suits my shape and all I do is hang it over the bunker on the left and let the green feed it into the middle. Darren Clarke had a hole in one here during the European Open.

Hole 15 — Par 4
Yards 446 — Pheasant Run

The most rewarding tee-shot here involves taking on the water down the right, from where you will get a good view of the target. But the hole normally plays into the breeze and I tend to favour a fade shot off the trees on the left. Either way, you have to commit to the shot and by this stage, players could be becoming a little jumpy. I can see players sacrificing length here so as to ensure keeping the ball in play.

They will then be faced with a very deceptive approach shot where it's not possible to see the bottom of the flag or even the green itself. This has to do in part with a ridge to the front which, if not carried, can throw an apparently well-hit shot, left or right. You must trust your yardage and after hitting probably half a club more than the eye would indicate, there is a decidedly tricky green with a severe diagonal movement, right to left and from front to back.

Hole 16   Par 5
Yards 606   Inismor

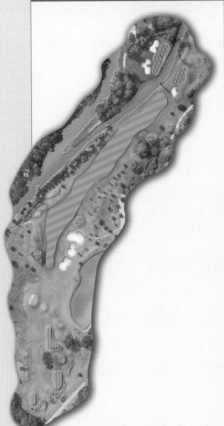

Hole 17   Par 4
Yards 424   Half Moon

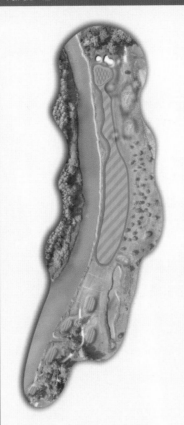

Hole 18   Par 5
Yards 537   Hookers Graveyard

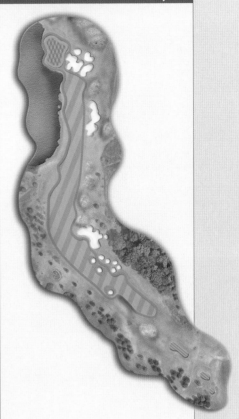

For me, one of the outstanding holes on the course. It demands a big tee shot and Woosie has put in some additional trees down the right, so as to force players further left. I would expect the middle tee to be in use here, which will make it very definitely a two-shotter. But it will take two, well-struck shots to reach the target.

With the prevailing wind, you're going to be taking it down over the right half of the largest trap. Then the big hitters may be using as little as a four iron for their second shot.

The green is 46 yards deep, and a very receptive target for a long iron. The right half has been raised so that balls don't fall into the Liffey and the left has been opened up with the addition of some new bunkers. The safe play is to fade the approach shot off those bunkers. It's a great par five, a great matchplay hole and a great start to the climactic stage of a match.

The 17th gets its name from the shape of the fairway, which follows a gentle bend in the river. In a fourball, if a player takes out the driver and launches one over the water to within 40 or 50 yards of this green, he has psychologically forced the opposition's hand. It's an 80 per cent chance the good player will make birdie from this position.

Under pressure, even a player of Tiger Woods' experience will be aware of the danger of pulling it into water or blocking the ball into trees on the right. So the fourball player who plants one straight up the fairway, has put down a huge marker. The green has a serious fall towards the Liffey where the bank will be shaved, which means that anything from the rough pitching low and hard into the front of the putting surface, will most likely finish in the water.

Appropriately, this is a gambling hole, which is likely to have a huge bearing on the destination of the trophy. Additional bunkers have been put in on the right to stop players driving over the corner. It means that where a hit of 290 would have carried the sand, it's now going to take a huge effort of 320 yards.

The change of angles is going to force players to hit more left, where they will reap the reward of having the green opened up. The only time this hole will be difficult is if the wind is howling left to right, which would mean aiming more left than you'd want to, ideally. In my view, a good drive is almost mission accomplished in terms of making a birdie. I don't think fours will win here: it will more than likely take an eagle, which we've seen in European Opens over the years.

Dr Michael Smurfit at The K Club, July 2005: "I've been taking stick all my life. Every major deal I did was supposed to put me under, but it was water off a duck's back. I had a dream and a vision here, which I've seen to fruition. Now it is for other people to judge."

Top left: Michael Davern who took over from Ray Carroll **(above)** as Chief Executive of The K Club in September 2005.

Clockwise: Scenes from the interior and exterior of the hotel which will house the respective Ryder Cup teams in 2006 including **(top right)** detail from *Leda y el Cisne* by Victor Villarcal de la Vega.

Below left: Former Executive Director of the PGA European Tour, Ken Schofield who showed himself to be a formidable negotiator.

Below right: Padraig Ó hUiginn, the mandarin who represented the Government's interests at all stages of the Ryder Cup process.

Top left: John McHenry, recently appointed Director of Golf and Head Professional at The K Club.

Clockwise: Scenes from around the course and the clubhouse including (main photograph) a view of the 18th green taken from the clubhouse. **Inset:** One of four stamps issued by An Post to commemorate Ireland's staging of the Ryder Cup.

Bottom right: Paul Crowe, former Director of Golf.

LADY CAPTAIN'S PRIZE

1996	MRS. M. O'CALLAGHAN
1997	MS. P.H.R. KEMP
1998	MRS. M. O'CALLAGHAN
1999	MS. P.H.R. KEMP
2000	MRS. K. O'CONNOR
2001	MRS. J. MURRAY
2002	MRS. A. FREYNE
2003	MRS. S.A. O'CONNOR
2004	MRS. G. BLAKE
2005	MRS. P. FURLONG

10th TEE

1st TEE

Éire 65c

THE K CLUB

"My wife Glen and I are absolutely delighted. The Ryder Cup has been a big part of our lives and it is a huge honour to be named captain of the European Team. It makes me feel very proud, especially as Wales has such a great tradition of producing Ryder Cup captains."
Ian Wosnam
European Captain 2006 Ryder Cup

"Sometimes you can never dream big enough and this is an honour beyond my wildest dreams. I consider the Ryder Cup to be the ultimate golfing experience, even greater than winning the Open."
Tom Lehman
USA Captain Ryder Cup 2006

Ian Woosnam (left) and Tom Lehman with the Ryder Cup at The K Club, June 2005.

RYDER CUP 2006

How Ireland landed golf's biggest showpiece

By Dermot Gilleece

Red Rock Press

RYDER CUP 2006

How Ireland landed golf's biggest showpiece

BY DERMOT GILLEECE

Red Rock Press
www.redrockpress.ie

Glengyle
Claremont Road
Howth
Dublin 13
Ireland

redrockpress@eircom.net

This edition published 2005

The author would like to thank *The Irish Times* and the various golf writing colleagues who generously helped in this project.

The moral right of the author has been asserted.

A catalogue record for this book is available from the British Library.

ISBN 0-9548653-2-4

Papers used by Red Rock Press are natural, recyclable products made from wood grown in sustainable forests; the manufacturing processes conform to the environmental regulations of the country of origin.

PRODUCTION
DESIGN AND PRODUCTION
Stephen Ryan
COPY EDITOR
Sean Ryan
PHOTOGRAPHIC COLOUR MANAGEMENT
Norman McCloskey for INPHO
INDEX
Mark Gilleece
PRINTING
Colour Books LTD, Ireland.
PHOTOGRAPHY
COVER
All photographs INPHO/Getty Images except: Dr Michael Smurfit, INPHO/Morgan Treacy. The K Club, Alan O'Connor.
SECTION I
Hole graphics by thegolfbusiness.com. All photographs Alan O'Connor except: 16th and 18th holes by Norman McCloskey/INPHO.
Dr Smurfit by Morgan Treacy/INPHO. Ray Carroll, courtesy The K Club. Ken Schofield, INPHO/Getty Images.
Padraig Ó hUiginn, The Irish Times. Paul Crowe, INPHO/Andrew Paton. Ian Woosnam and Tom Lehman, David Maher/Sportsfile.
SECTION II
All photographs INPHO/Getty Images
SECTION III
All photographs INPHO/Getty Images
SECTION IV
All photographs INPHO/Getty Images except Norman Drew courtesy UK PGA. Jimmy Martin courtesy Greystones G.C.
Paul McGinley celebration on the 18th green, Phil Sheldon.
SECTION V
All photographs INPHO/Getty Images

RYDER CUP 2006

How Ireland landed golf's biggest showpiece

THE CHAPTERS

THE PHOTOGRAPHIC SECTIONS

Foreword
By Arnold Palmer

I t doesn't matter how many Open Championships or titles you may have won, when you stand on the tee for a Ryder Cup match and play for your country, your stomach rumbles like a kid turning up for his first tournament. And there is simply no experience in golf quite like being part of your first Ryder Cup opening ceremony, unless perhaps it's the closing ceremony after your side has won.

The way things worked out for me, it wasn't in the Ryder Cup that I first represented my country. It was in the old Canada Cup, which later became the World Cup. And it brought me to Ireland for the first time, in 1960.

Only a few days after winning the US Open at Cherry Hills in June of that year, I was in Dublin where I was to experience links conditions for the first time at Portmarnock, with Sam Snead as my partner. So there wasn't much opportunity of celebrating what was my second major win of that year, following on a Masters success at Augusta National.

I learned I was a replacement in the American team for Ben Hogan, who declared himself unavailable. And I enjoyed the experience enormously. To the best of my recollection, Sam and I handled it fairly well *(they swept to an eight-shot win over second-placed England: DG)*. And I seem to remember Flory van Donck winning the individual award. And, of course, who could forget the local pro, Harry Bradshaw. A wonderful character and a fine golfer.

It's hard to believe we're talking about something that happened 45 years ago, but when you love the game as much as I do, these things become treasured memories. I happen to love golf and I happen to love people, which has proved to be a very rewarding combination. I believe it explains why I have had so much good fortune in my life. Because I talk to people. I find if you're nice to people, it always comes back to you, one way or another. Playing the Canada Cup in Dublin was especially important to me because I was devastated in 1954 when, after winning the US Amateur, I wasn't in a position to play in the British Amateur or the Walker Cup team. The simple fact was that I couldn't afford it. I had no money. I had gone to Wake Forest on a full scholarship – my books, tuition and room and board. And there wasn't money for any frills. So, instead of extending my amateur career, I turned professional towards the end of 1954 and joined the tour the following year.

Given where I came from, it seemed the logical path to follow. My father, Deke, was a professional golfer and a very tough task master. He was a fighter but also a guy who could be very sentimental. He liked people and he didn't like it when others did things that weren't nice. And he drove that home to me constantly.

Prior to the selection of the 1959 Ryder Cup team for the matches at Eldorado Country Club in Palm Springs, I had won the 1958 Masters and nine other tournaments since 1955. Had I not been serving an "apprenticeship" imposed by the PGA, I would easily have collected sufficient Ryder Cup points to make the team at a venue where my wife Winnie and I had a host of friends. I must admit that the injustice stuck in my craw for years.

Just think of it, if such a restrictive clause existed today, players of such world-class as Tiger Woods and Justin Leonard, wouldn't have made the Ryder Cup squad which went to Valderrama in 1997.

But I must admit that the hard feelings I privately nursed about the 1959 matches, vanished two years later when Winnie and I walked onto the quiet, hushed grounds of Royal Lytham and St Annes, along with other members of the American squad and their wives. What I remember most was standing with my team-mates near the first tee and feeling a lump rise in my throat and tears fill my eyes as the brass band played the "Star-Spangled Banner", followed by "God Save the Queen." To make it even more special, I had won my first British Open title only three months previously, down the road at Royal Birkdale.

Another great memory from 1961 was my first Ryder Cup singles against Peter Alliss, an elegant man and an accomplished player. Like most British players, he shaped his shots for control purposes. His preferred ball-flight was a controlled fade and he played the game with great precision and accuracy. And it says much for the man's tenacity that I had to work my tail off, simply to achieve a halved match.

By 1963, Ryder Cup participation had come to mean an awful lot to me, so it was a great thrill to achieve the milestone at East Lake, Atlanta, of becoming the last playing captain in the matches, from either side of the Atlantic. On this occasion, Peter Alliss beat me in the first series of singles, and I have to say that for a man whose Rolls-Royce bears the licence plate "3 PUTT", he sank more than his share of putts.

After a great run over the next five stagings, I had hoped to play my way into the 1975 matches at Laurel Valley, but it wasn't meant to be. But they made me captain, which

Arnold Palmer during his first Ryder Cup appearance at Royal Lytham and St Annes, 1961. It was to be the first of six consecutive appearances. He was playing captain in 1963 and captain in 1975.

Foreword

everyone knew was a deeply symbolic and sentimental choice. My record as a player in the event spoke for itself in that regard.

By that stage, no American had a better win/loss record in Ryder Cup competition than I had, but it was obvious that my better days on tour were behind me, as my mediocre tournament record from that year indicates. The only high-point was winning the British PGA Championship at Royal St George's.

I was deeply honoured to be selected captain. And what a team I had that year! It was golf's equivalent of the Dream Team and despite what they say about the 1981 line-up at Walton Heath, I believe the squad of 1975 was probably the best ever. Nicklaus...... Littler....Trevino....Miller.....Weiskopf....Floyd....Casper....Irwin....Geiberger....Dave Hill....J.C. Snead....Lou Graham....Bob Murphy. I challenge you to name better than that.

An unexpected blessing was the close friendships I made among the game's golf writers. On your side of the Atlantic, I had a special regard for Pat Ward-Thomas of *The Guardian*. We and our wives played quite a bit of bridge together and given his experience as a wartime pilot with the Royal Air Force, I was happy to allow him fly one of my planes.

Against that background, you can imagine how thrilled I am that the 2006 matches are being played at The K Club. And on a course carrying my name! My visits there in recent years have convinced me that it is going to be in fantastic shape for the big occasion. My design colleagues, Ed Seay and Harrison Minchew, have done great work there and the general updating will make it a great challenge.

I especially like the routing change which I understand has proved to be an outstanding success in the Smurfit European Open. Apart from the excitement the closing holes will generate, I feel it has ensured that the course will be very competitive for matchplay and I'm certain the players from both teams are going to love it.

It is very pleasing to me that my company's relationship with Dr Michael Smurfit has stood the test of time, despite the problems that arose in the early years of what was then the North Course. Michael talked about adversity bringing us closer together, which is probably true. But the really important thing is that we've got the job done. We're going to have a golf course worthy of a great occasion. I think it's marvellous in any sport that you can perform well enough to be asked to represent your country. That was among the things I told Tiger Woods when he came to me seeking advice before he turned professional back in 1996. I told him that because he was Tiger Woods, he was never going to be like anyone else. He would always be special. And because of having received so much, he had the responsibility to be nice to people and to treat them as he would like to be treated. And how he should act as a professional and control his emotions.

As far as I can tell, he's heeded that advice. In fact at this point in time I think Tiger has done a fantastic job. And it gives me a real kick to think of him playing in the Ryder Cup on the Palmer Course.

For me, the tournament was always about something far grander and more personal than income and money lists. It was about playing for your country, your people and therefore yourself, and it was pure joy to try and beat the best of Britain and Ireland in an honourable game. And I'm sure that facing a European team hasn't changed that feeling for the American players.

On a personal level, I'm proud of what the Ryder Cup did for me, and for what I contributed to my teams in six competitions. I won 22 matches against eight losses, with two ties and a total of 23 points. Nick Faldo passed my record at Valderrama, which is as it should be. Records are not meant to stand forever.

The game brings out the best in us and the best will always bring out their games in the Ryder Cup. Now, The K Club is about to add a treasured postscript to what has been a wonderful adventure.

Arnold Palmer

Arnold Palmer, October 2005.

Prologue

On the morning of Monday, September 25th 1989, Irish golfing nerves still tingled with the excitement of the previous afternoon, when a tie was sufficient to keep the Ryder Cup in Europe. Ronan Rafferty had distinguished himself with a singles win over reigning Open champion Mark Calcavecchia, and Christy O'Connor Jnr had claimed a place in golfing history through the majesty of a 229-yard two-iron approach to the 18th, which forced Fred Couples to concede hole and match.

Now, a bright future beckoned and British PGA officials turned their thoughts to the next European staging in 1993 and the most suitable host venue. In this context, their executive director, John Lindsey, was remarkably candid in admitting that "as it stands, the flatness of The Belfry course offers only limited viewing for spectators." It was an open acknowledgement of the fact that despite the undoubted thrills of the previous three days, many of the 28,000 all-ticket attendance had to rely on gallery-reaction around the greens, so as to assess the state of a match.

Departing skipper Tony Jacklin, whose leadership had transformed the biennial event from an American procession into a transatlantic battle of equals, made the point that, further down the line, Continental European venues should be considered. "I would like to think that when we decided in 1979 that we were going European, we meant it in all that that entails," he said.

In the meantime, however, there was little indication that such a radical move was being seriously contemplated for 1993. The likelihood was that the event would remain in Britain or Ireland, as it had done since the first "home" staging at Moortown, Leeds, in 1929.

Listing the venues by country, Lindsey read out Royal Troon, Turnberry and Carnoustie from Scotland; Royal Birkdale, Wentworth, St Mellion and The Belfry from England and Portmarnock, Ballybunion and the so-called County Kildare Club in Ireland. Then, in keeping with the spirit of Jacklin's remarks, we were informed that there would be an 11th application from Spain, probably involving Las Brisas or Valderrama.

When the names of the various venues had been digested, it suddenly dawned on us that the County Kildare Club hadn't even been built yet. We remembered that the 330-acre estate at Straffan, with its 19th century house, had been acquired by the Smurfit organisation only the previous October. Gradually it began to sink in that, in classic entrepreneurial tradition, Michael Smurfit was putting down a marker.

Perhaps a 1993 staging might be a trifle ambitious.

But who could tell what the future might hold?

Chapter 1

The Dream

Chapter 1 The Dream

hile finishing touches were being applied to contours at the embryonic K Club in the early months of 1990, a clever advertisement for a pocket tape-recorder, reportedly popular with politicians, was getting frequent exposure on American television. It involved Arnold Palmer making a characteristically slashing swing at a golf-ball against a backdrop of federal buildings in Washington DC. Watching the ball soar into the air above the US capital, Palmer exclaimed with boyish enthusiasm: "Whee! I might make it to the White House." Those with an eye on the golf scene, however, were aware that the popularity of the country's beloved King was undiminished, and that annual earnings of $9 million made a move into politics most unlikely.

Early on a Friday afternoon in April of that year, a sweltering Georgia sun was beating down as Palmer neared the end of his 36th appearance in the US Masters. Though at 60, he had got used to the idea of his challenge ending on a Friday, the disappointment of a second round of 80 was clearly etched in the familiar, weather-beaten face.

Three months later, in July, he would be back at Straffan to check on the progress of a major undertaking for the Palmer Design Company, which he had entrusted to his able lieutenant, Ed Seay. Palmer had already seen the initial earthmoving on a visit the previous July, when he stopped off for what became a highly-photographed walk in the Irish country-side, before continuing on his return trip to the US from the Open at Royal Troon.

Choosing a golf-course architect was one of the first decisions that confronted Dr Michael Smurfit and his business assistant, David Adamson, when the property had been acquired. As Adamson recalled: "We invited four leading companies who would each be paid $10,000 to submit a routing. Then we would decide."

The candidates were Seve Ballesteros, who had established a design company called Trajectory; Peter Alliss and Clive Clark; Dave Thomas and John O'Leary and the controversial American, Pete Dye. As the designer of Harbour Town and the fiendishly difficult Stadium Course at Sawgrass, Dye had many admirers internationally, but he declined the invitation to get involved at Straffan because he simply didn't work outside the US. Still anxious to have an American on board, Dr Smurfit came up with the idea of approaching Palmer, who had become very active in the design business by that time. Looking at other leading names, it was felt that Gary Player would have been too controversial, because of the continuing apartheid regime in South Africa.

Ballesteros didn't visit the site but the others did. And Adamson recalls the impressive presentation which Seay made, especially with regard to the technical support the Palmer company could offer. In the end, it came down to a choice between Palmer and Thomas and though Palmer was the more expensive, this was deemed to be offset by considerable advantages in the context of global marketing. In fact, it was the sort of thinking which had persuaded Tralee Golf Club, earlier that decade, to employ Palmer for the design of their new course at Barrow.

With their sights on the 1993 Ryder Cup and an official opening targeted for July 1991, time was of the essence. As luck would have it, the weather during the summer of '89 could hardly have been better for golf-course construction, with a welcome absence of traditional Irish rain, right up to September. Tanks of water had to be brought in to spray the site so as to keep the dust down. Meanwhile, Adamson became the first Director of Golf, and would later be followed by Ken Green, before the appointment of Paul Crowe who resigned in autumn 2005 when John McHenry became both Director of Golf and Head Professional.

For his part, Palmer returned for the official opening. And among distinguished colleagues who joined him on the day were Player and Lee Trevino, along with legendary European Ryder Cup representatives such as Brian Huggett, Bernard Hunt and Neil Coles. The Irish professionals in attendance included Paul Leonard.

In September 1992, Leonard was back at The K Club as captain of the European team which included fellow Ulsterman David Jones, for the biennial PGA Cup Matches against the US. This was the first international event to be staged there and was notable for some dramatic exploits by Brett Upper, a member of the American side which retained the trophy with a 15-11 victory. While winning all his matches, Upper gained the distinction of scoring three eagles at the 529-yard, par-five 18th. So it was that the spectacular finishing hole with water all the way down the left, to the green, passed its first matchplay examination with flying colours.

When the King and I met on that Friday at Augusta National in 1990, he reflected on the story so far, on how the casting vote of PGA chairman Lord Derby had made The Belfry a compromise choice for the 1993 Ryder Cup. "I realise that some people felt we were being over-ambitious in putting it (The K Club) forward for 1993, but it was an entirely realistic application," he said.

"In fact, I made it clear to the British PGA that we could have the course in play this fall, if we so wished. I believe it is a perfect setting for a championship venue, offering a top-quality test in delightful surroundings. I would like to think that if the Ryder Cup passes it by, it would be considered for other prominent events such as the Irish Open."

Straffan had long been accustomed to distinguished visitors. No less a figure than academy award-winning actor, Sean Connery, had seen the venue in two distinct guises. He had been there in the 1970s as a guest of Kevin McClory, the then owner of Straffan House.

Chapter 1 The Dream

And 20 years later he collected a prize at the Chris de Burgh Pro-Am, in a quartet which also included Christy O'Connor Snr, otherwise known as "Himself", Gerry McGuinness and the eponymous balladeer.

We are informed that the history of the estate at Straffan dates back nearly 1,500 years to 550AD, about a century after St Patrick was spreading Christianity in this fair land. Apparently a house or church then stood where the village is currently located.

It seems that there was nothing further of note about the place until the Norman invasion in the latter half of the 12th century when Richard FitzGilbert de Clare, better known as Strongbow, gave the lands at Straffan to compatriot Maurice FitzGerald, ancestor of the Dukes of Leinster. This grant was subsequently confirmed by King John of England, who signed the Magna Carta in 1215. As things turned out, however, the FitzGeralds were destined to be owners for only a century insofar as the Manor of Straffan was sold in 1288 to Sir John Fannyn (Fanning), a local who revelled in the title Chief Lord of Straffan. It then became the property of Richard de Penkiston and remained in his family until 1490, when it was sold to John Graydon, a Dublin merchant who was also known as Grayton.

After the ill-fated uprising of 1641, Cromwell's army landed in Ireland and proceeded to cut a swathe of destruction through the land. In the process the Graydons, a Catholic family, were wrongly accused of crimes against the Cromwellian state, resulting in the confiscation of their lands at Straffan. The 700 acres were acquired by Thomas Bowles in 1653 but returned to Graydon 10 years later, after be had been declared innocent of the alleged crimes. By that stage, however, the family were too poor to maintain the estate and were forced to sell it to Richard Talbot, the Duke of Tyrconnell, in 1679.

By the 18th century, for a reported outlay of £2,200, it had become the property of Hugh Henry, a banker who did much to develop the early banking system in Dublin. Having acquired lands on both sides of the River Liffey, he then proceeded to build his great house. Later, in 1774, one of the sons of the Henry family, also named Hugh, built another fine house in the village, Lodge Park House, which was designed by Nathaniel Clements, architect of what is now Aras an Uachtarain, the official residence of the President of Ireland in Phoenix Park. Incidentally, Lodge Park still stands as the home of Robert and Sarah Guinness who run the Straffan Steam Museum in its grounds.

We are informed that John Joseph Henry, the last of the Henrys to live in the great house at Straffan, was a remarkably generous and extravagant landowner, often to his own detriment. He planned a big extension to the house which was never built and he was eventually forced to flee the country and settle at Chaton near Paris, where he died in January 1846.

And so, the house changed hands once more, in 1831. This time it became the property of Hugh Barton (1766 to 1854), who was the grandson of Thomas Barton of Buttevant, Co Cork, the founder of a wine firm in Bordeaux in 1725. Hugh Barton had, in fact, been brought up there and managed to escape the worst excesses of the French Revolution, including a planned trip to the guillotine as a member of the wealthy, merchant classes.

It was alleged that the purchase of Straffan was by way of settling the wine debts owed by the Henrys to the Bartons. Either way, Hugh Barton commenced the construction in 1832 of a new, grand house for his family. And it was this house which would ultimately form the basic structure of what is the east wing of the present-day hotel. During the construction period, the Bartons resided at nearby Barberstown Castle.

The design was based on a great chateau in Louvesciennes, to the west of Paris. Indeed the outlines of the mansard roof, chimneys and windows can still be seen in the hotel. For Hugh Barton and his wife Anne, the daughter of a naturalised French subject of Scottish origin, Straffan became a haven of peace and serenity after the upheavals of France. Later on, as a final touch to the house, Barton added the Italian style campanile, still there today and similar to the tower built on Queen Victoria's estate at Osborne in the Isle of Wight.

Other refinements added by subsequent generations of Bartons were two suspension bridges to the island in the Liffey which is now home to the seventh green (the 16th as the course will be played for the Ryder Cup). The first of these bridges was built in 1847 and the second in 1907. Meanwhile, in 1963, the garden was given a parterre, linking the house with the river. Incidentally, 100 years ago, the house consisted of four storeys and had 30 bedrooms.

One of the present generation of the Straffan Bartons is Anthony, who runs extensive vineyards in the Bordeaux region. His father, Derick Barton, set down affectionate reminiscences of a childhood in Straffan in his autobiography, "Memories of Ninety Years." He noted that the estate looked especially magnificent in the spring of 1947, with its wild garden and flowering bulbs. Two years later, they sold it for what was even then a giveaway price of £15,000 to Mr and Mrs John Ellis, who owned woollen mills in Yorkshire.

They in turn, sold it in 1960 to Stephen O'Flaherty, a legendary figure in the Irish motor industry. A native of Passage East in Co Waterford, O'Flaherty had the foresight and business sense in the early 1950s to see the enormous potential of the Volkswagen Beetle, for which he originally acquired the franchise in these islands before selling off the British concession. He also became Irish concessionaire for Mercedes, among other leading marques, and founded Motor Distributors, which remains one of the most influential companies in the Irish motor industry.

He and his wife Dorothy divided their time between Straffan, their house in Killiney, Co Dublin, and their villa in the south of Spain. Then, in the mid 1960s, they sold the property

Chapter 1 The Dream

to Irish-American McClory, who will always be associated with James Bond. Among his movie credits are *Around the World in Eighty Days* (1956, associate producer), *The Boy and the Bridge* (1959 producer), *Thunderball* (1965 producer) and *Never Say Never Again* (1983 executive producer). It was at the screening of *The Boy and The Bridge* in 1958 that McClory first met Ian Fleming, who had unsuccessfully attempted to get all seven of his James Bond novels turned into movies. The closest he had come to success was in 1954 when he sold the rights to *Casino Royale* to CBS for the princely sum of $1,000.

It was McClory who suggested to Fleming that they take Bond into an underwater world, as well as creating a super-villain character. This nemesis would be a diabolical, intelligent and seemingly invincible mastermind with formidable henchmen, whose single-handed defeat would make Bond a cinematic super-hero. Fleming and McClory began to work on a script in early 1959 and were later joined by the well-known and accomplished British screenwriter, Jack Whittingham. The script marked the introduction of SPECTRE and Ernst Stavro Blofeld in what became known as *Thunderball*.

In 1963, McClory married Bobo Sigrist, a millionaire in her own right, and in 1977, he embarked on a second marriage, this time to Elizabeth, eldest daughter of celebrated horse-trainer Vincent O'Brien. His main addition to Straffan House was the impressive, indoor swimming pool which remains a key element of the hotel's amenities. But McClory is also remembered for the famous charity party he played host to there in 1968, which went on for days. Many friends from the film world came to the house, including Connery, Shirley MacLaine and Peter Sellers, then the owner of Carton House. Another noted visitor was the Co Clare author, Edna O'Brien.

When Connery returned to Straffan in the de Burgh Golf Classic, it was as a more than useful performer off a handicap of 11. In fact, he made an admirable contribution to the fourth-placed team which, as we indicated earlier, was led by none other than Christy O'Connor Snr, "Himself" as he is widely known, a long-time friend.

Renowned as a tough competitor who played off single figures for most of his golfing career, Connery displayed the sort of enduring talent which has endeared him to cinema audiences, with five net birdies and three pars in a team score of 88 points. This included an admirable par five at the treacherous 007th!

The McClorys departed Straffan in 1978 when it became the property of the ill-fated Najar Djahanbani. This air-force lieutenant-general, who was head of the Iranian sports federation under the Shah, was executed by the Khomeini regime in 1979 for allegedly "destroying national sports institutions." After that, it was acquired by property developer Patrick Gallagher, another controversial figure who was jailed for fraud in Northern Ireland, having spent £2 million on the place when he still had the Midas touch. The next owner was British mining millionaire Alan Ferguson, who spent even greater sums of money on it. By the time Ferguson had invested about £6 million in the property, however, his interest was deflected elsewhere. Thriving Canadian investments led him to put Straffan on the market at £7m in 1988.

As it happened, it was a time when a Dundalk-born hotelier named Ray Carroll, was chasing a dream. Educated by the local Christian Brothers, Carroll went on to gain a Diploma in Hotel Management at the Cathal Brugha Street College of Catering before joining the Forte Group in the UK as a trainee hotel manager between 1974 and '78. Now committed to the life of a career-hotelier, he took up appointments as general manager of the luxurious, Forte-owned Sandy Lane Hotel in Barbados (1979-'82) and general manager of the Grosvenor House Hotel in London, followed by ownership of the Cashel Palace Hotel. And by way of leisure, he enjoyed nothing better than exercising his modest talents as a golfer, followed by a steak and a bottle of wine.

Even in his capacity as owner-manager of the Cashel Palace, however, Carroll still harboured the dream of establishing a small, quality hotel in Dublin – what he lovingly described as a boutique hotel. "Around the middle of the 1980s, there was little or no hotel development taking place in Dublin," he said. "PV Doyle had done his thing with the Berkeley Court, the Burlington and various other, smaller hotels. Now, things were at a standstill.

"Around 1987, on one of his visits to the Cashel Palace, I met Michael Smurfit for the first time. Prior to that, I was aware of him only as a prominent businessman. I remember outlining my ambitions for a boutique hotel, pointing out that I saw a need for one and that I was looking for somebody to back me. A few months later, I got a phone call asking me to come up to Dublin to meet him. 'I think there's some merit in what you're saying and I'd like to pursue it with you,' he said.

"In the meantime, I had found a little property on Pembroke Road called Halcam Court, a lovely, preserved Victorian front on it and a big apartment behind. It contained 30 apartments: perfect. It would become Dublin's first boutique hotel. Though Michael Smurfit opted out of the deal, I went ahead with a Dubliner named Derek Quinlan, a financial expert who actually set up the first Government-sponsored Business Expansion Scheme, involving a hotel.

"It was agreed I could buy Halcam Court for £500,000 if I got planning permission, but the authorities turned me down. Despite my assurances, they were apparently concerned that if I received the go-ahead, there would be nothing to stop me turning it into a disco. So the plan evaporated." He paused before adding: "It was sold, incidentally, late in 2004 for €9.3 million."

Chapter 1 The Dream

But all was not lost. About eight months after the Halcam Court disappointment, Carroll was called back to Dublin by Dr Smurfit. On this occasion, he explained that he was interested in developing a golf resort. And since Carroll's other plans had fallen through, perhaps he would be prepared to offer his expertise, looking at properties that were either on the market or likely to become available. "I looked at a total of about eight estates including Adare Manor, Carton House and Straffan House. And I finished up recommending Straffan which, as things turned out, was put on the market by the owner, Ferguson, at that time."

Michael Smurfit takes up the story: "When I was in my thirties (1970s) and I saw the way golf was being played in America and in parts of Europe, I got the idea of building a country club here. In fact, I looked at one particular site and nearly bought it, but I simply didn't have the time for what was obviously going to be a very time-consuming exercise.

"In hindsight, it was probably fortunate that things worked out that way because such a venture would have been ahead of its time and probably wouldn't have taken off back then. Golf in Ireland had always been inexpensive for club members who had, dare I say it, facilities to match. Whereas my ambition was to build something of a truly international standard.

"I bought Straffan for £3.5 million which was a very inexpensive deal for 330 acres. Four years later, I took an option on an additional 220 acres, at a cost of between £2,000 and £8,000 an acre. Then there was other land that we bought, about 50 acres. But nowadays, land's gone mad around here. There was two and a half acres I wanted to buy and it was selling at €1 million an acre. And that was taking a chance on getting planning."

After the departure of the Fergusons, Straffan House had a lone occupant from the autumn of 1988. Adamson, who had been Dr Smurfit's personal assistant since 1972, had worked in Los Angeles from 1983 to 1988. Now he was to become a resident of Co Kildare. "During the early 1980s, Michael told me about his plans for a country club," Adamson recalled. "He was a regular golfer at that time, varying in handicap from 14 to 18, but highly competitive.

"When I moved into the estate on my own, I was told the house was haunted. People would look at me a little strangely and enquire if I had had any interesting experiences there, and I regret to say that in the course of six months, I didn't. In fact if was very pleasant accommodation, having been completely renovated by the Fergusons.

"It was a lovely old estate, still with some horses, though not many. Part of the first courtyard was already converted into offices. The original deal involved Tony O'Reilly and GPA's Tony Ryan and I remember the deal Michael had was that he would underwrite 50 per cent of it and the two Tonys would have 25 per cent each. And I can recall that one of the first things we did was to produce a brochure. Michael had done a budget for the development and it was going to cost in the region of £12 million. His plan was to sell 124 shares at £100,000 each, which would leave a small surplus after the development costs."

There would be a very exclusive golf course with a clubhouse of appropriate quality adjoining part of the main house. As it was at that time, the house had 12 bedrooms but a further 15 would be developed in the courtyard – still quite modest in scale compared to what it later became. As part of Dr Smurfit's contract with the Jefferson Smurfit Group, however, they would have first option on any venture he embarked upon. In this context, the Straffan deal had a particular appeal for the Group in view of a tourist expansion scheme which had been introduced by the Government involving significant tax breaks.

As Dr Smurfit recalled it, the purchase and development of Straffan Estate became essentially a tax-driven deal. "My original idea was to buy the place for myself," he said. "But it so happened that at the time, the (Jefferson Smurfit) Group were in discussion with the Irish Government for over a year, about the inequity of the tax regime. We were the first truly multinational Irish company and when all the double-taxation agreements were drawn-up in the 1930s and 1940s, no thought was given to outward investment, only inward investment.

"Meanwhile, 90 per cent of our operations were outside of Ireland; only 10 per cent of our earnings were in this country. But we paid our dividend in this country. And when we remitted money from America to our Dutch holding company and then to Ireland, it meant we were paying tax in America, Holland and here. Of every dollar we earned, we were paying 79 cents in taxes. The upshot of it was that we didn't bring the money back.

"As a consequence, we were building a cash hoard overseas and weren't permitted to deliver the money to Irish shareholders of which we had 12,000 at the time. So the whole thing was a mish-mash. Finally, the Government agreed to introduce what became Participation Privilege, provided we created 200 jobs. And since I couldn't create 200 jobs in packaging in this country insofar as I already had 50 per cent of the market, the country club offered an ideal solution."

Carroll's initial involvement during the planning stage was as a consultant. Then he became launch manager. But the first Gulf War prompted him to sell the Cashel Palace and shortly after that, when The K Club's first golfing year had been beset by drainage problems, he accepted the full time appointment as chief executive in 1993. "The brief at The K Club was simple," he said. "It was to create a five-star resort that would compete unapologetically with the world's other five-star offerings. The timing was almost perfect for making that level of investment in quality.

"Overall, the positive advantages of the property outweighed any drawbacks. The house and estate were about the right size and close to Dublin and its international airport. Mature trees offered very attractive design options for golf-course construction, while the River Liffey had fine fishing. And when work got under way, it was clear that Dr Smurfit wanted only one standard – the best." Though their relationship was often difficult, Dr Smurfit always held Carroll in the highest regard.

"I suppose Ray's great talent has been in the way he relates to people," he said. "He demands and gets the highest standards from his employees, which is hugely important when you're dealing so closely with the public."

The first stage in developing the resort cost £35 million. But as Dr Smurfit explained: "We put £77 million back into the economy. So it was a totally tax-driven deal. That's how it started. And before you can develop properties, you must have a product. So, this was a property as well as a golf-club deal. If we hadn't made money out of the properties it wouldn't have been the sort of financial success which has delivered a great return for the Smurfit Group.

"When we decided to bid for the 1993 Ryder Cup, we had a model made of the complex and an audio/visual presentation, as it was envisaged at that time. The golf course was being developed and the clubhouse was being built. Work was in train. And I was thinking Ryder Cup. I was absolutely convinced that the Ryder Cup would be coming to Ireland at some stage and when that happened, I wanted to provide the venue. So I discussed it with Arnold Palmer.

"The bid for 1993 was deadly serious and, quite frankly, I was disappointed it went elsewhere. Apart from The Belfry, there were very few stadium courses at that time. But it all worked out for the best. We got lucky. Portmarnock could have got the nod, in which case the Ryder Cup wouldn't have been coming back to this country for a long time, certainly not in my lifetime."

In May 1998, eight months before knowing whether they would get the Ryder Cup, The K Club announced a £10 million development, extending its facilities to 36 holes. Explaining the thinking behind the second course, on the south side of the River Liffey, Dr Smurfit said: "We needed 36 holes to make the facility cost effective, in terms of maintenance."

Formal application was made to Kildare Co Council for planning permission and since the development had been on the cards for some time, no hitches were anticipated. The new 18, with an overall length of 7,176 yards, had been entrusted to the Palmer organisation and, according to the then Director of Golf, Paul Crowe, would "complement the existing course. The idea was that in the long term, either course could be chosen by members or visitors or for a major event." (The accuracy of that assessment was borne out by the staging of the Smurfit European Open there in 2004).

It was also emphasised, however, that the development would not affect arrangements for the Ryder Cup, if the bid were to be successful. In the event, the new course would be totally self-contained with its own clubhouse. Perhaps most interesting of all was that good faith with the Palmer organisation had clearly survived some serious teething problems with the North Course, notably with regard to drainage.

"There was many a time I questioned what I had let myself in for, especially when we had those serious drainage problems," Dr Smurfit reflected ruefully. "But my business principles have always been: problem, solution, result. Identify the problem; produce the solution and then live with the result. If you can't change it; live with it."

By this stage, Straffan House had been transformed into Ireland's only five red-star hotel, not least through the architectural skills of Brian O'Halloran and the building expertise of Mick Holly. Construction work began in 1989 and was completed two years later, in time for the official opening on July 15th, 1991, by the then Taoiseach, Charles J Haughey.

In the early part of 1989, a series of studies was made with a view to finding the correct formula for the hotel. "After we had prepared the ground, I had a 45-minute meeting with Dr Smurfit on Good Friday of that year," recalled O'Halloran. "That was when I persuaded him that the best plan would be to go for a new wing to the existing house and bring all the hotel facilities under the one roof. He agreed, and work began."

Mick Holly, a native of Tarbert, Co Kerry, worked for a number of years in the construction industry in England, before returning to this country in the mid-1970s. The Cedar Building Company, of which he was part owner, did work for the Smurfit Group, including Dr Smurfit's house at his Four Noughts racing establishment in Co Kildare.

Certain parts of Straffan House needed considerable work, notably what had been the old ballroom on the second floor, where the floor was reinforced with steel beams and heavy timbers. New cornices had to blend in with the old and highly-skilled plasterers did the work by hand. The inside and outside of the old house were made to match exactly with the new wing, this identical look being especially in evidence in a façade faced in plasterwork.

So as to achieve the same uniformity with the roof, Bangor slates which had been quarried in North Wales, were salvaged from old, 18th century warehouses which were being demolished at that time at Alexandra Quay in Dublin Port. Some 80,000 of these slates were recovered, all in perfect condition, for use in the roof of the new wing.

Another example of careful preservation was the manner in which stables in the inner courtyard were converted into apartments, with craftsmen painstakingly preserving the limestone facades. O'Halloran referred to this area as having an Anglo-Irish atmosphere, by way of contrast with the distinctly French style of the main house. At the height of the transformation, about 180 people were employed on various aspects of construction throughout the estate, under the watchful eye of Dr Smurfit. The emergence of The K Club and Mount Juliet, which had no pretensions to being anything other than American-style courses set in Irish terrain, caused quite a stir among the country's golfing cognoscenti. They welcomed these demanding layouts as adding a crucial, new dimension to the Irish scene.

Tour operators were aware that visitors, especially from the US, liked the idea of playing a so-called menu of courses, ranging from traditional links to heathland and classic parkland and now there would be the sort of country-club challenge they were likely to encounter in their own country.

Prior to that, Irish golfers were most likely to have experienced these conditions on holidays to Spain's Costa del Sol or the Algarve in Portugal. And they delighted in such Robert Trent Jones classics as Sotogrande Old, Las Brisas, Los Naranjos, Mijas and Las Aves, before its nines were reversed and it became known as Valderrama, under the ownership of Jaime Patino.

So, on recognising that The K Club was very much in keeping with this type of development, a visit there moved high on every discerning golfer's wish list. Many were to leave severely chastened by the quality of the test, and there were countless tales of woe about precious golf balls being despatched to a watery grave, especially on what soon became known as the notorious 16th.

Overall, the development was welcomed as a significant boost to Irish golf, even if there was no indication at that stage of it playing host to the Ryder Cup.

But there were others who took a rather narrow view, even before it had a chance to prove itself. Notable among these was Frank McDonald, the environmental correspondent of *The Irish Times*. In an assessment of Mount Juliet and The K Club which had their official openings at the same time, McDonald wrote of the developments: "And though their centre-pieces are stately homes of one sort or another, they are likely to be given a wide berth by those with Old Money who will see them as vulgar stomping grounds for the nouveau riche." Later in the piece, he observed: "Ireland has never before seen anything like The K Club. It is as if a piece of West Palm Beach had been planted in Co Kildare without the guaranteed sunshine." There was also a swipe at "the Smurfit brochure" which mentioned erroneously that the Magna Carta had been signed in 1066.

In the event, Dr Smurfit showed a particularly keen interest in the hotel and was often seen climbing ladders so as to get a closer look at particular details. "His personal involvement was such that he was really the senior clerk of works on the project," remarked Mick Holly, in part jest but wholly in earnest.

For his part, Dr Smurfit said: "I've enjoyed this project, seeing it come to fruition. I admit that I had doubts about the second course a few years ago, when the world economy was not nearly as healthy as it is now. I indicated that if I had the decision to make again, I might postpone it. But things have worked out fine."

Initially, it was accepted that the hotel would have been too small, had the bid for the 1993 Ryder Cup been successful. So, the first new wing was built, bringing the accommodation up to 36 rooms. The next expansion was planned in 1999 after the venue had been officially awarded the Ryder Cup, and was completed by 2001. In that development, a further 33 rooms were added.

One last piece of the jigsaw remained to be put in place. And the grand plan was finally complete in November 2004, with the official opening of a luxurious spa. Offering separate memberships to Kildare residents and to members of The K Club, it was built at a cost of €7 million and located close by the hotel in what were formerly the indoor tennis courts where some memorable functions were staged, including appearances by Shirley Bassey and Burt Bacharach and his orchestra.

The K Club now comprised a 78-bedroom hotel, two championship-standard golf courses, significant housing costing up to €2.5 million per unit and two clubhouses, the newer of which measured a formidable 50,000 square feet. "People I respect in golf disagreed with the idea of two clubhouses, but I wanted to do something different," said Dr Smurfit. "Though it was a bit of a gamble, I'm satisfied now that we made the right decision. The interior and exterior design of the new clubhouse, which is intended to service 81 properties and the international memberships, is stunning. Meanwhile, the original clubhouse will remain as it is, ensuring that the two courses have distinct identities."

He added with a quiet smile: "That will give us an overall spend of €115 million. And that's it." Apart, of course, from the house he was building for himself to the left of the first hole on the new Smurfit Course. It would be called Straffan House and replace his former residence behind the first green on the Palmer Course.

In the meantime, Carroll was left to contemplate the challenge which the resort faced of playing host to Ryder Cup players and officials from both sides of the Atlantic. "The hotel will be taken over by the Ryder Cup," he said. "Both teams and senior officials will experience the usual standard of service and cuisine and they will leave the hotel with whatever rooms are left. The plan is to assign these to our premium, VIP customers, at roughly €1,000 per night. That would involve a premium of 20 per cent on our normal rates, which we would consider perfectly reasonable. And we would sell them only to people who were staying seven nights, or something like that. We don't want turnover."

When all of these plans were taking shape, it was assumed that Carroll would still be in charge. His intention was to retire after the last Ryder Cup guest had left, but there has been an enforced reappraisal of his situation. "For family health reasons, coupled with the recent change of ownership, I decided to stand down a year ahead of schedule," he said. "In fairness to my successor and other key members of The K Club staff, I didn't want to get involved too deeply in the Ryder Cup arrangements and everything that they entail."

Up to the time of his departure, however, he carried on as normal. Which meant he could be satisfied that "our Ryder Cup guests are going to experience the special ambience of The K Club, which is quality orientated yet fairly relaxed. Both sets of officials will be providing detailed requirements for each individual player for every meal – dinners, snacks etc. There will be 24 golfers and we could have 24 different menus for every meal. We've been told this. Whatever Tiger says he wants, he'll get. Whatever Darren Clarke wants for breakfast, he'll get. In normal circumstances, a taste of Ireland is brought in every so often, which would include bacon and cabbage and Irish stew, but nothing like this has been planned so far for Ryder Cup week.

"If the Americans want basic fast food, they'll get it and I'm sure there won't be any problem about that. The scale of the catering for the week of the tournament, the third week in September, will be relatively small, with about 80 as opposed to the normal complement of 140 sleepers every night, demanding all sorts of things. Our staff/guest ratio that week will be more than three to one.

"It will be interesting how the public areas of the hotel are finally allocated to the respective teams. They'll want to be separate, which could present difficulties. The Americans and Europeans will each have a team room where they can sit and relax and watch television. Each team will also have to have their own treatment room. The space is there, but how exclusive these areas can be made, is another matter. We have been informed that the teams will want as much separateness as possible and we've been working on that with Richard Hills, the Ryder Cup director. In fact, the logistics are hugely challenging.

"Obviously the challenge for the hotel staff will be to deliver the Irish dimension. They will be representing The K Club that week and I can visualise everybody getting caught up in the emotion of the occasion, which makes the Ryder Cup so special. Though I will no longer be directly involved, I've no doubt I will get a tremendous thrill seeing the event being broadcast all over the world. It will be wonderful for the resort, for the key members of The K Club Ryder Cup team, headed by my successor, Michael Davern along with David Adamson, Gerry Byrne (course superintendent) and John McHenry."

When The K Club opened in 1991, the future chief executive had a staff of 70. Of those, 27 still remain in key positions among the 250 people employed in the complex. "Together, we grew this business, but I like to think that the human touch wasn't lost along the way," he said with undisguised pride. "From my experience, a good hotel man can smell the atmosphere in his hotel. If there's something wrong he'll sense it. If a porter is tense you can sense there's a problem somewhere and you have to be aware of that and find out what it is". Carroll's staff still speak of the shock of seeing him get behind the bar to pull pints of Guinness during a busy night. "I've been known to experience a dull day," he has said with a hearty laugh, "but not very often".

In early September 2005, provided everything went to plan, Carroll expected to be sitting on a beach surrounded by his favourite food and drink. The beach in question wouldn't be ringing to the sounds of Caribbean rhythms, nor would the victuals be the sort one might encounter in a gourmet hamper from Fortnum & Mason.

It so happens that Carroll's desired destination was Donabate, County Dublin and the bill of fare would come courtesy of a splendid, local establishment named Macaris. "The best fish and chips in the world," claimed the CEO of Ireland's first five red-star resort. "And they go down a treat when accompanied by a gin and tonic". Then he paused, perhaps wistfully, before concluding: "The only difference is that I'll be doing it a year earlier than I originally planned."

Understandably, Dr Smurfit had a very different picture of the road ahead. As he explained: "From the time Madison Dearborn acquired the Smurfit Group in 2002, they accepted the contracts and agreements that we had in place, including our employees' contracts. And they didn't want to destroy the culture of the company. So, these contracts will be honoured. When they did their due diligence on the company, they took into consideration our commitments, including that of finishing the place. We were just starting the clubhouse at that time. These were all things that were discussed before the takeover documents were signed."

There was another agreement – albeit not a legal one, but still an agreement which he trusted – that they wouldn't sell The K Club until after the Ryder Cup. This had to do with contractual agreements with Ryder Cup Ltd and the European Tour, which were extremely complex. Anybody taking them over would have to honour those obligations and there was a clause in the contract stating that in the event of a change of ownership, those bodies had the right to renegotiate certain aspects of the deal.

Against that background, it seemed likely that nothing would happen regarding a possible change of ownership, until the dust of Ryder Cup 2006 had well and truly settled. But things didn't work out that way. In fact, the big event was still more than 14 months away when dramatic developments were finalised.

Dr Smurfit explained: "As we know, the value of the Ryder Cup after Spain (1997) rose

Chapter 1 The Dream

appreciably from the figure Ireland paid. Indeed it doubled within a few years and it more than doubled again, to the extent that I have heard a figure in the region of £Stg90 million mentioned for Scotland in 2014. In other words, its valuation has gone up significantly.

"At that stage, I had no thoughts of purchasing The K Club myself because, leaving aside any egotistical considerations, I couldn't see how I could make it financially viable. And for such a deal to happen, it would have to have made economic sense to me. Granted, I wouldn't like to have seen it go outside the family but if somebody were to come make a ridiculous offer for whatever reason, who was I to try and outbid them? Those sort of thoughts began to dominate my mind when I looked at the sale of Wentworth and The Belfry. On closer examination, however, I came to the conclusion that they couldn't be compared to what we have here.

"Either way, I had no intention of simply throwing money at the project. The K Club was certainly viable from a property point of view, but not very profitable in operational terms. We got clobbered by 9/11 when the Americans simply disappeared in droves. Then came the strong dollar. The combination of these events militated against us.

"There was the problem of being without things like a Spa, which has since been rectified. And between the demands of members and their guests, there was too much pressure on a single course. That, too, was rectified by the emergence of the new, Smurfit Course."

But it was a matter far removed from golf which eventually changed his thinking. In the autumn of 2004, trading conditions in the Jefferson Smurfit Group began to deteriorate as a result of excess capacity in the European market. He acknowledged this as a well-known fact, to the extent that he described an article in the *Sunday Business Post* under the heading 'Smurfits Boxed In', as being pretty much on the money.

"It was a cyclical thing," he conceded, "and, against that background, I realised that I had no pre-emptive rights to buy the place. Even though we're a private company, there are bond-holders to be considered and certain procedures to be gone through."

That was when Gary McGann, the company's chief executive, went to Dr Smurfit and told him they were going to sell The K Club and asked if he were interested. "Gary knew he couldn't actually sell it beforehand (because of Dr Smurfit's agreement with Madison Dearborn) and I, naturally, was also aware of that. But at the same time, there was the valuation of €115 million to be considered," he said. Meanwhile, because of the deterioration in trading conditions, the Smurfit Paper Mills, where Dr Smurfit started his career 56 years ago, looked as if it would be put on the market.

"It's right opposite our head office in Clonskeagh, a lovely site of a couple of acres. And I was very keen to buy it with a view to building a museum there. Which is what I did.

"The knowledge that I would need a property developer for the Clonskeagh site, led me into negotiations with the Group about buying The K Club. There were also 80 acres across from The K Club, apart from 20 or 30 apartments in the existing development still to be built. And I needed somebody who knew the business and who could take the heat out of the deal as far as the price was concerned. From an early stage, it was clear that the price of €115 million was non-negotiable, for the simple reason that that's what had been invested in the resort.

"So I needed a partner and I approached three or four people, all of whom expressed an interest when I gave them an outline of the transaction I had in mind – half by debt; half by equity. I obviously wanted to have some participation in the profits of the property going forward and, at the end of the day, the best and most attractive offer came from Gerry Gannon (of Gannon Homes). And though it's early days yet, I'm very happy.

"Though Gerry was a long-time member of the club, whose bona fides were already well known to me, I only really met him for the first time at The K Club's New Year's Party on December 31st 2004. He had always spent a lot of time here and, of all the people I had spoken to, he was unquestionably the most K Club-oriented. That became a huge factor from my standpoint. He's one of the biggest fans we have and I'd go so far as to say that he's in love with the place as much as I am."

Despite having property of his own close by, Gannon was a frequent guest at the resort's hotel, while his wife, Margaret, appeared to be equally enthusiastic about being involved there.

As a consequence of the deal, Dr Smurfit and his partner will have no concerns about outstanding contracts which were negotiated by the Smurfit Group. And the new owners forfeited all of the resort's Ryder Cup income, which could run to a couple of million euro.

"I imagine the Ryder Cup will add a considerable amount to our room-rate and to green fees," he said. "But on a broader level, it is our opinion that Ryder Cup Limited could have received far more income from both hospitality and tickets than that which they have achieved, as hospitality has been sold out as never before."

Monday, June 1st 2005 dawned bright and sunny when Dr Smurfit's helicopter touched down in The K Club. It was the first time he had landed in what he could now describe as his home place.

"Funny thing, but it felt no different," he said. Then, looking out from the second floor of the new clubhouse, he mused: "I've been taking stick all my life. Every major deal I did was supposed to put me under, but it was water off a duck's back. I had a dream and a vision here, which I've seen to fruition. Now it is for other people to judge.

"I believe Irish people take pride in this place in what is effectively a showcase for the

Chapter 1 The Dream

world. I've experienced the joy of having people grab me by the arm and say 'Good on ye. This is what we need in Ireland.' That means a lot more to me than anything complimentary which might be written about the place."

Thinking back to the beginnings in 1988, the shadow of a smile flickered across his face, as if he were remembering a private joke. Then he murmured: "Seventeen years. It all went so quickly."

♦

Chapter 2

The Glory

Chapter 2 The Glory

merican reaction to events at Oakland Hills in a memorable staging of the 35th Ryder Cup matches, told us more about the mood of a nation than even the remarkably lop-sided scoreboard could have done. It was all there in the report by Tom Spousta of *USA Today*, who suggested on Monday, September 20th 2004 that the determination of Padraig Harrington to ease a 25-foot, downhill putt into the 18th hole for a win over Jay Haas, was "overkill, perhaps."

Of course the trophy had been retained some time before Harrington hammered home the final nail. But the fact that the Americans should have been somewhat peeved by his intent on achieving the biggest possible margin of victory, represented a significant come-down for a nation accustomed to golfing dominance.

Imagine European newspapers producing a similar reaction in 1981, when the most illustrious of all American Ryder Cup teams won by the same record margin at Walton Heath! It would have meant chastising the great Jack Nicklaus for demolishing Eamonn Darcy by 5 and 3 in the final singles of that particular staging. Unthinkable.

Just as the Bear had done, Harrington went about finishing the job his captain had assigned him. But, unlike Nicklaus, he was moved to admit: "We couldn't have expected anything like this. We were hoping for a very tight match all the way through the weekend. If that had materialised, who knows what could have happened over the last couple of holes. But, as things turned out, we had the momentum from the start."

Arguably the only plus to emerge from the debacle, from an American standpoint, was the contribution of a most unlikely assistant captain.

It was widely acknowledged that 81-year-old Jackie Burke made a lasting impact on the young 'uns he had been brought in to help. Accorded the sobriquet of Socrates by skipper, Hal Sutton, Burke won many hearts, among them fellow Texan Chad Campbell's, who described him simply as "incredible."

A superstitious leader would probably have steered clear of Burke, given that a year after capturing the US Masters title, he gained the unwanted distinction at Lindrick in 1957 of becoming the only US Ryder Cup captain in the post World War II period, to lose to a British and Irish line-up.

But Sutton revered him as a long-time mentor. And a less well-known credit concerns the influence he had on a celebrated American astronaut. In fact, it could be said that the co-founder, with Jimmy Demaret, of the Champions Club in Houston, played a significant role in one of the most historic shots in golfing history.

Among the advantages of being a US astronaut at the Johnson Space Centre in Houston during the 1960s, was the opportunity it afforded of meeting golfing luminaries such as Burke. "I'd be out there practising and Jackie would come along and give me a hint from time to time," said Alan Bartlett Shepard Jnr, in an interview in 1996, two years before he died.

Shepard, who was a 15-handicapper at the time of Burke's intervention, went on: "I think what he tried to tell me was that, as an engineer, I was too regimented; that I should relax and enjoy the game."

And such was the enthusiasm for golf instilled into him by Burke, that Shepard made it a memorable element of the Apollo 14 mission in 1971, with the aid of a retractable instrument which was used to collect dust and rock samples from the moon.

It was towards the end of his second lunar walk that the astronaut pulled out two golf balls and the instrument with a six-iron clubhead attached to it. Executing one-handed golf-shots, he shanked the first into a crater about 40 yards away. With the second one, however, he kept his head down and the result was a flush contact which sent the ball "at least 200 yards," down-sun and against a black sky which allowed him to easily follow its trajectory.

"It happened to be the direction we paced out 200 metres, for our experimental field, and it landed just past that area," he recalled. "Of course I said it went for several miles, which was a slight exaggeration. I folded up the club, with the clubhead, put it in my pocket, climbed up the ladder, closed the door and we took off."

In February 1971, a telegram was despatched from the Royal and Ancient at St Andrews, with the message: "Warmest congratulations to all of you on your great achievement and safe return. Please refer to Rules of Golf section on etiquette, paragraph 6, quote – before leaving a bunker a player should carefully fill up all holes made by him therein – unquote."

Three years later, Shepard donated the makeshift club which had executed a shot literally out of this world, to the USGA Museum in New Jersey.

Before his death, aged 74, on July 22nd 1998, he remarked: "I'll forever be remembered for playing golf on the moon." And though US Masters and USPGA Championship triumphs in 1956 were among Burke's tournament successes, he is likely to be better remembered, certainly by the current generation, for a scathing postscript to events at Oakland Hills.

Karl MacGinty, golf correspondent of the *Irish Independent,* had breakfast with him at the Champions Club, in the aftermath of the 2004 Ryder Cup. His subsequent report included the observation: "If his (Burke's) appointment (as Sutton's assistant) caused surprise abroad, nobody was more stunned than Burke himself by what he saw behind the scenes at Oakland Hills."

MacGinty continued: "Burke fears for the future of the game of golf in the US and he isn't only talking about the US team's record defeat in Detroit as he states: 'When the commerce

Chapter 2 The Glory

side in golf is so much bigger than the art side, you are going to get your ass handed to you.' While paying tribute to Bernhard Langer and his team for the quality of their performance, Burke's overwhelming concern is with a generation of American players which, he says, 'have never had to work hard; never had to teach golf or never had a (waiter's) napkin over their arm in their goddam lives.

"'We used to play 16 events a year for a total of $160,000 but the guy that finished 27th the other day made more than that. To these guys, the Ryder Cup is almost an interruption to life, they are so long on the Tour and the money is so big. I've never been around a group like them before. They were like a frat house at a college. I've never been to college but I'm sure that's the way it was. Marine Corps boot camp, that's where I went to college.

"'While the European team ply their trade across several continents, America's most wealthy professionals don't leave the comfort zone of their own tour very often.' Remarking on one of the most obvious differences between the two sides in Detroit, Burke said: 'The Europeans all went home in one plane but our team went home in 12 jets. I don't think they'd even know about being a team. They don't talk about that. They don't talk about this being one force going somewhere. They are very much individuals and they don't hardly speak to one another.'"

Burke went on to reveal that he disagreed with Sutton's decision to pair-up his two top players, Tiger Woods and Phil Mickelson. "Hal was on about Tiger and Phil having to bond, so I said to him: 'Are you running a church here or is this a golf tournament we're in? What the hell is this?' I don't give a damn about players bonding or if they don't like each other, but Mickelson and Woods shouldn't have been paired together. Spread 'em apart and you might win two points. Pair 'em together and the best you're going to do is one."

In the endless post-mortems which followed Oakland Hills, it became abundantly clear that competing egos placed an impossible strain on Sutton's dream pairing. According to Colin Montgomerie, Friday's defeat of Woods and Mickelson in the opening fourballs and also in the afternoon's foursomes, became a huge factor in Europe's ultimate success. Indeed Monty described the afternoon foursomes win by Darren Clarke and Lee Westwood as "a massive point for Europe."

Though most observers would find it difficult to imagine a pre-Ryder Cup switch from Titleist to Callaway woods being highly significant for a player of Mickelson's skill, the fact remained that he hit an unbelievably wayward drive down the last hole of that match. Indeed it was truly shocking to see such a fine player block a three-wood 40 yards off line to within a foot of the out-of-bounds fence. "Even for an amateur, a shot that badly off line simply wasn't on," said Montgomerie. "But the real damage was to be seen in the look on Tiger's face, when the camera moved in on him."

The Scot was referring to an expression which ranged from puzzlement to utter incredulity. It was really quite something to behold and with Woods taking a penalty drop from the fence, the upshot was that Clarke and Westwood, who had been three down after five, won the 18th with a bogey for a most improbable point. Referring afterwards to his dream duo, Sutton pleaded: "Who'd a bet they'd a lost that lead? We'd all be broke."

Back at The Belfry in 1993, when a rampant US team were demolishing Europe in singles combat, skipper Tom Watson urged a colleague to "listen to the silence. Isn't it beautiful?" On that Friday afternoon at Oakland Hills, swirling winds carried precious few cheers from a strangely muted home crowd. Sutton was so angered by Mickelson's performance that he denied the player the courtesy of telling him before the official announcement, that he was dropped from Saturday's fourballs.

There was no mistaking the impact of what had been a shattering experience for Sutton, as Europe raced to their biggest opening-day lead of 6½ to 1½, since the Continentals joined the Ryder Cup fold in 1979. Was he surprised at the quietness of the crowd? "Well, they would have been cheering pars and bogeys if they had been cheering, you know," he replied dryly. And what was the atmosphere likely to be in the players' room? "When I get really mad at myself, I don't want somebody patting me on the back and lovin' on me. I can assure you I won't be lovin' on them."

By his own admission, the former USPGA champion conceived the idea of putting Woods and Mickelson together from the moment he had been handed the captaincy two years previously. He thought it was something the American public deserved – the prospect of seeing the country's two best players as Ryder Cup partners.

Was Sutton justified in such thinking? He certainly appeared to be, given Woods's comment in a television interview a month before the Ryder Cup. When asked about the process of coming up with the correct pairings for foursomes and fourball matches, the then world number one replied: "Friendship is fine and chemistry can help, but even if you have two players who hate each other, if they both happen to play well, they'll win."

This point was given rich emphasis by John McEnroe later in 2004, when he was interviewed about his hate-hate relationship with arch tennis rival Jimmy Connors. Referring to one of the few Davis Cup ties which they played together, McEnroe said: "We played the whole tie, never practised together and didn't talk. And we won 5-0. When we played, we trashed each other on the change-overs. Jimmy called me a baby and I told him what he could kiss."

Perhaps Woods and Mickelson might have performed better had they verbally abused each other. As it was, they hardly exchanged a word during that fateful Friday. And their shambolic performances led to a severe and, in my view, totally unfair roasting for the embattled skipper

Chapter 2 The Glory

from the local media over the course of the weekend. *The Detroit Free Press* reported: "Sutton failed miserably because he ignored the basic components of Ryder Cup chemistry – you find it; you don't force it." For his part, Woods argued: "I thought we gelled (as a team). We just didn't make enough putts."

Like a good ole son of the south, Sutton was also cussin' his luck about those pesky Euros slotting heaps more than their share of birdie putts, especially during the 12 singles on the final day. It was enough to move the heart of any fair-minded follower of the fairways. Except that it wasn't true.

An analysis of the singles matches showed that the Europeans did rather well in securing a combined total of 38 birdies, with the bonus of an eagle from Harrington. And what about the home side? Well, actually, their haul of birdie putts was also precisely 38. And they, too, had the bonus of an eagle – from Woods. An even match!

Which obviously meant that the Americans dropped a lot more strokes, otherwise they couldn't have lost by such a crushing margin? Again not true. In fact, their aggregate of two over par for the 12 matches, happened to be six strokes better than Europe's. So what went wrong for the US? The answer lay partially in the fact that nine US birdies came in clear-cut, no-pressure wins by Jim Furyk and Campbell and a further nine were not good enough to save Jay Haas and Stewart Cink from defeats by Harrington and Paul McGinley at the tail of the order. And when the squeeze was applied in earnest in other tight matches, the visitors got the birdies that really mattered.

In assessing the overall performance of the US skipper, I'm reminded of one of the many memorable comments from the former Nottingham Forest soccer manager, Brian Clough, who died in September 2004. "Players, not tactics, lose games," said Cloughie. "There's so much crap talked about tactics by people who barely know how to win at dominoes."

Most successful managers these days mould millionaire players into a successful unit either through fear or greed: only in exceptional circumstances do they place their trust in loyalty. With no money involved for Ryder Cup players, greed was out. And not even Alex Ferguson could strike fear into Woods and Mickelson et al. So, having appealed largely to their loyalty and team-spirit, Sutton was short-changed on both counts.

Meanwhile, Mickelson's equipment change made a fascinating story in its own right, not least for its timing, a mere two weeks prior to the event. In fact, he played with his new woods in only one tournament, the Canadian Open, before going to Detroit. Then there was his decision to opt out of practice on the Wednesday before disappearing on the Thursday, too, apparently so as to practise with Woods's Nike ball on the North Course, in anticipation of foursomes combat. Why would this highly successful player do such a thing? As in most things to do with professional sport, the answer is money. In the wake of his US Masters triumph earlier in 2004, Mickelson sought an increase in his endorsement deal with Titleist, only to be refused on the grounds of difficult market conditions. Enter Callaway, who offered him a 10-year deal reported to be worth between $7 million and $10 million per year. The immediate change involved only woods and ball, to be followed later by Callaway irons.

Would Sutton have done such a deal at that particular time? "No," the captain replied, "I wouldn't have done it. But I'm not Phil Mickelson and I believe he's capable of playing golf with anything."

Some time later, Sutton's assistant was marvelling to MacGinty about the plush treatment accorded the US Ryder Cup party. "With the wardrobe for each player costing $15,000, gosh, where does the game come into it," Burke remarked. "It's easy to forget what you went there for." It was certainly very different from the Ryder Cup battles he had had with men like Dai Rees and Harry Bradshaw during a total of five appearances, including his ill-fated one as player-captain at Lindrick.

"I've never owned an Oxford suit in my life," he went on, "but I was given a tuxedo (in Detroit) that cost $3,100. I told my wife you can bury me in that one, with a blade putter in case they have the greens fast up there. The hotel we stayed in wasn't five star, it was 10-star. And everything was gold. We had a whole floor, and the Europeans had the floor underneath.

"There was this main room with food, ping-pong, a pool table and game that you sit in a chair and little cars go runnin' all over the place. I asked the guys, 'can you really see (Ben) Hogan sitting here playing with these things? I feel like I'm on a cruise.' The wives had a lot to say about a lot of this stuff. They brought a jeweller in from Hollywood and those girls were down there buying bracelets for $15,000. Every morning, there was a present for Robin (his wife) outside the door."

It was suggested to Burke that the decision of the PGA of America to spend an estimated $80,000 per couple on entertaining and clothing the American players and their wives/partners, was probably born out of guilt at not paying the combatants a share of the huge profits generated by the event. To which he replied angrily: "If you've got to pay the players to play for this country, I'd cancel the son-of-a-bitch. I'd tell them they don't need to play and pick the next 12 or try the Nationwide Tour just to get somebody up there who wants to play."

Burke concluded: "If money's your problem pal; if playing for your country's an inconvenience, then you shouldn't be on the team."

Whatever about the home side, one suspects that such concerns were far from European minds as they remorselessly ground the Americans into total submission. In this context, it is said that the secret of good health is to pick one's parents well, and Montgomerie graciously

Chapter 2 The Glory

acknowledged his good fortune in the Ryder Cup partners he'd had.

Among an elite group, Harrington stood apart. Montgomerie succeeded in gaining one and a half points on the opening day in partnership with Nick Faldo in 1993, Paul Lawrie in 1999 and Bernhard Langer in 2002. His partnership with the Dubliner gave him a bigger return than these "major" champions could deliver.

On Friday morning, Harrington produced four winning birdies and five in all, as he and Montgomerie covered the 17 holes in a better-ball of five under par. Then, in the foursomes, their two-under-par figures for 16 holes were the best of the afternoon, by a stroke, over the only American winners, Chris DiMarco and Jay Haas.

Perhaps the most fascinating statistic of a remarkable day, however, was that by Friday evening, Montgomerie had completed the staggering sequence of 115 holes without ever going behind, since his opening shot at The Belfry in 2002.

According to Darren Clarke, the sustained nature of a magnificent European effort was attributable to a confidence which never threatened to slide into complacency. This approach was undoubtedly helped by the view from many astute observers that the Americans were logical favourites to regain the trophy which they had relinquished two years previously. Among them was the great Nicklaus, who anticipated a US win, "simply because I felt we had the better side."

"By the time we were holding the trophy aloft on Sunday evening, it seemed a lifetime since we gathered together in the team-room on the Thursday night," Clarke recalled. "We all got around this massive table – the 12 players along with our captain Bernhard Langer and his assistants, Anders Forsbrand, Thomas Bjorn and Joakim Haeggman. My over-riding impression was of a definite air of confidence as we talked about what we were going to do.

"Everybody spoke their mind. It wasn't a question of bowing to everything that Bernhard said, though there was never any dissent. We made certain suggestions and, as far as I could see, they were taken on board. All the while, our various practice sessions through the week had confirmed to us that we had a very, very strong team. And that we had a great chance of retaining the trophy."

Within 24 hours, European optimism had received a resounding endorsement, as a normally tense opening day developed into one of almost total dominance by the visiting side. Could it be that the match was effectively over before it had begun in earnest? "Going into Saturday, Bernhard was hoping for a 4-4 split, which would have meant a European lead of 10½ to 5½ entering the singles," said Montgomerie. "I remember feeling anxious that we shouldn't let our advantage slip."

Clarke reflected: "Obviously the lead was impressive but I can assure you there was no sense of complacency among the European players when we gathered on the Friday evening. It never crossed our minds that we had put ourselves into a position of having everything to lose. We simply never considered the possibility of blowing what had clearly become a terrific chance of winning.

"This was where the balance of youth and experience in the European team came into play. I was among those who had reason to remember the bitter lesson of Brookline. Having been there before, myself and the other old hands ensured that the rookies were made aware of what could happen if we let out guard down."

Indeed Clarke's sense of caution remained, even when an unprecedented lead of six points was carried into Sunday's 12 singles. "Brookline was always there, not as something that worried us, but as a valuable lesson, painfully learned," he said. "And I could imagine the concern of European fans when a lot of red (for the US) went on the scoreboard early in the afternoon. I don't know about the other guys, but I can assure you that I wasn't unduly bothered. I just looked down through our playing order, noting the terrific strength we had in depth. And everybody was playing well. There was also the point that, with the exception of Tiger's match (against Paul Casey), the gap in most cases was only one hole, that sort of stuff.

"We weren't sure where Sutton would play Woods, except that it was likely to be fairly high in the order in the hope of getting early points on the board. So people are wrong in assuming that Paul Casey was thrown in at number one in the belief he would be facing Tiger. As it turned out, Sutton led from strength, right down the order, but to be honest, it didn't really matter to us how he arranged his line-up."

At Brookline, where the Europeans had taken a four-point lead into Sunday's singles, the advantage was wiped out by a stunning American resurgence. Lee Westwood at number one and Clarke at number two, were both beaten. And when the three rookies, Jarmo Sandelin, Jean Van de Velde and Andrew Coltart, fell at three, four and five, the Americans had not only wiped out the deficit, but had swept into what proved to be a winning lead.

"Looking back to Brookline, Lee and I were playing well enough to be convinced that one of us, if not both, would win our singles," said Clarke. "So we never considered the possibility of a collapse. That's why it came as such a shock when it actually happened. Five years later, however, it was to become priceless experience."

So, the marvellous Europeans provided us with an absolutely riveting spectacle through the weekend. When I talked some time later to Nicklaus about those heady days, he admitted to watching only very brief snatches of the telecast. "Probably 15 minutes in all," he said. "I just stopped by the television when I was passing, to see what the score was."

One can only imagine that, after Friday, he had no wish to pursue the misfortunes of a side

Chapter 2 The Glory

which contained nine players from the US President's Cup line-up he captained in South Africa the previous November.

In the event, any prospect of a spirited US revival was unceremoniously scuppered by the audacious skills of Casey and David Howell, who raised many an eyebrow and broke countless American hearts by beating Jim Furyk and Campbell on the 18th in the Saturday morning fourballs. Further pain was inflicted in the afternoon, when the irrepressible Sergio Garcia teamed in foursomes with Luke Donald to beat Furyk and Fred Funk, again on the 18th. And we had the only all-Irish pairing of the weekend, Harrington and McGinley, gaining a 4 and 3 win over Woods and Love.

Harrington hit the foursomes tee-shots on all the odd holes, which happened to include the four par-threes at Oakland Hills. And who could forget the thrilling birdie chance he set up for Montgomerie at the short ninth on Friday afternoon against Davis Love and Fred Funk? "On all the par-threes, Bernhard came up to me, told me the club to play, the place to hit it and why I should hit it there," he said of his captain. "And while it wasn't like he was telling you to do it, you were definitely aware that he was advising you."

For his part, the skipper took a predictably pragmatic view of such advice. "It just helps the players to have a second opinion from someone they respect," he said some months later. "When they're in a little doubt, if you tell them to take that club and hit it there, they will react 'that's what I was going to do anyway, but now I know for sure.' That kind of thing. As for Padraig: I'm proud of the way he has progressed in the game. He has certainly moved up a few notches in the last couple of years."

In terms of leadership qualities, Langer met Napoleon's requirement of his generals – that they be lucky. I believe he was extremely fortunate in the extraordinary success of rookie partners, Casey and Howell, whose crucial victory must have been beyond his wildest hopes.

When considering McGinley's contribution to the European effort, we should remember the thorny path of Ryder Cup qualification he had trod, just as Darcy did in 1987. And how determined he was that the spectacular, nine-foot putt he sank at The Belfry in 2002 wouldn't become the defining moment of his Ryder Cup career. "I remember being asked by an American TV station at the start of the week in 2002, what I would I do if I had a putt to win the Ryder Cup," he recalled. "My response was that I'd love to have the opportunity. And having done it once, I can't wait for the chance of doing it again."

So to Sunday, when none of us saw any great significance in the placing of Harrington and McGinley at 11 and 12 in the singles order, other than the possibility of an Irish player finding himself in a critical role, in the unlikely event of an unprecedented US comeback.

"There always seems to be an Irishman in a key role," British scribes have frequently observed during Ryder Cup weekends. They said it at Oak Hill in 1995, when Philip Walton was required to deliver a trophy-winning victory over Haas. And they said it at Brookline where Harrington, placed seventh in the singles order, seemed to have been cast in the same situation until a dramatic collapse by Jose Maria Olazabal against Justin Leonard, culminated in that outrageous, 45-foot putt on the 17th and ensuing mayhem.

Some weeks after Oakland Hills, I learned that Langer's strategy in placing Harrington and McGinley in positions where they could draw on huge Irish support in the event of a tight finish, was not as inspirational as it seemed. In fact it was the brainchild of none other than Caroline Harrington, Padraig's wife.

The notion struck her as she watched wildly enthusiastic Irish supporters cheer every stroke her husband and his partner executed in Saturday afternoon's foursomes, in which they thrashed Woods and Love by a crushing 4 and 3 margin. "Imagine the sort of support you would get from those fans if you were playing in successive singles tomorrow," she told the two players. So it was that at the players' meeting that night, Harrington and McGinley put the notion to Langer who thought it was a terrific idea.

"Much as I'd like to take credit for Sunday's arrangement, I have to admit that it was Caroline's idea," said McGinley. "I only wish I was that clever."

In the event, with the overnight score at 11-5 in Europe's favour, Casey set off at noon local time in the opening singles match against the world's number two. At 3.20pm, Woods completed a 3 and 2 victory over the young Englishman, so narrowing the match score to 11-6. Four minutes later, Furyk crushed Howell to make it 11-7.

Surely we weren't about to be hit with a repeat of Brookline? It seemed unthinkable, yet a sea of red on the scoreboards throughout the course was not especially comforting for European hearts. All lingering concerns disappeared at 3.30, however, when Mickelson fatally carved his approach into the water at the 16th, allowing Garcia to post his side's first singles point in a 3 and 2 victory. With the match score at 12-7, the good ship Europe had been steadied.

Less than 30 minutes later, Clarke capitalised on a chip-in birdie on the short 17th to set up a halved match with Love. Yet pockets of US resistance remained and by 4.11, Campbell had closed the gap once more, before a win by Westwood, recorded at 4.26, restored the European lead to five points. Now, only one more point was needed for victory and it came at 4.35 when marvellous Monty holed a treacherous four-footer on the last for victory over Toms.

But was this actually the decisive moment? In a piece the following Sunday under the headline "This man won the Ryder Cup not Monty", the *News of the World* claimed that Ian Poulter should have been hailed as the Oakland Hills hero. It reported: "... we have found the real drama went almost unnoticed three holes back. Seconds before Montgomerie's ball dropped, Poulter's birdie three at the 15th guaranteed him at least half a point against fellow rookie Chris Riley – enough to win the 35th Ryder Cup outright."

The *News of the World* went on: "That took Poulter to three up with three to play and put the icing on the cake after Lee Westwood's win over Kenny Perry sealed the 14th point Europe needed to retain the trophy. A par at 16 gave Poulter a 3 and 2 win. He went to join the celebrations at the 18th, where Monty was being hailed as the hero – but events proved everyone wrong.

"Course commentators recognised Poulter's feat, but feared being left with egg on their faces had something untoward then happened to him."

(BBC) Radio 5 Live golf correspondent Iain Carter, at the 18th, explained: "My editor said Poulter was three up seconds before Monty hit his putt. Then Colin's putt went in – you can imagine the situation. To have over-ruled his achievement would have been like trying to deny Alan Shearer a goal that went in off a defender.

"In any case, Poulter had not officially finished his match. For all anyone knew he might have been disqualified."   Mind you, it is impossible to think of any circumstance in which Poulter could have been disqualified, but either way, Thomas Levet, Harrington and McGinley completed the rout, for a final score of 18½ to 9½.

For his part, Montgomerie said: "It doesn't matter who holes the winning putt. I'm here as part of a team. Whatever part I play in the Ryder Cup, I'll always be that." It was a situation which brought to mind a memorable line from the 1962 movie *The Man Who Shot Liberty Valance*. After it was revealed that John Wayne's character and not James Stewart's actually shot the eponymous villain, a newspaperman was told: "When the legend becomes fact, print the legend." So it is that Monty will be remembered as the man who despatched the decisive putt of the 2004 Ryder Cup.

Meanwhile, Irish observers had much to mull over during an eventful, Sunday afternoon. Like whether Clarke was really trying to hole the four-footer he had for victory against Love on the 18th, after the American had sportingly resisted the temptation to take relief on his approach shot. The Tyroneman's reaction afterwards reflected mixed emotions. "I'm disappointed at missing that putt," he said, "but I think a halved match was a very fair result for both of us." Then there was the superb effort by McGinley, who was always in command when easing to a 3 and 2 victory over the winner of the NEC Invitational at Firestone only a few weeks previously. Nominated as one of Sutton's wild-card choices, Cink entered the Ryder Cup

Oakland Hills

II

♦

This page clockwise from top: The two teams on parade at the opening ceremony of the 35th Ryder Cup. Colin Montgomerie launching his drive at the opening hole of the first match on Friday 17 September. Montgomerie partnered Padraig Harrington (left of frame) to a 2&1 victory over the dream pairing of Tiger Woods and Phil Mickelson. Caddies and players taking stock of Oakland Hills during practice. Hole 1 detail. Fans line the fairways with the latest in viewing technology. Thomas Levet, who played in three matches, collecting one point from his singles match against Fred Funk on Sunday. Ian Poulter guides a mid-iron shot to the target during practice.

Above: Paul McGinley signing autographs. **Below left:** Security was tight during the week. At the gala dinner before battle commenced: Caroline and Padraig Harrington; Darren and Heather Clarke; Paul and Alison McGinley; Tiger Woods and Elin Nordegren. **Below left:** Fred Funk's shoes. **Bottom left:** Former US President George Bush spectating. **Below:** Stewart Cink framed by foliage while **(bottom right)** Elin Nordegren (left) and Amy Mickelson out on the course supporting the USA.

The Tiger Woods/Phil Mickelson partnership (right), signalled by Captain Hal Sutton as the bedrock of the United States challenge, fell apart on opening day. They lost to Padraig Harrington and Colin Montgomerie in the morning fourball match and then to Clarke and Lee Westwood in the afternoon foursomes. Main photograph: Tiger Woods. Below left and clockwise: Europe team captain Bernhard Langer sees only good news unfolding on the scoreboard. Lee Westwood and Darren Clarke celebrate their victory over Mickelson and Woods in the afternoon foursomes on day one. David Howell and Darren Clarke up close. Paul McGinley and Tiger Woods framed during the second day foursomes match. McGinley and Padraig Harrington defeated Woods and Davis Love III by 4 and 3. US Captain Hal Sutton contemplating his side's collapse. Rookie Luke Donald (centre) in action in his second day foursomes match with Sergio Garcia. when they beat Fred Funk and Jim Furyk one up.

35th RYDER CUP MATCHES

STATUS	Europe	HOLE	U.S.A.	STATUS
2 & 1	MONTGOMERIE HARRINGTON	F	MICKELSON WOODS	
5 & 4	CLARKE JIMÉNEZ	F	LOVE CAMPBELL	
ALL SQUARE	McGINLEY DONALD	15	RILEY FINK	ALL SQUARE
5 UP	GARCIA WESTWOOD	13	FUNK FURYK	

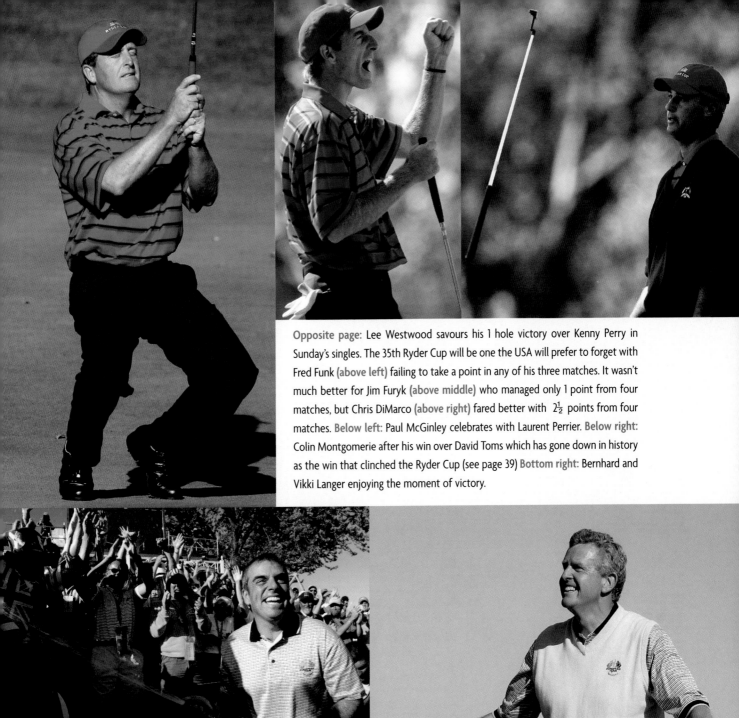

Opposite page: Lee Westwood savours his 1 hole victory over Kenny Perry in Sunday's singles. The 35th Ryder Cup will be one the USA will prefer to forget with Fred Funk (above left) failing to take a point in any of his three matches. It wasn't much better for Jim Furyk (above middle) who managed only 1 point from four matches, but Chris DiMarco (above right) fared better with $2\frac{1}{2}$ points from four matches. Below left: Paul McGinley celebrates with Laurent Perrier. Below right: Colin Montgomerie after his win over David Toms which has gone down in history as the win that clinched the Ryder Cup (see page 39) Bottom right: Bernhard and Vikki Langer enjoying the moment of victory.

That every day would be like this: Ian Poulter in ebullient mood with the trophy. The rookie took one point from two outings beating Chris Riley by one hole in Sunday's singles.

as statistically the best putter in the US, yet he was outscored 5-4 by McGinley in terms of successful birdie putts.

After the hero of 2002 had secured this latest victory, he joined his colleagues behind the 18th green, waiting for Harrington's match to finish. There, in expressing delight at a great European effort, he was happy to credit Montgomerie with sinking the winning putt, just as he himself had unquestionably done two years previously. "Nobody was more deserving than Monty," he said.

Soon, another winning putt, this time from Harrington, rested in the bottom of the cup on the brutally difficult 18th green and the three Irishmen found themselves in the middle of a party, singing and dancing with flag-waving Irish fans. It was the scene which prompted an American scribe to observe that the match climaxed "in a mist of champagne and Irish folk songs."

And it was beautiful to behold. Nobody enjoyed it more than McGinley, whose battle to make the team became one of the great sports stories of the year. The revellers also included a certain, middle-aged man wearing a distinctive, bright orange wig. "He's my caddie's (Darren Reynolds of Delgany) father," the player explained to fascinated American journalists. "Tony Reynolds is his name. In fact, Darren's girlfriend was bumped off the plane to make way for him. Mind you, he didn't board it dressed like that.

"It's funny, he's had two or three girls come up to him this week, giving him their cards. So he's been lucky. He's a character; obviously a passionate Irishman." Paying special tribute to the fans, he added: "It was like half came from such main Irish centres here as Chicago, Boston and New York and the other half from Ireland. And they met at Oakland Hills and called it home. We might just as well have been in the middle of Ireland."

Those who doubted Clarke's Irishness had only to observe his willingness to be wrapped in the tricolor with Harrington and McGinley. And there was a ready smile when he chided them: "Make sure I'm under the orange bit." Which he was, in a memorable shot which received considerable exposure in Irish newspapers and magazines during the ensuing months. The waving of the tricolor by Irish supporters in a meaningful, celebratory sense, made a pleasant change from Athens, where it was done sympathetically for Sonia O'Sullivan, who was lapped in the final of the Olympic 10,000 metres.

Not for the first time, Irish golfers had done the country proud, especially in the Ryder Cup. Between them, the trio at Oakland Hills contributed to no fewer than 10 European points, either as partners in foursomes and fourballs or as individual performers in the final day's singles. In the process, they exposed as meaningless hogwash, the notion that in competitive sport, taking part is enough. Distraught at being beaten at tennis, Snoopy, the lovable cartoon beagle, got it right when he was imagined to remark: "It doesn't matter if you win or lose, until you lose."

It seems that every time the Ryder Cup comes around, we're fed the traditional line about the wonderful friendships it creates among the combatants. Yet we know that, after Europe had the effrontery to wallop the Americans at The Belfry in 1985, winning became the only thing.

Meanwhile, Dr Michael Smurfit had other, crucial matters to consider after his trip to Detroit. Everything he saw at Oakland Hills made him acutely aware of his forthcoming role in the 2006 matches. So it was that with pen and paper in hand, he took extensive notes, one of which concerned the space accorded to corporate hospitality. "The scale of things here is much bigger than I imagined," he said.

This had become a familiar reaction since the biennial showpiece took off in earnest at The Belfry in 1989. That was the year the US Open was staged at Oak Hill, and when club officials came to The Belfry in 1993 to see how they should prepare for the Ryder Cup in 1995, their first discovery was that the '89 media centre would have to be doubled.

So it was at Oakland Hills. Over 320,000 square feet were dedicated to corporate hospitality over the weekend, compared with 148,000 for the US Open there in 1996. And that didn't take account of the huge corporate parties organised in the gardens of homes rented along nearby Maple Road.

On site, a total of 60 chalets, each accommodating 100 people and costing $350,000 for six days, were sold out three years previously. There were also 50-person chalets situated along the first, 10th, 11th and 16th holes, at $175,000 each. Companies which couldn't afford a chalet, settled for 10-person tables at $60,000 each, inside three giant, so-called Champion Club tents. There, 225 tables costing $60,000 each, were all sold out in the year. Each tent contained bars, buffets and 40 television sets.

"It's fantastic," enthused Dr Smurfit during the course of the weekend. "Apart from the attractiveness of their structure, the overall quality of the chalets is outstanding. And the security is excellent: efficient but unobtrusive. In fact, there's a touch of class about the whole place. They have been able to create an impression of space through making full use of both the North and South courses here. This prompts me to conclude that the European Tour should look very carefully at using more space on our second course.

"I think it's safe to say that the scale of the Ryder Cup in Ireland will be on a par with what we see here. So we're going to have to re-think. A certain amount of space has already been allocated on our second course but if they need more, we will happily supply it. We don't want to have a congested event."

It was estimated that the City of Detroit made revenues close on $180 million from their staging. So, how would The K Club measure up? "I'm confident we will do something to make Ireland proud," replied the man who dreamed of landing this coveted prize, even before The K Club was officially opened in July 1991. "It should do wonders for the country's image abroad, especially where golf tourism is concerned."

These observations prompted the thought that heroic deeds in the Ryder Cup are not always limited to the combatants inside the fairway ropes. Men like Jaime Patino of Valderrama and Michael Smurfit of The K Club had the vision to transform the wild hope of staging such a thrilling event, into marvellous reality.

Meanwhile, in the wake of Oakland Hills, Americans continued their painful search for some explanation of their team's amazing collapse. And when Love claimed that part of the answer might be found in the playing of President's Cup matches (launched in 1994) and Ryder Cup matches in successive years, he found a powerful ally. "It takes some of our edge off," Love had claimed. But he also conceded that "the rest of the world are getting better at golf." "Who's the number one player in the world?" asked Love. "He's from Fiji."

These views were strongly supported by an American icon who could speak with some authority, having captained both their Ryder Cup and President's Cup sides. "I agree with Davis," said Nicklaus, who was largely instrumental in bringing about the formation of a European team in 1979. "I've been saying this for years. It definitely makes a difference having to get up for an important team event every year as opposed to doing it every two years, like the Europeans.

"A possible solution, which I believe could work, would be to create a new tournament, a sort of 'King of the Hill' event involving the US, Europe and the Internationals. And if, say, the US beat the International side in one year, they would qualify for a decider against Europe a year later. Or if Europe beat the US, as happened last weekend, they would get a crack at the International team."

But the Bear added: "The only problem with such an arrangement is that there would be a conflict of interests here in the US, where the Ryder Cup is controlled by the PGA of America, while the PGA Tour run the President's Cup."

What about the match itself? Was he surprised by the outcome? "Yes, I was," he replied. "Though Europe have some fine players who obviously performed very well, I honestly thought our's were better. I never imagined they would lose by such a margin, especially at Oakland Hills, which I expected to be better suited to our guys. But we must also consider the fact that foursomes golf was an entirely new experience for some of our guys. The only chance you get of playing foursomes over here (in the US) is in the President's Cup or the Ryder Cup. And, of course, the Walker Cup, which was my first experience."

Chapter 2 The Glory

He then offered words of sympathy to the beleaguered Sutton. "Captaining is not easy," said Nicklaus. "Tony Jacklin did a wonderful job for Europe on four occasions (1983, 1985, 1987 and 1989). And there was a suggestion over here that I should take over captaincy of our side on an ongoing basis. But what if something like last weekend were to happen? How long would I stay in the job then?"

On this point, McGinley offered the interesting observation: "You know where you read that if you took an average player and put Jack Nicklaus's head on his shoulders, how good a player that guy would become? Being with Bernhard was a little like that. He gave us advice about course management and club selection and pin positions all the way around."

Yet, for a fleeting moment on the morning after the event, it seemed as if Langer were already in need of a job. Beside a headline proclaiming "Euros' Heroes", the front page of the *Detroit Free Press* informed us in another headline that "Bernhard is off the list for key GM post." Surely this was something of an over-reaction in Motor City to the achievement of the European skipper? Happily, the attached story referred to a certain Wolfgang Bernhard of Chrysler, not our favourite German. Drive on, Herr Langer!

As for his US counterpart: my view regarding Sutton's captaincy was that whatever about the wisdom of some of his decisions, the inescapable truth was that his players let him down. They simply weren't up to the challenge. For all the pre-tournament talk about their supremacy with the blade, they putted only as well as their nerve permitted. Which, in most cases, didn't match that of their European counterparts. This became critical on surfaces which were described by eminent architect Rees Jones as "greens within greens." In fact, Jones remarked: "With all those contours, if you're not fairly close to the hole, you don't have much chance of a birdie."

For all the abuse that was hurled at him by the American media, Sutton lost with dignity, just as another proud southerner, Lanny Wadkins, had done at Oak Hill in 1995. Indeed Sutton paid the ultimate tribute to the triumphant Europeans when, in putting his own embellishment on the familiar catchphrase of the USPGA Tour, he said: "You know, these guys are darned good."

♦

Chapter 3

The Mandarin

Chapter 3 The Mandarin

Shortly before it was officially announced at Valderrama that Ireland was to play host to the Ryder Cup in 2005, a European Tour official called me aside and asked if I could write the name of Padraig Ó hUiginn for him. The Gaelic spelling of Higgins posed understandable difficulties for an Englishman and the Tour weren't about to insult a man whom they viewed as having been central to the Irish bid.

Yet I was to learn later from Ken Schofield, that the joyous Irish news from Valderrama might never have happened. "If Lord Derby, the late chairman of the PGA, had sought mediation or compromise, the Tour would have supported Ireland at Portmarnock, for the 1993 matches," said the executive director of the European Tour. "That's factual, because in terms of suitable venues, it was too early in the days of what became wonderful proprietorial clubs. That was certainly the view of Bernard Gallacher and Tony Jacklin. Instead, it went back to The Belfry through his (Lord Derby's) casting vote, which was a great disappointment to us, because we were originally supporting Spain."

The golfing life of Kenneth D Schofield CBE, effectively started at Gleneagles in his native Scotland. He had gone there for the staging of the Dunlop Tournament, in which one round was played over the Queen's Course and another over the King's, before the cut was made. As he recalled: "I was 14 years young at the time and as a lad who couldn't afford the entrance – there were no silver spoons in our family – I knew how to get into Gleneagles without having to pay. Which I did. And I saw Himself (Christy O'Connor Snr), who was in his pomp at that time. And I saw John Panton, Harry Weetman and Ken Bousfield. And if memory serves me correctly, I also saw Fred Daly play.

"I was old enough to realise that I was seeing some of our greatest players and it was an experience which sparked a love-affair with the game. Ten years later, my second big connection with Irish golf cemented the bond."

Clearly relishing the memory of rather special times past, Schofield recalled: "Together with my wife Evelyn, I took the ferry to Dublin, where we were spectators at the Alcan Golfer of the Year tournament at Portmarnock. Bruce Devlin won the main event and I can recall Paddy Skerritt being carried shoulder-high from the 18th green by the delighted members of St Anne's GC (club captain, Tommy Eglington, among others) after winning the Alcan International.

"It was September 1970 and we stayed at the Grand Hotel in Malahide. By that stage, I had already gone into banking and Evelyn was pregnant with our first daughter, who was born the following January.

"These experiences had the effect of getting me more and more into golf. As things turned out, I applied for a job 11 months later, working as assistant PR and pressman with George Simms and John Jacobs on what would become the PGA European Tour. So, there is no doubt but that Ireland, and the feel for the game I acquired as an observer at Portmarnock, became highly significant in shaping my career in golf."

An enduring affection and admiration for the quality of Irish tournaments through the years, could be gleaned from vivid recollections not only of Portmarnock, but of Royal Dublin, where the Irish Open found a welcoming home from 1983 to 1985. What he described as "the Seve-Langer days", when Europe's dynamic duo dominated the event, with Ballesteros winning in 1983 and '85 and Langer capturing the one in between. All of which contributed to what became for him "a 40-year love affair with Irish golfers and a 30-year love affair with Irish golf.

"Later, my eyes were opened enormously by what seemed to happen in Ireland overnight. Having attended the first Irish Open under the Carrolls banner at Woodbrook in 1975, I witnessed the move to Killarney in 1991 and '92 and from there to Mount Juliet, the first of these splendid new venues to play host to the national championship.

"I first visited The K Club for the PGA Cup matches in 1992. I remember it was the week of Black Wednesday, when (Norman) Lamont (Chancellor of the Exchequer) took Britain out of the European Monetary Union and interest rates went through the roof. Through John O'Leary, I was introduced to Fintan Drury, a man of considerable substance and influence. And we got very close to getting a sponsor for an Irish Masters, but like so many things, the sponsor in the end decided that the time was not right.

"This was all part of a process which had caused me to look seriously towards Ireland as a future Ryder Cup venue. We had seen the massive efforts Spain had made through the Turespana series in the run-up to their bid for the Ryder Cup in 1993, before they successfully got it four years later. In any one season, Spain were generating six, seven or maybe eight golf tournaments. Now, we wanted to give this message to Ireland, or anybody else who cared to listen.

"I have a signal moment in mind. When Murphy's took over from Carrolls and we had the Irish Open at Mount Juliet in 1994, I can remember a number of things becoming very relevant. Through the help of Laurence Crowley of Carrolls, Murphy's agreed to take over the tournament by assignment, which was very nice. Then, through John O'Leary and David Adamson, we brokered arrangements whereby The K Club would play host to what would become the Smurfit European Open.

"So, with The K Club coming to the fore and Mount Juliet already on board since the final Carrolls, these were clearly venues with wonderful potential. And in the background, I was

Chapter 3 The Mandarin

aware of Padraig Ó hUiginn's ambitions for Irish golf."

In Schofield's view, Ireland, as a nation, usurped from Spain the position as Europe's number-one force in golf, several years ago. "A key element driving the growth of Irish-based tournaments was the wonderful investment in quality courses," he said. "There was the run which Dr Tim Mahony gave us with the Irish Open at Mount Juliet from 1993 to 1995, followed by four wonderful years at Druids Glen. And when we went looking for venues for the AIB Seniors', along came St Margaret's, Tulfarris, Powerscourt and, more recently, Adare and The Heritage. It has been a case of Irish golf reaping the rewards of their major investment in the game.

"The golfers are following suit. Darren Clarke became Europe's first world champion by beating Tiger Woods at La Costa early in Millennium year. And how proud we all are of Padraig Harrington and his outstanding performances on both sides of the Atlantic. And the exemplary manner in which he handled that awful situation (in the Benson and Hedges International) at The Belfry a few years ago. Not many guys, whatever the sport, would have taken such a blow so graciously. Then, of course, there has been the wonderful play of Darren, Padraig and Paul McGinley in the Ryder Cup."

He went on to acknowledge the contribution which a former Irish Open champion has made to the administration of the European game. "John O'Leary played in the first Ryder Cup I attended in the States in 1975 (at Laurel Valley)," said Schofield. "John's playing career, encompassing his memorable Irish Open win at Portmarnock, speaks for itself. But as a director of the tour, it is incalculable what he has put back into the game, through consistent support of everything we have tried to do over the years, characterised by the commonsense he brings to board decisions."

Recalling the beginning of his involvement in Ryder Cup affairs, O'Leary said: "It coincided with the decision to award the event to Spain in 1997. When that happened, Seve (Ballesteros) withdrew because of an obvious clash of interests. He also wanted to do other things in Spain at that time. I had served for several years on the Tour's Board of Directors and as chairman of the Tour's Tournament Committee, so I suppose I was an obvious replacement for Seve."

With reference to the well-documented casting vote against Portmarnock for the 1993 matches, O'Leary said: "Lord Derby was a very special man, as was reflected in the fact that he held the positions of Chairman of the PGA and President of the Tour at the same time. I first met him when I was learning the ropes on tour and finished runner-up in an Under-23 Championship which he sponsored. And I was fortunate in having a marvellous rapport with him from then until his death.

"He was a tremendous man for golf and I'm sure it upset him greatly when the Tour separated from the PGA in 1975. That was when the PGA moved to The Belfry and the Tour stayed at offices at the Kennington Oval before moving to its present home at Wentworth in 1981. The split was inevitable in that the Tour had to become independent. A measure of the esteem in which Lord Derby was held was that he remained as President of the Tour until his resignation immediately after that famous Ryder Cup meeting in 1993. Having thrown in his lot with the PGA, he felt he had no option but to relinquish his Tour position, which was typical of the man.

"I was fairly certain that the Ryder Cup would be coming to Ireland in 1993. But it is ironic to think that if it had gone to Portmarnock, we wouldn't be looking towards the 2006 staging at The K Club. And whatever about the rights and wrongs about what happened over 1993, I have always considered the Smurfit Company very deserving of the honour. They have been very supportive of golf for many years, going back to the launch of the Smurfit Junior Series and later to their sponsorship of the Irish Professional Championship. Then, their sponsorship and running of the European Open greatly enhanced their standing with the Tour. It seemed a perfect fit and I'm delighted with the way things have turned out."

From Schofield's standpoint, the Tour experienced difficult times in the wake of the first Gulf War. Among other things, they lost very strong European Open sponsors in Panasonic and General Accident. "I'm not suggesting that the European Open was entirely in jeopardy at that time," he said. "But from a position where it was in danger of being under-resourced and understrength, to get that marriage with the Smurfit organisation at a custom-built venue close to the capital city, was a wonderful boost for us.

"It meant that the European Open could rank alongside the (BMW) PGA Championship as a flagship event of the Tour. Who can forget the European Open going to The K Club for the first time in 1995 and Philip Walton disembarking from Concorde at Dublin Airport holding aloft the Ryder Cup trophy that was won back at Oak Hill? It wasn't a bad way to announce a new venue, was it?"

The emergence of the Smurfit European Open became a fascinating story, as Adamson was keen to point out. Ironically, the spark was lit by the failure of the Smurfit Irish Professional Championship at The K Club in 1992, when the venue received seriously adverse publicity because of the sodden nature of the course. Clearly, it would have been unwise to stick with the plan of holding it there on an annual basis. Nor could it be moved to another Dublin venue without losing face. So it was decided to move it around the country, which meant stagings at such venues as Galway Bay, Slieve Russell and Belvoir Park.

Meanwhile, a close friendship between Carrolls chief, Laurence Crowley, and Dr Smurfit,

Chapter 3 The Mandarin

seemed certain to result in the Irish Open coming to The K Club in 1994 and 1995. But fate took a hand. After both men had reached agreement on the move, Carrolls was taken over by Rothmans, which effectively scuppered the move. "As I remember it, Murphy's were interested in taking up the option for 1995, but they were seeking an increased venue fee," said Adamson. "But we refused, with the result that the event stayed at Mount Juliet until and including 1995.

"There was another coincidence which worked in our favour. This concerned the difficulties which the European Open faced through the withdrawal of their title sponsors, General Accident. It meant the Tour had to step into the breach for 1994 and there was no sign of a replacement sponsor for 1995. At the same time, Smurfits made a major acquisition in France, of a company which had operations all over Europe. And I remember being approached by Paul Holland of Drury Sports asking if we would be interested in sponsoring the European Open. It was at this point that I met with Ken (Schofield) and John (O'Leary) and we discussed title sponsorship and whether it could become economically feasible.

"With the title, Michael knew we could stage the event at various venues throughout Europe, if we wished. So, when I put it to him, his reaction was: 'We'll do it.' He considered the title sponsorship was better value for money than being a subsidiary sponsor. Among other things, it afforded us the opportunity of promoting The K Club viz a viz properties etc. And, as he put it: 'It will put us on the inside track with the European Tour regarding the possibility of landing the Ryder Cup in 2005.' So we did the deal, which was how the decision on the venue was made. Our position was later strengthened when we acquired 50 per cent of the European Open. It was at this point that we informed the Tour that staging the Ryder Cup was a crucial part of our future golfing strategy. And that was well before 1997."

Dr Smurfit's recollection of events was: "Being a pan European company, which we had become at the time, it made sense to spend a certain percentage of our income on sponsorship. How do you brand-name a packaging company? We had already got great value from Cheltenham (horse racing) and from the St Leger in its early years. Since then, the St Leger, which we won twice with Vintage Crop, has lost a bit of its cachet.

"So, looking at what we have here (at The K Club), how were we to attract more visitors, more members? It struck us that sponsoring a tour event would deliver a relatively good return for our investment. Looking at the events which were available, the one which was very obviously going nowhere at the time, was the European Open. And having acquired it, we successfully set about raising its profile throughout Europe."

Returning to Schofield, it is no secret that he swears undying allegiance to the St Johnstone soccer club. Some would argue, probably unkindly, that such loyalty betrays a serious lack of sporting judgement, yet he was appointed as the First Secretary and Executive Director of the European Tour in 1975. Fiercely protective of its remarkable growth during distinguished years of service until his retirement at the end of 2004, he remarked generously: "To those who would hold the European Tour in some esteem, I would say: 'Look no further than Ireland.'"

By comparison, Ó hUiginn would have been seen by many golfing observers as something of an aloof, enigmatic figure. Born in Cork, which is still evident in his accent, he went on to become a career civil servant, working both nationally and internationally. From Local Government, he left these shores for posts in Geneva and New York and, almost inevitably, he also worked in Brussels.

On completion of a stint in the United Nations in New York, he took up golf on his return to Ireland, "when the children had grown up a bit." That was when he was made managing director of An Foras Forbartha, before going to Europe in 1973 on Ireland's accession to the then EEC. And he can recall returning home from Brussels at weekends, when he would play at Edmondstown GC on Saturday mornings, with John Healy and Michael Mills, the country's most famous political commentators of the time. That was before Mills left *The Irish Press* (since defunct) and became Ombudsman.

"By 1979, I was in Economic Planning and Development which was wound up when Charlie Haughey came in as Taoiseach," he said. "It meant my being transferred into his (Taoiseach's) Department, as assistant secretary in charge of economic and social planning. Ultimately I became secretary of the Department, twice under Garret FitzGerald and twice under Haughey."

One of Ó hUiginn's most arduous and, ultimately, rewarding tasks was to write the Programme for National Recovery in 1987, which, as chairman, he then negotiated with the unions and employers on behalf of the Government. He also became involved with Europe in the disbursement of regional fund money, largely from a tourism perspective. Indeed so valued was he at the highest level that Haughey decided to keep him on past his retirement age until 1993, when the then mandarin was 69.

Ó hUiginn recalled: "On my eventual retirement in 1993, Charlie McCreevy, in his capacity as Minister for Tourism and Trade, asked me to become chairman of Bord Failte. Prior to that, I was asked by Dermot Desmond to advise and help on the possible staging of the 1993 Ryder Cup at Portmarnock. I remember one of the problems was parking and they identified the former Baldoyle Racecourse as an ideal solution.

"So I negotiated with Brian Lenihan, the then Minister for Defence, that Baily-Bridges could be built across the estuary to Portmarnock. That particular presentation was a good

Chapter 3 The Mandarin

effort, but the fact that the Irish Open was our only tournament at the time, we didn't have a very big standing with the European Tour. Successful though it was, there was no way it was going to give us an inside track."

As chairman of Bord Failte, a position he held for three years before going on the board for a further five, he looked at those deficiencies, though, by his own admission, the Ryder Cup wasn't a major consideration at the time. As he saw it: "There was no great hunger for the event, but I still thought it appropriate to change the promotional strategy of Bord Failte. I saw golf as one of the country's tourism strengths. From being a regular visitor to Ballybunion over the years, I could see the impact of the marketing they were doing, for instance in becoming the first people to promote the idea of overseas members. And they were very critical of the absence of support from Bord Failte at that time, especially in the US.

"It meant that club officials themselves were forced to go out to the US where they visited the main golf clubs over there, selling Ballybunion. It was a classic example of targeted salesmanship, which impressed me enormously. You must always distinguish between marketing and salesmanship. You can market something as a general concept but as a salesman, you must knock on the door and ask will you buy this. Two different styles are required. One is based on catching the attention of the customer; the other is selling them a product. Ballybunion became salesmen."

A measure of Ó hUiginn's administrative expertise and negotiating skills was the manner in which he succeeded in furthering the cause of Irish golf through three different Governments. The first of these was a Fianna Fail led administration which came into office in March 1987; then there was the so-called Rainbow Coalition, led by John Bruton's Fine Gael party in January 1993 and this was followed by another Fianna Fail administration in June 1997, when Bertie Ahern became Taoiseach. Of particular significance was that the last of these three Governments actually came to power only two months before the Ryder Cup announcement at Valderrama in September 1997.

As Bord Failte chairman, Ó hUiginn went to the 1993 World Cup of Golf at Lake Nona, Florida, where he explored the idea of bringing that event to Ireland. But he claimed that in talks with the European Tour, he was told that before there could be any chance of success, the country would first have to stage another tournament.

"From a promotional perspective, our one tournament was clearly good, insofar as we were getting four days' coverage from the BBC," he said. "But I thought we should get editorial control of the film, particularly the highlights. With that in mind, I started to make a contribution to the event, as chairman of Bord Failte. At first, we gave about £200,000 to the Irish Open. That, in turn, opened the door to contact being established with the European Tour, through Ken Schofield. Our officials went over and met him and his officials.

"A condition of putting up the money was that we would get an input into the commentary. This allowed us to provide speaking notes to the commentator on promoting Ireland. And on the highlights' film, we could intercut footage of what Ireland had to offer in golf. Once the Tour saw we were interested, they approached us with a view to supporting another tournament. And when I put this to Charlie McCreevy, he agreed. Our contribution this time was £250,000, which became instrumental in the launching of the Smurfit European Open. Now we had two tournaments.

"It meant we also had another film promoting Ireland abroad and again, we had editorial input. Thirdly, we did the Seniors (AIB Irish Seniors Open) and in between we did the Irish Ladies. This was all part of a policy I had formulated, distinguishing between marketing and salesmanship in our attempt at getting more people to book golfing holidays in this country. At one stage we were supporting four European Tour events – the Irish Open, the European Open, the Double-badge (North West of Ireland Open) and the Irish Seniors. And we had the Ladies. And the Ladies World Cup. All the while, there was an awareness that, wherever possible, these events should travel around the country."

Given the clear, precise manner in which he outlined these details, there seemed little chance of Ó hUiginn's views being disputed by contemporaries. Schofield certainly had no difficulty in agreeing with his account of those critical days in the development of tournament golf in this country. "I wasn't at Lake Nona in 1993, though I remember it, and the essence of what Padraig says is true," he said. "In fact, I would suggest that anything Ó hUiginn said to you, would be pretty close to the mark.

"Those were heady days. All the things that Padraig had helped to stimulate were now there for all to see. It was also a time when respective Ministers like Enda Kenny and Charlie McCreevy were meeting us and talking about the possibilities of getting the Ryder Cup. And I have to say that our perception in dealing with Government Ministers was that they were effectively operating like chief executives of Ireland Inc. That made all the negotiations very much easier.

"I should also point out that Mark Mortell, in his capacity as chairman of Bord Failte, was an excellent person, a man of substance. He looked after the detail where Ó hUiginn made the decisions, having been given the power to do so on behalf of the Government, which was totally helpful. There was belief that the Ryder Cup in Spain, the first 'double-language' staging of the event, would be hugely successful and having had that success, the Spaniards would want it again. My recollection is that the deal was finalised by Ó hUiginn because of his astuteness, doggedness and intuition."

Chapter 3 The Mandarin

Schofield then said: "A few weeks before the '97 Ryder Cup, Padraig reached me in my bedroom during the British Masters at the Forest of Arden. That was when he met the kind of ball-park numbers that we considered to be fair and reasonable. In the process, he effectively took any other challengers out of the race."

When the Fianna Fail/Labour Coalition Government went out of office, Charlie McCreevy was replaced as Minister for Tourism and Trade by Enda Kenny who would later become leader of Fine Gael and who, as it happened, was equally keen on golf. Bernard Allen became Minister for Sport. Kenny declared: "While I cannot speak for a future Minister, my view is that he or she would be very much off the mark if they were to undo the process we have set in motion. In fact, I couldn't envisage a future Minister for Tourism failing to lend full support to the idea of bringing the Ryder Cup here."

Like his predecessor, part of Kenny's familiarisation with the professional golfing scene was through the reasonably tolerable chore of attending the US Masters at Augusta National. He and Ó hUiginn played Pine Valley together and Kenny was fully supportive of the policy which the mandarin had initiated. So, in a golfing context, the transition was effectively seamless, even if there were occasions when rival politicians insisted on playing games.

Notable victims of this politicking were the Irish Ryder Cup Committee, set up in 1996 by Minister Allen, so as to ensure continuity. Chaired by former amateur golf international Hugh Mackeown, a Cork-born member of Portmarnock, the eight-member committee also included Des Smyth, Irish Permanent chief executive, Roy Douglas, former Irish international and national team captain, George Crosbie, PR consultant Pat Heneghan, PGA Irish Region secretary, Michael McCummiskey, Aidan Marsden of the Department of Education and Marc Howard of the Department of Education. Though Mackeown had no wish to be quoted on the committee's limited activities, he made it clear that the experience was not among his most cherished golfing memories.

In the event, in the wake of the formal announcement at Valderrama, Allen accused his successor as Minister for Sport, Dr Jim McDaid, of sacking the committee in order to "grab the glory" of Ireland's successful Ryder Cup bid. McDaid counter-claimed that Allen was being "disingenuous" in making such accusations.

Meanwhile, in the view of Ó hUiginn, the most significant political development in the context of ultimate success was when McCreevy came back into Government as Minister for Finance. "I informed him that I believed sport was an ideal way to sell Ireland," he said. "The result was that I got £5 million a year for five years for sports tourism, which was used for all kinds of events, including golf. He then extended that to 2007 in order that we could bid for the Solheim Cup, which we did. Unfortunately, it didn't work out."

This was a rare failure for Ó hUiginn and the reaction of Failte Ireland (previously Bord Failte, which was reconstituted in 2001) spoke volumes for his ongoing influence on tournament golf in Ireland. In January 2004, they pulled the plug on the Irish Ladies Open, by way of a public reprimand to the Ladies' European Tour. And the LET were left in no doubt that Government support was unlikely to be renewed, until they had something to offer in return, like for instance, the 2007 Ladies World Matchplay Championship.

The official line from the LET regarding the absence of the Irish event from the 2004 schedule was that Failte Ireland "were unable to commit to funding" the tournament. But money was not the problem. Rather was it a case of Irish officials, especially Ó hUiginn, being extremely angry regarding arrangements for the 2007 Solheim Cup.

With a substantial offer on the table, arranged by Ó hUiginn, negotiations took place in good faith for a staging at Killarney, which seemed to impress members of the Solheim family as a prospective venue when they visited it the previous summer. They also noted a successful staging of the Curtis Cup at Killarney in 1996, quite apart from two Irish Ladies Opens, one on the Lackabane Course where Iben Tinning emerged triumphant and the other at Mahony's Point where the title went to Sofie Gustafson.

Then, when a rival Welsh bid petered out, the Irish negotiators understood, quite reasonably, that the 2007 Solheim Cup was effectively secured. But unknown to them, the LET had done a reported £Stg7 million deal to keep the event in Sweden, where it was unquestionably a resounding success at the Barseback course near Malmo in autumn 2003.

Relations with the European Tour, however, remained decidedly cordial, not least for the fact that Ireland actually played host to four European events, during the critical run-up to the Valderrama decision. "By that stage, it was clear to me that they (European Tour), saw Ireland as a credible place for the Ryder Cup," said Ó hUiginn.

It may be appropriate to point out the inhibiting situation which Scotland's negotiators found themselves in when attempting to bring the Ryder Cup to their land for a second time. From a decision-making standpoint, their Minister McLeish was representing only a regional parliament and the sort of major spending that a Ryder Cup would entail, meant it being referred to Chancellor Gordon Brown, at Westminster. The Welsh situation was markedly different in that their bid was effectively coming from a private citizen, Terry Matthews, the owner of Celtic Manor.

How important was it then, from an Irish negotiating standpoint, to have direct access to Finance Minister McCreevy? "That was everything," replied Ó hUiginn. "We could get a decision in five minutes as opposed to the system with regional parliaments, where the process would be entirely different. As advisor to the Minister (McDaid) I could go directly to the

Chapter 3 The Mandarin

Minister for Finance and get his commitment to the necessary funds. It meant that everything was done speedily: red tape was kept down to the very minimum."

By way of launching the negotiation process in 1997, Ryder Cup officials dealt with Bord Failte chairman, Mortell, and Ó hUiginn. The former civil servant had, in fact, two roles, as a director of Bord Failte and as a special advisor to Dr Jim McDaid, the then Minister for Tourism and Sport.

"One of my main concerns was obviously to build up a strong relationship with Schofield," said Ó hUiginn. "Of course Richard Hills (Ryder Cup director) was also involved. I go back a long way with Schofield. I remember him inviting me over to Britain to play golf with himself and Neil Coles and we had discussions about getting more tournaments in Ireland. Later, I got the impression that he was imbued with a desire to reward Ireland for the commitment we had made to his tour, though those decisions were obviously in our own interests, as a strategy towards boosting golf tourism in this country.

"The important thing was that Schofield's feelings of goodwill made him favourably disposed to our getting the Ryder Cup. He knew the time was right and that we could run it successfully.

"When he and I got down to the serious talking, I have to say that I found him to be a very open, honest and straight negotiator. I never had any difficulty in understanding what he meant and what he was seeking. And despite all the stories about him, he wasn't particularly tough, in my view. Indeed we reached agreement fairly quickly, mainly because we had interests which converged. I remember putting the two of them (McDaid and Schofield) together on the phone and there were no arguments.

"The Tour wanted to base an agreement on annual payments up to 2005, but the total figure they put on the table was unacceptable to us. It was too high and I made it clear in my dual capacity that the Government could not pay all the money, whatever figure we decided upon. We were attracted to their idea of annual payments but I asked them if they had any objection to the presence of private assistance.

"It was a genuine difficulty for us, going to the Department and Minister for Finance for the sort of money that was being talked about. When I discussed the matter with the Minister for Finance, he agreed with me and, in answer to an approach from the European Tour, he said the same thing to them.

"Eventually, we came up with what became the final figure of £7.5 million (punts). I thought this was a reasonable figure spread over seven or possibly eight years. When I went again to Minister McCreevy to explain the situation, he asked how much I wanted. My response was: 'Would you be prepared to give us £4 million?' His answer was: 'Yes.'

"So, I reported this back to Jim McDaid with the rider that we would have to find £3.5 million from other sources. I then went to Smurfits, Waterford Crystal and Aer Lingus and asked each of them for £1.5 million. They all agreed. And when the Minister and I went to Valderrama to announce the agreement, we had those three on board.

"When we announced it, we deliberately stayed out of the issue of where it would be held. Though we were aware that a number of courses were interested in staging the event, we considered that the precise venue should not be a concern of the Government or Bord Failte. We could not be seen to have a favourite. Indeed I remember telling the Minister that our job was to bring the event to Ireland. After that, commercial bidders would come in.

"We remained completely neutral even though I always suspected that it was going to be very hard to beat the Smurfit organisation, given the quality of their course and the fact that they had a share in the European Open. Interestingly, Michael Smurfit came to us and said that if he got the Ryder Cup at The K Club, it would involve very big expense. So he couldn't afford the additional expense of being one of the three commercial supporters.

"This left us temporarily stuck, but fortunately we got AIB on board to take Smurfit's place. Further problems arose when Aer Lingus got into difficulties and felt they had no option other than to drop their share of the sponsorship. We spoke to them and suggested that the European Tour would be prepared to forego payments until Aer Lingus had got out of their present difficulties. That they could pay it all at the end. To be honest, it seemed like a good deal to us, but they said no. Which I have to say was a big worry for us."

"Regrettable but necessary," was how an Aer Lingus spokesman described the decision to scrap their Ryder Cup involvement on November 9th, 2001. By that stage, the state airline had already paid over roughly half of their financial commitment of £1.1 million to the tournament. But withdrawal would save the company a further £600,000 in repayments and considerably more in terms of their projected spend between then and 2006.

A major promotional campaign at a cost of about £2 million, was envisaged, right up to the event itself. The decision also had an impact on the European Open to which Aer Lingus contributed £50,000 per year, along with an additional £10,000 in travel vouchers as a prize to the leading Irish professional in the event. "In all cases, we believe we got value for money," the spokesman concluded.

With a view to filling the gap left by Aer Lingus, an approach was made to Philip Lynch, chairman of Bord Bia (1995 to 2005) who had been very much involved with Ó hUiginn in the Irish Golf Trust, to which the board contributed. Lynch brought the proposal to his board, who agreed that the sponsorship would be a natural fit for Bord Bia in terms of targeting key export markets such as the UK and the US. So it was that the decision was taken to transfer

Chapter 3 The Mandarin

the sponsorship to Bord Bia, effective from November 2001. With that, Bord Bia officially became one of the Ryder Cup partner sponsors.

Meanwhile, as part of the annual payments, Bord Failte and the partner sponsors would be granted publicity at all qualifying events, with signage on every course. Given the obvious expense involved in such an undertaking, however, they considered it more prudent to choose the larger, more accessible tournaments for an actual presence, though the current Ryder Cup table would be publicised at every qualifying event. On top of that, there were deals about Ryder Cup tickets and so on. These sort of details were handled by Bord Failte while there were other deals on merchandising.

"When it was all agreed, I thought it was a fantastic deal," enthused Ó hUiginn. "Even more so now, when you look at what Wales are paying." (In the aftermath of the 2002 staging at The Belfry, Michael Smurfit estimated it would cost £stg 50 million to get the Ryder Cup to this country at the values of that time). Ó hUiginn continued: "From an Irish perspective, the 1997 staging at Valderrama was not as big as we ultimately imagined it could be. The important thing for us was that the potential was clearly there. And when placed in the context of the going rate at that time, I believe we did very well at £7.5 million. All the publicity and the fact that the State was carrying only £4 million of the overall outlay."

Was there a sense of achievement at landing such a cherished prize? "Oh yes," he replied, unhesitatingly. "We were hugely gratified at having clinched the deal and my feeling was that we got it because we were great supporters of the European Tour in Ireland. (American Express were also committed to a 2002 staging at Mount Juliet). Our strategy clearly paid dividends."

And Schofield? "Where the Ryder Cup was concerned, Spain marked a significant departure for us in that it was the first time we were dealing at national level," he replied. "In many respects, Spain set the marker. The Spanish government's input was to support a package of tournaments through the Turespana series, and Ireland learned from them.

"But the Irish deal was different. Apart from the additional tournaments which brought Ireland into the frame in the first place, our eight-year deal gave the Tour a pot of money we could use to develop. This meant that both sides effectively got what they wanted."

Was he pleased to have seen such a momentous deal for the Irish being completed during his tenure at the head of the European Tour? "Most definitely yes," he replied. "We believe that good deals leave something on the table for both parties. We believe that's the case with Ireland, who have delivered what we asked.

"The alternating process between the PGA and the Tour meant that we were going to be coming back to The Belfry in 2001. So '05 was our call. And it could have been Spain, while the Swedes were also making noises at that time. But they never got to the level Ireland were at. The evidence was there in Ireland's pioneering the double-badge event (North West of Ireland Open, launched at Galway Bay in 1999); support by Nissan and Failte Ireland for the Irish Open and AIB's sponsorship of the Irish Seniors.

"The fact was that if Ireland met what we wanted, the answer was yes. We didn't believe in the idea of horse-trading. There was also the belief that Ireland deserved the Ryder Cup, not only because of the Government's financial commitment, but because of the nation's passion for the game. We knew instinctively they would deliver a welcoming venue for a visiting team and the thousands of supporters for whom the Ryder Cup is now one of the world's truly great sporting occasions."

Speaking like a businessman, Dr McDaid put it rather more succinctly. "The bottom line in securing the deal was money," he said after the announcement at Valderrama. Meanwhile, on being asked which venue was likely to be successful, Schofield gave the typically political answer: "There are five or more courses, possibly as many as 10, capable of holding the Ryder Cup in Ireland," he said. "The two main criteria which the committee (Ryder Cup) will assess in reaching a decision is the quality of the venue itself, and a course that is also able to provide a challenge to the players."

And amid all the excitement, it was interesting to note that the Tour did, indeed, spell Ó hUiginn's name correctly.

Six years later in 2003, a handsome postscript was written to his career in the field of golf diplomacy, when he was accorded the distinction of being made a Life Vice President of the PGA European Tour "...... in recognition of his pivotal role in cultivating professional golf in Ireland."

◆

Chapter 4

The Deal

Chapter 4 The Deal

The executive director of the British PGA was seething. And Sandy Jones didn't mince words when expressing an acute sense of abandonment to Derek Lawrenson of the *Daily Mail*. "We will not be bullied over the Ryder Cup," he said. "We would rather see the trophy in a museum than that happening." The "that" to which he referred was the disclosure in the *Mail*, totally unknown to him, that the 2009 (now 2010) Ryder Cup would be going to Celtic Manor in Wales and not to a Scottish venue, as was widely anticipated.

"It could be the most damaging thing that has ever happened to the Ryder Cup, apart from the American players and their wives running on to the 17th green at Brookline," added Jones. Later in the article, which was published in May 2001, Lawrenson wrote: "Jones found it impossible to disguise his disappointment that (Ken) Schofield, a fellow Scot who he has known for 20 years, should have given the story to this paper. 'I thought we were friends,' he (Jones) said. When somebody suggested to him the old adage that you should never do business with your friends, he nodded knowingly."

Jones's position was greatly weakened, of course, by the fact that in the same year, the European Tour officially took management control of an event which had been the property of the British PGA since its launch in 1927. A new, limited liability partnership company was formed with a 60-20-20 shareholding ratio between the Tour, the British PGA and the national PGAs on the Continent.

So it was that for the first time on American soil, Europe's involvement in the matches at Oakland Hills was managed completely from the headquarters of the PGA European Tour at Wentworth. Among other things, it represented quite a change from 1989, when the Tour had to settle for a so-called facility fee of £100,000 along with relatively modest television revenues from the BBC.

None of this would have come as a surprise to Dr Smurfit, who was very familiar with the business skills of Schofield. From the meetings they had had over sponsorship of the European Open, he knew that the Scot drove a hard bargain. And he expected nothing less when they sat down to discuss the possibility of the Ryder Cup going to The K Club. Dr Smurfit was, after all, a man well used to handling major business deals in his own right; a man renowned for his vision, and acknowledged as Ireland's leading businessman of recent decades.

It has been said of him that he has a great talent for seeing where he wants to go and what he needs to do to get there. And once he sets out on that road, there is a single-mindedness which is very difficult to shift. His objective normally represents a very high bar; he is painstaking about details and can instantly see what others might not comprehend in a week.

As a business associate put it: "You know when you talk to him that there's no room for bullshit. Tell him what you think he wants to hear and you'll get blown away. In business, he's hard-nosed, concentrated and leaves no room for flim-flam."

He is also known to be hugely disciplined and if he agrees an appointment for 7.30, he means it. If a meeting is set for eight in the morning and if he says the meeting will finish at 8.10, it will finish at 8.10, by which time he will have accomplished what he set out to do. Even avowed adversaries would acknowledge that it took huge vision and a brilliant mind to take a tiny little Irish family business, based in a factory in Clonskeagh, and build it into a multi-national business with an annual turnover of close on €4 billion. In Irish business, only Tony Ryan of Ryanair and Sir Anthony O'Reilly could be compared with him.

"It was clear to me from the outset, that his (Schofield's) primary concern would be the interest of the European Tour," said Dr Smurfit. And as PGA chief Jones learned to his cost, this remained valid, even if it happened to impinge on a close friendship.

Not even the hugely powerful Mark McCormack escaped his wrath, even though McCormack's International Management Group were entrusted with organising the Heritage Tournament in Schofield's honour at Woburn during the week following the Ryder Cup at Oakland Hills. "I had a real rant," said Schofield. "I blackballed one of his (McCormack's) World Matchplay Championship dinners. I gave him the silent treatment as opposed to the hairdryer treatment.

"I have always seen my primary function as promoting the Tour, even if it might have appeared that I was being slightly disloyal to my native Scotland. I felt that simply because Scotland were getting the Open every second year or two years out of three, paid for, incidentally, by all of our visitors, they hadn't a God-given right to be number one in golf. Other countries like Ireland were investing heavily with a view to taking that banner away."

Alluding to the dynamism of his former boss, his successor, George O'Grady, said: "There is no way you could live your life if you saw Ken Schofield every day. We think similarly, but when the going gets tough, I like to think I have him on my side and I would like to think that he thinks the same." Jaime Patino, owner of Valderrama, observed: "He's very opinionated and he doesn't like criticism, though over the years he has accepted it. He has upset certain people but, overall, the European Tour and European golf owe him a great deal of gratitude. Ken Schofield has brought the European Tour to the forefront of world golf."

This view was roundly endorsed by Royal and Ancient secretary, Peter Dawson, when he said: "It's his determination to see the Tour grow that is so striking. He is never one to take 'no' for an answer. When obstacles present themselves, he won't lie down. He just goes through, around or over them." Add these characteristics to what the Tour's chief referee, John

Chapter 4 The Deal

Paramor, described as a man "consumed by golf" and one gets a ready picture of a formidable adversary across a negotiating table.

Against their respective backgrounds, it is clear that Dr Smurfit and Schofield both brought enviable skills to this process. And there was unquestionably a high level of mutual respect.

Most observers felt the Scot would continue in his post until after the staging of the Ryder Cup in Ireland, but he retired at the end of 2004, handing over to his long-time assistant, O'Grady. By way of explanation, he said at the time: "I have asked myself, given that I do not want to do this job forever, do I want to do other things? The answer is 'yes'. I don't want to walk away and put my feet up. They have asked me to do a serious consultancy for the Tour and I will do that."

When I was in Schofield's office in Wentworth during his last year at the helm, he revealed details of what remains one of the most staggering deals in the history of the European Tour. Effectively, it came down to a commitment from Dr Smurfit that in return for getting the Ryder Cup, his company would sponsor the European Open all the way up to 2015 – 10 years on from the original date of 2005.

"I'm amazed at what's happened to the Ryder Cup," Schofield mused with typical enthusiasm, "especially when I look back to my first one, which was Laurel Valley, Pennsylvania, in 1975. It was actually my first visit to the United States and within 24 hours of arriving there, I found myself being invited to Arnold Palmer's home. And via Arnold Palmer, I flew in a private plane with Colin Snape, my counterpart in the PGA at that time, to see Jack Nicklaus's emerging development at Muirfield Village.

"I remember the opening foursomes match in which Brian Barnes and Bernard Gallacher, a trusted pair for us, were roundly beaten (5 and 4) by Jack (Nicklaus) and Tom Weiskopf. And I can recall Tom apologising to Jack for missing a fairway. I also remember Eamonn Darcy playing foursomes on the second day with Guy Hunt. And I remember some great American judges commenting on Eamonn's technique, while pointing out how beautifully he got through the ball. Of course the high point of that staging was Barnes beating Jack twice in the one day."

Watched by no more than a few thousand spectators, it was all pretty innocent stuff compared with the vast commercial undertaking which The K Club were attempting to bring to Co Kildare. And the disclosure of the European Open deal nailed the widespread, cynical view, certainly among Irish observers, that success for Dr Smurfit was always a foregone conclusion. Rather did it illustrate graphically the extent to which the Irish businessman was prepared to go to realise a cherished dream. And though the Smurfit company has since been taken over by Madison Dearborn, there is an assurance that the contract will stand for the full term. Among other things, Schofield explained why he waited 16 months after the September 1997 announcement of Ireland as the destination of the Ryder Cup, before naming the successful venue. "During that time, we visited our friends at Portmarnock GC and told them we were not going to insult a great club by asking what we had decided was then the commercial, going rate," he recalled. "And we believe they accepted that.

"At the time, many traditionalists argued that, surely, Portmarnock should be the place. But we had witnessed not only the development of The K Club and their sponsorship of the European Open; we had seen what Tim Mahony had done at Mount Juliet. And we'd seen what Hugo Flinn and his son Donal had done at Druids Glen.

"Let's be clear about this, we're talking commercialism, unashamedly as far as I'm concerned. And yes, the Tour was using leverage we had access to only once in every eight years at that time, given the way the European stagings were rotated between ourselves and the PGA." (The way became open for this change when, in a final compromise with the British PGA, it was agreed that the event would go to Scotland in 2014, after the Welsh staging in 2010.)

From an early stage, Portmarnock recognised that they faced an uphill battle. When Ireland's successful bid was announced at Valderrama, Dr Jim McDaid, the then Minister for Sport, was visibly taken aback when questioned on the so-called women's issue. On being reminded that Portmarnock was an all-male club and that tax-payers' money would be funding the Ryder Cup effort, he said: "The Government will make them (Portmarnock) quite aware of our policy on equality."

Still, the club's honorary secretary at the time, Moss Buckley, indicated that his members had no intention of bowing-out without a fight. "With the approval of our members, we would be prepared to seek sponsorship for the necessary money," he said. "As the country's premier club, we believe it is incumbent on us to do so."

By the time negotiations had reached an advanced stage, however, Buckley and his members were beginning to feel the financial heat, especially when confronted by a so-called venue fee of £750,000. So it was that the honorary secretary effectively opted out of the bid by declaring that Portmarnock had no wish to engage in a Dutch auction.

For his part, Schofield then concentrated on the proprietary clubs which, he believed, were best positioned to give him what he wanted. He recalled meeting Dr Smurfit on the 17th hole at Valderrama in 1997 after the announcement was made that Ireland had landed the Ryder Cup. Indeed I, too, was on Valderrama's 17th that day and heard Dr Smurfit remark wistfully: "Just imagine all of this at The K Club."

During the ensuing months, Schofield met, in turn, with Druids Glen, Mount Juliet and

Chapter 4 The Deal

The K Club which, in his view, were the only three venues in contention. "One of these was going to be successful," he said. "At one of these meetings, I remember Michael Smurfit putting the question: 'When do you feel you will have lost your leverage regarding the next Ryder Cup; when will you be at your weakest?' And I replied that it would be on the day after the decision was made, because you have only one go at getting what you want.

"By that, I meant that when the announcement was made, we could lose the other two applicant clubs as future business associates on the grounds that they were interested only in the Ryder Cup. Or one of them might make me look like a fool by disclosing that they would have doubled what the successful club had offered.

"With that, Michael took a sip of wine, looked at his company colleague present and said 'Ken makes a fair point.' He then eye-balled me across the table and said: 'How would 10 years of the European Open after 2005 do?' And I replied: 'I think that would be very seriously considered, Michael.'"

Was it an offer Schofield couldn't refuse? Ever the canny Scot, he said: "Let's just say we certainly didn't refuse it, given that where Druids Glen and Mount Juliet were concerned, the other key areas were all going to be fairly similar."

It had become a custom for Dr Smurfit and a K Club colleague to meet with Schofield in London during Cheltenham race week and on this occasion the get-together was at fashionable Annabel's. David Adamson, who accompanied Dr Smurfit, recalled: "As it was getting closer and closer to Ireland being chosen, we badly wanted the Ryder Cup. John O'Leary proved very approachable as a member of the Ryder Cup committee; Failte Ireland were doing their thing and we were doing ours.

"On the way to Annabel's, I remember Michael asking me in the taxi: 'Just tell me Dave, what's it going to take?' And I replied: 'A fee, probably £1 million. And we'll have to maintain our commitment to the European Open.' I knew the last thing the Tour would want was that we would get the Ryder Cup and then bugger off, as it were. 'How long do you think we'd have to do?' Michael asked. 'I would think five-plus years,' I told him.

"While we were talking, Michael was taking notes, which is his way. Then he turned to me and said: 'This is what we'll do. We'll do 10 years from 2005.' I remember noting how Schofield, as only he could do, hid his excitement. Both of them remained dead-pan. There was also a commitment that the European Open prize fund would increase incrementally over that period."

This has clearly been reflected in the development of the tournament in recent years. For instance, the prize fund for the 1999 event, which was staged seven months after The K Club was awarded the Ryder Cup, was €1,357,142 of which the winner, Lee Westwood, received

€316,660. By 2005, the fund had risen to €3,336,288, with €556,048 going to the champion. This represented an increase of €145,056 on 2004 alone. It also meant that the total prize money for the European Open under the Smurfit banner from 1995 to 2005, amounted to €22,016,012.

Commenting on those figures, Dr Smurfit, said: "The European Open is a truly international event, as our list of champions clearly indicates. To remain at the forefront of the European Tour it is important that our event gets the prize fund it deserves. In that context, I would like to thank all our support sponsors and in particular our partners, Fáilte Ireland, Budweiser and Lucent Technologies for their continued backing of the Smurfit European Open."

Meanwhile, it was hardly surprising that Dr Smurfit should have retained a vivid recollection of that decisive, London meeting. Was a commitment to the 10 European Opens after 2005 not rather excessive, when he had only to tilt the balance over his rivals? "On the face of it, yes," he replied. "But not when I asked myself if I wanted to sponsor the European Open for 10 more years purely as a business proposition, outside of the Ryder Cup.

"Once I decided that I did, then the obvious thing to do was to make a splash that was certain to sink everyone else. Effectively, it followed from my business decision.

"You could talk about the European Open being our trump card, but in my view it went beyond that. We've been sponsoring junior golf in Ireland for nearly 40 years. And we still do. And we sponsored the PGA Irish Championship for many years. So there was no doubting our commitment to helping golf in this country, as opposed to being motivated simply with buying the Ryder Cup, as has been alleged in some quarters."

Then, focusing directly on a cherished dream, he said: "Getting the Ryder Cup was always going to be a battle. I saw Ken Schofield as a shrewd cookie. I'd known him a long time and I knew he was going to play his cards as closely to his chest as I was playing mine. Frankly, I was very disappointed when it went to Spain in 1997. Why Spain before Ireland? Compared with us, Spain were latecomers to golf.

"That was when I became aware that there was a lot of politics going on and I had yet to learn the political game. The main runners for the 2005 staging were: here, Mount Juliet, Druids Glen and Portmarnock and I was conscious that the traditionalists in the PGA would want to go to Portmarnock. That was the players' view as well, and it was definitely a runner before the women's membership issue broke.

"There was also the fact that while they had been generous in making their course available for the Irish Open, they hadn't been great supporters of the European Tour in recent years. But I would always acknowledge and respect the traditionalist view. In fact, my son

Chapter 4 The Deal

Michael's father-in-law (Frank Muldowney) is a trustee there.

"Tim Mahony, of course, I saw as a very real rival. But given the location of Mount Juliet, I didn't think he could get enough hotel rooms in the area. And it would have been a nightmare to get people from Dublin in large numbers. To be honest, once it was coming to Ireland, I felt quietly confident that we were the frontrunners. Even with Ken (Schofield) trying to convince me that we were simply one of four, I felt we had the inside track.

"We'd had a number of Americans over such as Tiger Woods, Mark O'Meara, Tom Lehman and the late Payne Stewart, among others, and we asked their genuine opinion. Most of them didn't know Portmarnock, though I gather O'Meara played there in the Irish Open (in 1987). Either way, their response was very encouraging from our perspective. There was always the danger, of course, that such support by Americans for our course would not necessarily help our bid. But that was for the Ryder Cup committee to decide.

"Let me put it this way: I saw us as 4/6 favourites. But there was still a doubt there. Absolutely. Up to the last minute."

In respect of venture capitalists Madison Dearborn, who acquired the Jefferson Smurfit Group in 2002, he pointed out that they had accepted all the contracts and agreements which Smurfits had in place at the time of the takeover, including employees' contracts. "They have no wish to destroy the culture of the company," he said at the time. "So, these contracts will be honoured. In doing their due diligence on our company, they took into consideration our commitments, including that of finishing this place (The K Club), insofar as we were just starting the new clubhouse at that time. These were all things that were discussed before the takeover documents were signed.

"Clearly, the K Club is potentially for sale after the Ryder Cup. Who will buy it? Who knows, it may even be sold beforehand. I wouldn't like to see it go outside the (Smurfit) family but if somebody were to come along with a silly price for a trophy asset, who am I to stand in their way?"

For his part, Schofield had reason to be pleased with the fruits of his discussions with Dr Smurfit. As a negotiator, he had learned well, from such masters as Mark McCormack and from John Jacobs, his predecessor on what was then the European Tour Players Division (ETPD).

As he told me: "It was the way Michael asked that question. In negotiation, you've got to create at least a perception, if not a reality, that there is a race. And you know that when decision-day comes and the announcement is made, you can't knock on a bidder's door again and say 'I've got it wrong. I needed 40 million instead of 20.' McCormack taught us that.

"On the day I came into this job in January 1975, John Jacobs urged me to see Mark

McCormack, soon. 'Introduce yourself,' he said. 'He'll argue; he'll debate; he'll negotiate fiercely. But my experience of him is that once you've done a deal, he'll never break it.' And he never did."

I told Schofield of an interview I once did with McCormack in his suite in the Old Course Hotel at St Andrews at the ungodly hour of 7.30am. And of my curiosity as to how he determined what the going rate was for a contract in the international market place. "You keep asking for more until somebody shouts stop," he replied, without, as they say, batting an eyelid. Schofield nodded. "I think that's our job," he claimed. "We feel we're in a very successful sector and our objective is to maintain it; to get to what is sustainable. And if that means using prime tournament dates as a lever, so be it. For instance, I never imagined that we'd have a prize fund of €3 million for the French Open.

"I remember being at The K Club at the Smurfit European Open in August of that year, and having a drink with Payne Stewart, who played in the tournament. His career was in something of a trough at the time and I remember he went to Vancouver the following week, rather than the World Series, for which he hadn't qualified. And he finished second in Canada, which started him on the road back, culminating in his victory in the US Open the following June.

"That was when we signed the contract for the Ryder Cup. So yes, we knew for four months what we were doing, before we announced it. The only reason I can recall for delaying the announcement was to get the season out of the way. There were also negotiations to be completed with Bord Failte. Everything else was in order. From March to August was five months so we had had plenty of time to deliberate on Michael's offer, which had been huge."

He then talked about the two unsuccessful venues. "We decided they had to know of our decision before it was made public, so on the night before the announcement, we visited with Tim Mahony and his colleagues in a Dublin hotel," he recalled. "When I broke the news to Tim, he thanked me before adding 'you will not expect me to agree with your decision, but it's your decision. Come have a drink.' (As Dr Mahony remembers that particular meeting, it was he who insisted on Schofield buying the drink. "And I asked for a large whiskey," he said with a half-smile).

"Where Druids Glen were concerned, we had problems tracking down Hugo and Donal or their manager, Denis Kane. Eventually we got them by mobile phone and they were grateful for the call. Hugo then suggested that when their hotel was up and running, we might consider using it. Which we certainly will."

There was no doubting Dr Mahony's disappointment. As early as October 1996, he stated

Chapter 4 The Deal

that he was ready to pay "whatever it takes" to bring the Ryder Cup to Mount Juliet, which was designed by Nicklaus and officially opened in July 1991, the same time as The K Club. My understanding was that Dr Mahony's commitment would extend to £5 million, if necessary. Five years after the venue's opening, he had said: "There are probably three leading Irish candidates – ourselves, The K Club and Portmarnock. It would be invidious of me to comment about The K Club which, as it happens, I don't know well enough to make direct comparisons.

"Portmarnock, meanwhile, is highly regarded internationally, with a wonderful tradition of staging important events such as the Canada Cup, the Irish Open and, more recently, the Walker Cup. But for logistical reasons, it is simply not suitable for an event of this nature. Traffic has always been a major problem and a comparison between the stagings of the Irish Open there and at Mount Juliet tells us all we need to know in that regard. We cleared all the car parks in less than 90 minutes." Dr Mahony could speak with some authority about the traffic situation at Portmarnock, given that he lives down the road in Sutton.

But the die was cast. In the course of a press conference in Jury's Hotel, Ballsbridge, Dublin, in January 1999, it was formally announced that the 2005 Ryder Cup would be at The K Club. "Your population may be small but your impact on golf is enormous," declared Schofield, in a direct reference to the significant investment which had ultimately landed golf's great prize.

"The Ryder Cup is the single most important asset to the European Tour. It's a vital piece of our business and has enhanced the funding of many of our tournaments. In that context, Mount Juliet and Druids Glen, which have staged the Irish Open in the 1990s, stood ready to play host to the event. But it is going to The K Club whose support of the European Open (since 1995) pre-dates the decision to bring the Ryder Cup to Ireland."

Though the European Tour had clearly played a powerful role in the exercise, technically the decision was made by the six-member Ryder Cup committee. It comprised the 1982 Irish Open champion, John O'Leary, Neil Coles, Phil Weaver, Angel Gallardo, David Huish and Brian Anderson.

"It will give us a solid base on which to promote the event in earnest," was how Mark Mortell, chairman of Bord Failte, reacted to the announcement. "From now until 2005 (2006), we will set about achieving the major rewards which the Ryder Cup is certain to deliver for Irish tourism."

Though Mortell was kept fully informed about the pending announcement – for which, incidentally, many of the Government and Bord Failte top-brass were otherwise engaged – he claimed not to have known the identity of the successful venue. "Our objective was simply to get the Ryder Cup to Ireland," he said. "We accepted that the venue would always be in the gift of the PGA European Tour."

Minister for Sport, Dr Jim McDaid, was among those unable to attend the announcement. But he said: "I regard my negotiating this holding of the Ryder Cup matches as a major feature of my tenure of office. I must also thank Enda Kenny and Bernard Allen (ministers in the previous Government) who, in their tenure of office, did much to advance Ireland's case."

Meanwhile, there was a generous response from Denis Kane, the chief executive of Druids Glen. "We wish The K Club every success and are confident their effort will enhance the status of courses such as ourselves, Mount Juliet, Portmarnock and Ballybunion in Irish golf."

Dr Smurfit was understandably delighted. Speaking from Venezuela, where he was on a business trip, he said: "It has been our ambition to build a complex worthy of staging the most prestigious golfing competition in the world. The importance of this event for Irish sport, Irish tourism and for the country as a whole, cannot be overstated. All our clubs will benefit from this decision and I feel it will lead to more great courses being designed and developed here."

Arnold Palmer was equally pleased. "There can be no greater accolade than to have our creation played by the elite of world golf, the Ryder Cuppers," said the great man, who retains the distinction of having been the last playing captain of a Ryder Cup team, when he led the triumphant American line-up at East Lake CC, Atlanta, in 1963.

Amid all the congratulations and general sense of well-being in the hotel that day, however, Schofield struck a discordant note with regard to the Republic's premier links course. "Portmarnock's time as a Ryder Cup venue would have been for the 1973 matches, which went to Muirfield," he said. "We're in a timescale in which a proprietary establishment as a sound business resource is a powerful factor in choosing a venue."

Among those who strenuously disagreed with that view was a former Ryder Cup player who, as a gifted broadcaster for the BBC, has become acknowledged as The Voice of Golf. The very mention of the Ryder Cup got Peter Alliss really fired-up about money. "I was just reading where one of your lads, Roy Keane, is not too pleased with being offered 40,000 quid a week to play for Manchester United," he said, adroitly switching sports in the wake of the Ryder Cup announcement. "Apparently it's an insult to his talent – for kicking a bag of wind around.

"So I'm thinking 'Oh! The bloody world's gone potty.' Christ, in these times of crisis in the (British) Health Service, we could pay three nurses a year's salary each, for what some of these Premiership players get for kicking a ball about each week. The whole thing's silly."

These observations seemed a world away from Ryder Cup images of friendship, triumph and heartbreak against American rivals – until Alliss supplied the context. "The greatest course

Chapter 4 The Deal

to stage the Ryder Cup for the first time in Ireland would have been Portmarnock," he declared.

"I say this because of its history, the majesty of the links, the very feel of the place and the memory of almost 40,000 delirious fans cheering John O'Leary to victory in the 1982 Irish Open. But we know money dictates that things should be otherwise. The PGA European Tour have sold it to the highest bidder. And with it their souls.

"As someone who cares passionately about the Ryder Cup, I find it all rather sad. Everything nowadays seems to be reduced to money, money, money, money, money, with the result that a competition which was always tough and bloody and wonderful, has been stripped of much of the charm. But I'm enough of a realist to know that in this Roy Keane society, life must go on and the bills must be paid. Still, it doesn't lessen the disappointment."

The Alliss family, father and son, have been synonymous with the Ryder Cup almost since its inception in 1927. "We played 11 Ryder Cups between us (Percy 3 and Peter 8) and my father wasn't eligible to play on a couple of occasions," recalled junior. "Our feat of playing in the Ryder Cup as father and son has been equalled by the Garridos (Antonio in 1979 and Ignacio in 1997) but they've got a bloody long way to go before they catch up with us.

"Against that background, it is to be expected that I would have a great passion for it. But naturally, I am conscious of the fact that the BBC don't do it on television any more, which means that mass audiences don't get to see it any more. Money. That's why Sky have all the golf: nearly all the sport if it comes to it. They've just bought their way in. So the public's interest in the Ryder Cup has become somewhat detached, long-range.

"Then there are the venues. In the years when my father and me were in the team, we played on traditional links courses like Southport and Ainsdale, Royal Lytham and at Birkdale, where I had my swansong in 1969. For a variety of reasons, many of the traditional courses are no longer capable of staging an event like the Ryder Cup. But I believe Portmarnock certainly could, provided the access was improved.

"Dubliners won't thank me for this but getting down that narrow little road to the Portmarnock clubhouse was horrendous, even when I played there 30 years ago. I often thought they might put a footbridge across the little inlet towards Joe Carr's old house (in Sutton). Any sort of access to the area of the first hole would do the trick.

"But, of course, as a members' club Portmarnock couldn't get among the big bidders. Looking back at the history of the Ryder Cup, it seems almost unthinkable that it's been played only once in Scotland. And with classic irony, this happened largely because the Scots didn't want it. Turnberry and Carnoustie were too far out of the way, St Andrews didn't want it because it's owned by the public.

"Where else were you going to go? Troon? No, no. The members wouldn't have it. Too much of a disruption. So it went to places like Ganton and Lindrick and Wentworth. But it didn't go to Ireland, where it should have gone long before now." In this context, Alliss insisted he was not necessarily promoting a return to old-style traditional courses of the links variety. Indeed he acknowledged that there were a number of aspects to be considered, other than the actual playing arena.

As he pointed out: "The traditional courses in these islands are all owned by the members. And if your course happens to be on the Open rota, you're going to have to accept major disruption every seven or eight years. There's increasing resistance against this.

"On the other hand, new, proprietary courses are specifically geared for major events and The Belfry, where the Ryder Cup is returning in 2001 (2002), has come to be acknowledged as one of the best venues for any tournament in Britain. It has a hotel with close on 500 bedrooms; is readily accessible on the outskirts of Birmingham; you can park a million cars there and you can get plenty of people on the golf course.

"People tend to forget that on the first two days, Ryder Cups only have four matches on the course. So, in an attendance of 30,000, you could have upwards of 8,000 following a particularly attractive match. Against that background, The Belfry has become a great success. Then there is the question of crowd security. Crimes like kidnapping, terrorism and common assault have to be considered. These are things we never had to think about 30 or 40 years ago and which are far more manageable at a modern, purpose-built venue.

"So I don't have any hang-up about places like The K Club. As far as the Ryder Cup in 2005 is concerned, however, the case for Portmarnock is overwhelming. Top of the list is that, unlike the other leading, traditional courses in these islands, it has the advantage of being close to a capital city, an international airport and a broad choice of hotels.

"The lone staging of the Ryder Cup in Scotland became special because it was at Muirfield. And with the greatest of respect to The K Club, I believe Portmarnock would have had a similarly special appeal for what could be Ireland's only Ryder Cup. Provided, of course, that they were to overcome the access problem."

Alliss then turned his thoughts to The K Club. "I've been there several times and it's not the easiest place to get to," he said. "But it is a lovely set-up. Early drainage problems have been overcome and the general quality of the venue cannot be questioned. The house is magnificent and there are those delightful, man-made gardens. Good luck to Dr Smurfit.

"I have no doubt but that their staging of the Ryder Cup will be a triumph as far as Irish attendances are concerned. And it will be a financial success, which should make the Tour happy. And if the Europeans win, everything will be wonderful. And that's the end of the

Chapter 4 The Deal

story.

"All the boys in the blazers can turn around and say 'there you are, we went to Spain and you said it was going to be crap and we won. Wasn't it wonderful? And wasn't it terribly wrong of you to be criticising us the way you did.' Ah the boys with the blazers. When I started in tournament golf, there were only a handful of people around the whole of the PGA. Now you pick up their handbook and there's dozens of people with European blazers on and dozens of people with PGA Belfry blazers on. And you think everyone must be on fairly good salaries and you wonder how we can afford it all."

So, had we reached the stage whereby the Ryder Cup had become an uncontrollable monster, increasingly out of touch with reality? "In a way that's true," he replied. "But whatever we may feel about it, I believe it is now destined to run its course. And all the while, we'll have its appeal softened for us by being told that personalities like the Azingers and the Faldos and the Seves are not really angry with each other and all of that.

"The key is that it remains competitive. I remember as a boy when the Wightman Cup tennis for women was a great thing but they (the Americans) kept on winning, so it was scrubbed. That won't happen to the Ryder Cup, at least not in the foreseeable future.

"Some writers would have had us believe that it was on the verge of extinction years ago – a notion I never subscribed to. Anyway we had Nicklaus being hailed as its saviour by suggesting that it be extended to three days and with the Europeans joining the British and Irish and all that. All good politics."

Alliss concluded: "The Ryder Cup has always been precious to me. Down the years from my father's day, it has been a wonderful competition and I want it to remain a showcase for the best of European golf. But I resent what I see as the greedy attitude of the European Tour. The sort of attitude that says 'Who's paying us the most? Fine, we'll go there.' Somehow, it doesn't seem to sit so well with the image of dear old Sam Ryder and what he had in mind when he started it all, 72 years ago."

Alliss's views in *The Irish Times* received a resounding endorsement in the next issue of the British magazine *Golf World,* the cover of which informed its readers – 'The Ryder Cup: Why The K Club is the wrong choice.' Inside, Peter Masters wrote about 'The 750K Club', a reference to the fee required by the European Tour before any aspiring venue would be considered. Other headlines read: 'The Ryder Cup might never go back to a traditional links, now that it has been sold to the highest bidder in 2005' and 'It is an event that deserves respect but you can't help feeling that it is being sold down the river.'

After quoting Alliss liberally through the piece, Masters concluded: "The European Tour are running the Ryder Cup in the interests of their members (the players) and the interests of good business. They are not running the Ryder Cup to protect it for what it stands for. The Ryder Cup Committee, which includes members of the European Tour and the British PGA, weighed up the options and plumped for The K Club which, pound for pound, seemed the best choice."

As a keen follower of sport, Schofield would also have empathised with much of what Alliss contended. But in his European Tour role, he couldn't afford such philanthropic views. It certainly wouldn't have sat well with his image of being a noisy, pugnacious terrier for what he pursued. Meanwhile, his preference for a Welsh deal over that of his native Scotland for the 2010 Ryder Cup matches, proved that he is primarily a pragmatist.

Thus, several years after those heady days around Dublin and its environs, the great dealmaker could permit himself a satisfied smile when reflecting on his role in bringing the Ryder Cup to Ireland and ultimately to The K Club. "I believe 2006 will be a fantastic event, combining the best in how the event has developed on both sides of the Atlantic," he predicted with typical self-assurance. "In fact, the Ryder Cup is coming to Ireland at the right time for everybody".

But the timing wouldn't be quite as he had originally anticipated.

♦

Chapter 5

The Wait

Chapter 5 The Wait

s a gesture to the City of St Louis on the occasion of its bi-centenary, the US Open went to Bellerive Country Club in 1965. Though long and demanding, the course, designed by Robert Trent Jones, was rather raw, having been opened only five years previously. Yet it gained a special place in golfing history as the venue where Gary Player joined Gene Sarazen and Ben Hogan to become only the third winner of golf's four major championships. Twenty-seven years later, the course was lengthened marginally to 7,148 yards as the setting for another major triumph by a South African-born player. This time, Zimbabwe's Nick Price captured his first USPGA Championship there.

Now, as a venue of proven status, Bellerive was to play host to the American Express Championship of 2001. Mike Weir, who celebrated the millennium as the surprise winner at Valderrama, would have to contend with the formidable challenge of Tiger Woods, who, in April of that year at Augusta National, had become the first player in history to hold all four major trophies at the same time.

My plan for September 2001 was to head for St Louis after an American holiday with my wife, cruising down the Ohio River. But there would be no trip to Bellerive. Instead, I am left with vivid recollections of the catastrophic events which caused the tournament's cancellation. And how Woods, with all aircraft grounded, actually made the journey by road from St Louis back to his home in Orlando, Florida.

He later described it as the longest drive of his life. And he did it alone. "Some people might think I'm nuts for driving halfway across the country by myself, but it seemed like the thing to do," said the world's most valuable sportsman. "Besides, negotiating 1,000 miles would require concentration, something I welcomed after the events of the day before."

Woods prepared for the trip by stocking up on protein bars and bottled water. He also relied on music from the car's radio/CD player and on mobile-phone calls to friends in his native California. Though he didn't eat dinner, he had four stops for petrol, when he also went to the toilet and, remarkably, was never recognised during the 13½ hour trip.

"I learned a long time ago how to limit pit stops on long trips," he added. "The key is not to overload with liquids. I sipped just enough water to keep the protein bars from tearing up my stomach." Averaging 75 mph, he eventually pulled into his driveway at the Isleworth resort at 6.00 am. "Home never looked so good," he said.

Ben Crenshaw, the triumphant US Ryder Cup captain at Brookline, faced similar problems with the same equilibrium. "I was stranded like everybody else, just me in my car, listening to the radio," he said. "Those were some of the happiest and most uplifting moments I've ever spent. The way this country responded was just magnificent."

Even at this remove, I find the horror of September 11th 2001, or 9/11 as it has come to be known to Americans, difficult to comprehend, possibly because my particular experience of it seemed to border on the bizarre.

On the shimmering, wide waters of the Ohio, the steam-driven paddle-wheel of the *Delta Queen* turned lazily under a burning sun. Tree-lined banks were broken only at lengthy intervals by a riverside town or the sight of barges close by an industrial plant. We were among 170 passengers, cruising the 470 miles from Pittsburgh to Cincinnati in the sort of classic, 19th century luxury immortalised by Mark Twain. Without phones, newspapers, radio or television, it seemed that nothing could intrude on the idyll. Until Tuesday morning.

The *Delta Queen* had berthed at the town of Marietta, Ohio, when an announcement came at 9.15am on the boat's public-address system. At first, the information was extremely sketchy. Something about New York's World Trade Centre being hit by an aeroplane. An unfortunate accident.

It was only while walking through Marietta in the heart of America's conservative midwest, that we gained any real sense of the enormity of what had happened. In shops, schools and other workplaces, locals huddled in groups, listening intently as the news unfolded on radio and television. Some people sobbed quietly. The entire town seemed to come to a standstill.

On returning to the boat a few hours later, a television had been installed on the main deck for the benefit of the passengers. Mobile phones, which had been inconspicuous since the start of the cruise, were now being used openly. Individuals found a quiet place and wept. In the women's toilet, my wife comforted two passengers who were physically ill because of what they had heard and seen.

Yet, as the only non-Americans in the group, we felt very much at a loss as to how to respond to the devastating developments. What could we say or do by way of comfort? What would happen to the daily entertainment schedule? The following 48 hours provided a fascinating insight into the American psyche.

Firstly, it was decided at the cruise company's headquarters in New Orleans that everything should continue as normal. So it was that when we had all held hands and observed a minute's silence after dinner on the evening of September 11th, the resident band struck up and couples took to the floor and danced.

Initially, the spectacle prompted a decidedly uncomfortable feeling. But gradually such reservations were replaced by admiration for the irrepressible optimism which seems to characterise Americans, whatever the circumstances. In the darkest hour these people had ever known collectively, here they were, determined to get on with living, in the frontier spirit

Chapter 5 The Wait

which shaped their great nation.

At every lock we encountered on the river, the delightful custom of playing traditional American airs such as *Oh Susannah* and *Camptown Races* on the boat's steam organ – the calliope (pronounced cal-i-o-pee) – was maintained. And as normal, people waved enthusiastically from the shore.

"I will find it hard to believe that I was out here, surrounded by so much beauty, when this terrible thing happened," said Ned Ruffin, a Pittsburgh attorney on honeymoon with his wife Sally. "Sure, we are all hurting, but we'll get through this. It's in our nature to get on with things. We have to look forward to a new day."

On the floor where we had danced on Tuesday night, we gathered the following morning for a deeply moving prayer service at which one of the passengers, a Methodist minister, officiated. To this outsider, the scene was reminiscent of a John Ford movie, as voices were raised in singing *Shall We Gather at the River?* Then, in sharp contrast, passengers assembled shortly afterwards in response to an announcement for "Picnic time in the Orleans Room."

Meanwhile, there was conflicting news from St Louis. Initially, it seemed that the event might go on, but as the full horror unfolded, it became clear that tournament golf would be unthinkable. And what would happen to the Ryder Cup, which was scheduled for The Belfry later in the month?

When the boat eventually berthed in Cincinnati at lunchtime on Thursday, people who view travel as a right rather than a privilege began the great scramble for onward connections. My wife and I stayed there until Saturday when we were fortunate to get a flight back to London.

In the meantime, while Ireland held a day of mourning on the Friday, we availed of the opportunity of attending a special, inter-denominational service held in the open in the centre of Cincinnati. And there were poignant scenes as shattered citizens consoled each other, trying desperately all the while to understand why this terrible thing had happened in their country.

For us, of course, there was the opportunity of removing ourselves physically from an environment of profound sadness and leaving the Americans to grieve. And as our plane climbed into the Saturday-night skies over Cincinnati, our hearts remained with them, hoping they might find a way to cope.

From our experience on the *Delta Queen,* we sensed they would. Time would help the healing.

Having kept in touch with Ned and Sally Ruffin, we met up with them again in the autumn of 2004, when they came to Dublin as part of an extended Irish visit. Apparently it was something they had wanted to do as individuals: now they were doing it as a pair. Though

The Archive

III

◆

Clockwise from far left: Walter Hagen, playing captain of the US in the 1929 Ryder Cup at Moortown, points out some of the London sights to fellow team members from the roof of the Savoy hotel. Hagen's team was beaten 7-5 by Great Britain whose captain, George Duncan, is photographed receiving the trophy from Samuel Ryder (left). Samuel Ryder (right) with his daughter Joan at Waterloo Station, London, en-route to South Africa. The great Henry Cotton (both photographs below) who captained the team on two occasions, 1947 and 1953, and who played in the 1929, 1937 and 1947 Ryder Cups. Scoreboard at the 1933 Ryder Cup at Southport and Ainsdale Golf Club where Great Britain won $6\frac{1}{2}$ to $5\frac{1}{2}$. Bottom left: Samuel Ryder flanked by Walter Hagen (left) and George Duncan. Byron Nelson (below left) in action in the 1937 Ryder Cup at Southport and Ainsdale Golf Club.

Top left: Peter Alliss photographed during the 1953 Ryder Cup. Alliss would form a great friendship with Christy O'Connor Senior, (above right) seen here playing in the 1965 Ryder Cup at Royal Birkdale. Right: Possibly the most famous "gimme" of them all. Jack Nicklaus concedes Tony Jacklin's two-foot putt for a half on the 18th green in the 1969 Ryder Cup at Royal Birkdale. As a result, the overall match was tied at 16-16 with the United States retaining the trophy. Above: taking a break during the 1961 staging. Above middle: Eric Brown out of a bunker in 1957 and (left) Welshman Dai Rees who played in eight Ryder Cups and who captained Great Britain and Ireland on five occasions. The 1969 Great Britain and Ireland team comprising of from left, Brian Huggett, Maurice Bembridge, Alex Caygill, Christy O'Connor, Brian Barnes, Bernard Hunt, Eric Brown (non-playing captain), Peter Alliss, Peter Butler, Tony Jacklin, Neil Coles, Peter Townsend and Bernard Gallacher.

Far page: Two legends of the game, Jack Nicklaus and Tom Watson, confer during the 1981 Ryder Cup at Walton Heath. It was Nicklaus who got the "European" team concept rolling following a succession of one-sided encounters for the United States which undermined the credibility of the Ryder Cup. Europe came close in 1983 but had to wait until 1985 before the team made the winning breakthrough at The Belfry where future US captain Hal Sutton (left) lost his singles match to Bernhard Langer by 5 and 4. Below: Paul Way, Sam Torrance and Ian Woosnam savour Europe's $16\frac{1}{2}$ to $11\frac{1}{2}$ victory. It was Torrance's putt on the 18th (below left) which sealed victory. Bottom left: Woosnam chases down a putt against Craig Stadler in his 1985 singles match which Woosnam lost 2 and 1. Bottom right: Team Europe celebrate: Back row: Jose Rivero, Bernhard Langer, Nick Faldo, Torrance, Tony Jacklin, Sandy Lyle, Way, Seve Ballesteros. Front: Howard Clarke, Woosnam, Jose Maria Canizares, Manuel Pinero and Ken Browne.

Ian Woosnam coming out of sand during his final day's singles match against Fred Couples at Kiawah Island, 1991. Woosnam halved but Europe lost $13\frac{1}{2}$ to $14\frac{1}{2}$.

Far left: Seve Ballesteros and Jose Maria Olazabal, who became known and feared as the Spanish Armada, began their remarkable partnership - widely acknowledged as the greatest in the history of the competition – here at Muirfield Village in 1987 where Europe had their first victory on US soil by a margin of 15-13. The United States regained the trophy in 1991 at Kiawah Island (photographs this page). Above left: Corey Pavin and (above right) fans at Kiawah Island. Left: Mark O'Meara and Payne Stewart look on as team captain Dave Stockton pushes Pavin into the water as the USA celebrate on the beach after victory. Below: Jose Maria Olazabal in action.

In full flow and at the top of their games are Nick Faldo and Colin Montgomerie. (See following pages)

Nick Faldo and Colin Montgomerie, both of whom have left an indelible mark on Ryder Cup history, seen here playing together on the opening day of the 1993 Ryder Cup at The Belfry. Faldo made 11 consecutive Ryder Cup appearances from 1977-1997 while Montgomerie has made seven consecutive appearances since 1991.

Tony Jacklin whose captaincy dominated the 1980s. He captained Europe in 1983, 1985, 1987 and 1989 and his record of two wins, one half and one loss led to a renaissance of the competition. Here he is hugging the trophy following the 1989 tied match at the Belfry which insured that the trophy stayed on the Eastern side of the Atlantic.

we talked over dinner about September 11th and the *Delta Queen*, it was more as an acknowledgement of a shared experience, than a conversation piece.

Ned and Sally's innermost memories, remained locked in their hearts.

So many hearts were crushed by the events of 9/11, that it might be considered selfish to seek a purely golfing dimension to the tragedy. But there are no degrees of heartbreak, as the story of David G Sezna Jnr illustrates.

On Thursday, September 13th, David Sezna showed a friend a photograph of his favourite foursome. As Michael Bamberger wrote movingly in *Sports Illustrated:* "Three boys and their father, all in shorts, polo shorts and smiles, standing on the 14th tee at Seminole in North Palm Beach, Florida, the Atlantic Ocean behind them and nothing but years in front of them."

The father was on the far right, looking suitably proud. Turning to his friend, he started to identify his boys. "That's Willie next to me," he said. "He's a senior in high school; plays to a three (handicap). That's Deeg on the left. Between them, that's ......" Words failed the 48-year-old.

Teddy, the youngest of the three boys, was only 15 when he died in a boating accident on the first Saturday of July in Millennium Year. Father and son were cruising in a 30-foot motorboat when they collided with a steel pole. It took two hours for rescuers to find Teddy's body. Now, David Sezna had lost another son.

On September 11th, Sezna Senior was playing golf at Pine Hill, a public course in southern New Jersey, just down the road from Pine Valley. His 22-year-old son, who carried the same first name but was affectionately known as Deeg, had arrived for work a little after 7.0am in a financial services company named Sandler, O'Neill and Partners, in the South Tower of the World Trade Centre. It was only his sixth day in the job.

Bamberger takes up the story: "Somebody pulled him (Deeg's father) off the course when the first plane smashed into the North Tower of the World Trade Centre. He was watching the terror unfold on TV when the second plane struck his son's building. 'I knew Deeg was on the 104th floor,' said the father. 'The plane hit, an hour passed, the building crumpled. A friend drove me home.'

"My father used to say 'A golfer is a gentleman.' I raised my sons to understand that. The first time I brought Deeg to the course, he was five. As we left, he said 'Was I a gentleman today, Daddy?'" On Wednesday September 12th, he went to the ruins of the World Trade Centre to search for his son. Now he was at home, struggling desperately to come to terms with an awful truth about Deeg, who had once got his golf handicap down to four.

When phoned by Tom Fazio, the renowned golf-course architect and a fellow member of Pine Valley, the father said, almost in a cry of anguish: "They can rip off your arms and legs,

Chapter 5 The Wait

Tom. You just don't want them taking your children." The remaining son, Willie, now has an annual date with his father in the Pine Valley Father-and-Son Tournament. And they compete in Deeg's memory.

On the other side of the US, players relinquished highly-prized tee-times at Pebble Beach and gathered in the Tap Room where they watched television. "Everyone was in such a state of shock," recalled one club official. "Some people decided to go out and play because they were here; they were helpless; there was nothing they could do. But a lot of people were glued to the TV. I don't recall the Tap Room being so crowded."

While a desperate scramble to recover bodies from the rubble of the World Trade Centre continued, New York mayor, Rudy Giuliani, urged the citizens of his stricken city to go out for a meal and, perhaps, take in a Broadway show. But it would have been fanciful to imagine that the Ryder Cup, scheduled to be played less than two weeks away on September 18th to 20th at The Belfry, could offer a comparable distraction to a grieving nation. Postponement was inevitable.

On September 13th, Jim Awtrey, Chief Executive Officer of the PGA of America, issued this statement: "Like the rest of America, we are deeply mourning the tragic loss of life and the series of events that will change the way we live. These changes also have an impact on the upcoming Ryder Cup matches, which are to be played in England. We continue to have discussions with US captain, Curtis Strange, and have communicated to a number of players that the safety of the team and their families is of utmost importance.

"It is our desire for the Ryder Cup matches to go forward. Having said that, the magnitude of the matches requires many logistics which are impacted by the events of this week. We are reassessing every logistic connected with the matches – a process which will take a number of days and which will require input from our government. When our assessment is complete, we will make further announcements as appropriate."

On the same day, Ryder Cup spokesman, Mitchell Platts, issued this statement on behalf of the PGA European Tour: "We continue to discuss and review the situation regarding the Ryder Cup.

"From the outset, all security and transport planning arrangements for the Ryder Cup 2001 have been formulated to address anticipated or potential requirements for an international sporting occasion of the stature of the Ryder Cup Competition. That said, the tragic events of the last 48 hours are without precedent and quite obviously we are currently reviewing all of our plans in the light of the current situation.

"This is an ongoing process and we are working closely with the Police and other security services to ensure we are taking every possible step to maximise security and safety for all concerned. For obvious reasons, we are not releasing in detail what those actions are."

On Saturday the 15th, Ken Schofield eventually arrived back in London after an ill-fated attempt at flying to St Louis for the American Express Championship. He and four European Tour colleagues – Keith Waters, Peter Adams, Gordon Simpson and Ben Watson – had taken off from Heathrow on the morning of that fateful Tuesday.

They were on a direct flight bound for St Louis, but they never got there. In fact, they never set foot on American soil. "The way things panned out, the transatlantic flight was a lot shorter than it should have been, which suggested to us that we weren't anywhere near St Louis," Schofield recalled. "Yet there was no mention of any change in the flight plan.

"From my seat next to Keith Waters, I saw through the window that we were landing in some place strange. Still, there was nothing over the intercom. Not a word. It was only when we had touched down and the plane was taxiing to a halt that we began to suspect something was seriously wrong. That came from overhearing Americans on the plane making mobile phones calls to their home, business, friends or loved ones."

They had landed in the Canadian airport of Moncton, New Brunswick, the next stopping-off point beyond Newfoundland travelling west. They had been in the air about five hours which meant it was around mid-day local time, about three hours after the World Trade Centre had been hit.

According to the City of Moncton Annual report 2001, at approximately 11.00am local time, public emergency vehicles were alerted that, due to "these acts of terrorism upon the United States", and the uncertainty of further attacks, all international flights destined for North America and domestic flights then in North American air space, were ordered down to the closest airport on their flight paths.

So it was that in the hour and a half between 11.30 am and 1.0 pm, 12 planes and more than 2,200 passengers were diverted to the Greater Moncton Airport. The report also informs us that over the next few days, Monctonians and all people of Greater Moncton showed an overwhelmingly warm and caring response to this unprecedented occurrence, by opening their hearts and homes to citizens from France, Holland, Germany, the UK and the US, as well as to fellow Canadians, whose flights were ordered down due to what were now confirmed acts of terrorism.

"Gradually, we began to piece things together," Schofield went on. "I'll never forget arriving there. We were taken into what could best be described as an airplane hangar – pretty basic. There, a Canadian Mountie named Joe Gallagher – for obvious reasons, his name will always stay with me – spoke to us. By this stage, up to 13 or 14 planes were grounded and we were one of three plane-loads of passengers in the hangar at this time.

Chapter 5 The Wait

"In addressing us all, Mountie Gallagher spoke of his sadness in attempting to convey some desperate news. He went on to tell us to watch a television set where CNN would inform us in words and pictures, better than he could, what had happened and why we were there. Then the Red Cross arrived on the scene.

"Soon we were looking at horrific images on CNN of planes diving into the Twin Towers. Later, when the extent of the devastation had begun to sink in, we were informed that due to the lack of hotel space, we were being assigned accommodation in a certain house which happened to be owned by a local firefighter." Given the heroism of his colleagues in New York he and his wife, who was a qualified nurse, had greater reason than most to respond to an appeal from the efficient Red Cross Response Team. We're told that local businesses showed immense generosity in donating food, toys and personal items.

Assuming that the five of them would be split up, Schofield and his colleagues were surprised that they were all housed together under the one roof of what was a normal family home. "In we trooped in our blazers and European Tour ties," he recalled. Two of them had to double up in the same bed and Simpson was assigned a child's bed. But they had no complaints.

In fact, they began to feel decidedly at home when, on rising for breakfast on the Wednesday morning, they looked out the window to discover that their lodgings were located opposite the corner of streets named Muirfield and Oak Hill.

Schofield went on to describe how, during three days in Moncton, they made numerous friends from different nationalities. Each day, they were summoned to the city's Coliseum-Arena Complex, a large ice-hockey arena which took the form of a local hall and became the official receiving centre for the unexpected guests. There, they were kept up to date on the latest developments, and the ladies of the Salvation Army Moncton Citadel Community prepared and delivered hot meals, of which a ham dinner was especially tasty.

Telephone communications were difficult for a while, to the extent that there was a virtual blackout for probably about 24 hours. From a golfing standpoint, Schofield's first concern was to contact his USPGA Tour counterpart Tim Finchem. Any discussion with the PGA regarding the Ryder Cup would be addressed a few days later.

"I eventually contacted Tim Finchem who was in St Louis and it was probably Wednesday night before we learned that the tournament had been cancelled," he said. "In the meantime, we passed the time with a variety of activities, including five-a-side soccer games with other passengers in the car-park outside the ice-hockey arena. There were Italians and Germans along with us Britons. Looking back on it now, there was a surreal quality to the entire experience."

When officials were finally in a position to address the mammoth task of getting stranded passengers to their destinations, or airport of origin, the quintet from the European Tour travelled by taxi from Moncton to Halifax, Nova Scotia. They then flew from Halifax to Reykjavik and from there back to London. "That was when Jim Awtrey contacted me, after Richard Hills had made the arrangement for Sandy Jones and myself."

The day happened to be the seventh birthday of Richard Hills's daughter, Fionnuala, and by way of celebration, father and daughter went to the ski run at Aldershot. "That was where I received a phone call to the effect that Mr Awtrey needed to talk with Ken and Sandy (Jones). A postponement of the Ryder Cup was now very much on the cards," Hills recalled.

In the course of transatlantic phone calls, the European Tour were informed by the PGA of America that "the scope of last Tuesday's tragedy is so overwhelming that it would be impossible for the United States' Ryder Cup team and officials to attend the matches this month." This led to a crisis meeting of top European Tour officials being called for 7.30 on the morning of Sunday the 16th. By 5.00 that afternoon, they were ready to announce officially that Ryder Cup 2001 was postponed.

Sam Torrance, the European skipper, spoke for all responsible golf fans when he said: "The decision to postpone the Ryder Cup matches this year is one of commonsense. What happened in America has put the Ryder Cup and everything else into perspective. I am desperately heartbroken for all the people involved in this terrible tragedy. All I can feel at the moment is an immense sadness. There will be time enough to talk further about the 34th Ryder Cup matches taking place next year."

When Awtrey attempted to apologise to the European Tour and the British PGA over his country's withdrawal, he was almost rebuked for thinking that way. He recalled: "I'll never forget ..... They said 'Jim, don't do it. Don't even go there. It's going to be such a mess, let's start working toward next year.' "

There was a proposal that the 34th and 35th Ryder Cup matches be staged in successive years, 2002 and 2003. But, on September 19th, the European Ryder Cup Board issued this statement: "The 34th Ryder Cup matches, which were postponed out of necessity following the enormity of the tragedy in the United States on Tuesday, September 11, have been rescheduled for The De Vere Hotel, Sutton Coldfield, England, from September 27 to 29, 2002.

"The European Ryder Cup Board announce that the inevitable consequence of the decision to postpone the matches in 2001 and reschedule in 2002 is for the immediate matches to be played in the even-numbered years. Consequently, the Ryder Cup matches will be played at Oakland Hills CC, Bloomfield Hills, Michigan USA in September 2004; at The K Club, Straffan, Ireland in September 2006 and at Valhalla GC, Louisville, Kentucky USA in September 2008.

"The European Ryder Cup Board would especially like to put on record their appreciation to the De Vere Group Plc for their superb support in The De Vere Belfry remaining the host venue, following the decision that the matches be postponed.

"Furthermore, the European Ryder Cup Board wishes to acknowledge the superb and immediate response of the Irish Government and The K Club in agreeing to stage the matches in 2006. Ireland Inc represents a partnership between the Irish Tourist Board (Bord Failte) and three private-sector companies – AIB Bank, Aer Lingus (later replaced by An Bord Bia) and Waterford Crystal.

"Clearly, the rescheduling of the matches has resulted in a variety of logistical challenges. The European Ryder Cup Board are especially grateful to the Birmingham and West Midlands Hotel Community, the National Exhibition Centre and the Ground Transportation Providers in recognising these challenges and standing alongside us in seeking to achieve all that is possible to ensure that the 34th Ryder Cup matches move ahead at The De Vere Belfry.

"The Ryder Cup Junior match will also now take place in 2002 with the European team seeking to retain the trophy against the United States at The K Club, Straffan, on September 24-25."

In the meantime, it fell to Ryder Cup director Hills to set about what was obviously a sharply different salvage operation on this side of the Atlantic. On Sunday the 16th, lawyers, insurers and the European Tour themselves began the process of assessing the implications of a postponement. "There were some very difficult phone calls to be made," he recalled. "Most of us have had to fill out an insurance claim at some point, but on the Monday morning, I had my first encounter with our loss adjuster. This was Shaun Coyne, who happens to be a very nice chap from Cavan.

"Our first formal meeting with the loss adjusters was on Thursday, September 20th. The insurers behaved impeccably, but it was still 10 months later before the claim was settled for a figure of £Stg17.5 million. Though there were a few gaps here and there, it transpired that we had a good policy. But even at that, it inevitably took time for matters to be finalised. All the suppliers and contractors had to be compensated and we came to an agreement with the hoteliers in the Birmingham area. Then there was the matter of trying to salvage as much as possible from the merchandising. So as to assist the insurers as best we could, it was agreed after consultation with Sam Torrance that the 2001 logo would be retained for 2002. Overall, the postponement wasn't something I'd wish on anyone but I have to say that the attitude of our insurers made a difficult job very much easier."

Failte Ireland received compensation of £Stg178,000 as part of the overall package. In this context, a significant amount had to do with merchandising. For instance, in common with other members of the media, I received Failte Ireland gifts of an umbrella, shirts and caps bearing the logo "Ryder Cup 2005" which, incidentally, I plan to cling to for dear life, on the assumption that they may one day be worth significant loot. "You're not alone," said Chris Kane, Director of External Affairs for Failte Ireland, since retired. "People keep telling me similar stories. From our perspective, the postponement raised the more important issue as to whether the annual promotional and publicity deal which was already agreed, would be extended to include 2006, without an additional cost to us. Which is what's happening.

"As for merchandise: we produced quite a lot of shirts, hats and videos, quite apart from printing and display material. Anything with 2005 on it had to be replaced and was covered by the insurance."

It should also be noted that earlier in 2001, a process began whereby the European Tour would officially take management control of an event which had been the property of the British PGA since its launch in 1927. A new, limited liability partnership company, with a 60-20-20 shareholding ratio between the Tour, the British PGA and the national PGAs on the Continent, was formalised by 2003.

Meanwhile, as the prospective host for 2005, Dr Smurfit took a positive, pragmatic view of the one-year postponement. "The reality of the situation was that the organisers had no choice," he said, reflecting on the phone call which he received at his home in Monaco from Schofield. "The alternative of having two Ryder Cups in succession would have been too much. On balance, I believe it would have taken from the unique character of the tournament. The right decision was taken in the circumstances and the important thing was that golf's premier event was still coming to Ireland: it was just going to be one year later than we thought.

"I wasn't disappointed about having to wait a further year. On the credit side, the extra time helped us with our preparations, not, I hasten to add, that we hadn't enough time already. And the additional publicity associated with an extended build-up was clearly of a considerable benefit for all of us in this country.

"As somebody who happened to be in Los Angeles during 9/11, my initial reaction was dismay. And when my thoughts later turned to the Ryder Cup, I felt certain it couldn't take place as scheduled. Sport had to act responsibly in such circumstances. Because of the raw emotions following the Twin Towers atrocities, I don't think it would have been a match in the accepted sense of the term. The American people simply didn't want to be involved in sporting activities. Golf courses were deserted; people stayed at home to follow events on television. While hoping that the US would soon return to some form of normalcy, I

Chapter 5 The Wait

remember fearing that the Ryder Cup might have been cancelled, rather than deferred. Then, where team rivalry was concerned, there was always the danger that one or more players from either side would endure a dramatic downturn in form over the following 12 months, rendering them non-competitive in September 2002. There wasn't any mechanism in place to deal with such an eventuality.

"Looking back on 9/11, the best analogy I could draw was with the suffering of the British people during the Blitz. During the nightly bombing of London, they never lost heart. In fact, they came through the ordeal triumphantly. I felt confident the same thing would happen in America and that they would be all the stronger for the experience."

From a financial standpoint, the postponement meant a loss of "only a few thousand pounds" to The K Club. "That was all we had spent on stationary and promotional material for 2005," said then director of golf, Paul Crowe. "Serious expenditure would not have started until the summer of 2002."

Whatever the amount, it seemed that the money simply didn't matter, not even to the British PGA and the PGA European Tour, which stood to share £Stg10 million from the 2001 staging. Indeed much of the PGA's money had already been earmarked for various projects aimed at developing the game. Instead, their thoughts were dominated by America's tragedy. There was a profound sense of golfing people everywhere pulling together, wanting to do the right thing.

As Padraig Ó hUiginn put it: "One could have taken the cynical view that, in a way, it gave us further exposure in that it extended the build-up period to the 2006 matches. But it was impossible to think that way in the wake of 9/11."

Meanwhile, there was a growing awareness among the three main support sponsors that they had bought into something special. As Jim O'Kelly of AIB observed: "In any sponsorship, what you're trying to do is to get something your competitors can't copy and your customers can't buy. That's one of the rules and the Ryder Cup fits it perfectly."

Around the mid 1990s, AIB became aware that the involvement of financial institutions in golf was essentially of a modest character. For instance, they themselves supported the Men's East of Ireland Amateur Championship; the Ulster Bank sponsored the West of Ireland the Bank of Ireland sponsored the "South." That was about as far as it went.

"In our sponsorship department, myself and Walter Coakley decided to change things. That was when we decided to take up sponsorship of what became the AIB Irish Seniors Open and to support the Smurfit European Open. Against a background of considerable talk at that time about the possibilities of Ireland landing the Ryder Cup, these were our first strategic steps towards building a relationship with the PGA European Tour."

After Tommy Horton had triumphed in a successful staging of the inaugural AIB Irish Seniors Open at St Margaret's in 1997, it meant that the bank were well positioned when Ó hUiginn went in search of a replacement Ryder Cup sponsor for the Smurfit Group, when they pulled out later that year. And when the call came, their response was immediate. As O'Kelly recalled: "If the biggest golf team event in the world was coming to Ireland, the largest financial institution in the country wanted to be involved in it. It was a big opportunity for us to link our brand values with a major event for which tickets and hospitality will be so highly valued."

So it was that the bank became official sponsors of the European team for the Brookline staging in 1999. They were also involved at The Belfry in 2002 but the real pay-off will come when they are the official bank to the Ryder Cup at The K Club. Given the ongoing changes in banking, the precise nature of that presence has yet to be finalised, but from their perspective, the important thing is that they will be the only financial institution on site.

Then, early in 2005, the bank further strengthened their links with the event by signing Christy O'Connor Jnr for what they describe as their Ryder Cup ambassador. O'Connor will be working with AIB in a broad-based programme of initiatives in the build-up to September 2006.

The involvement of Waterford Crystal in golf world-wide gained rich emphasis on the Sunday of March 13th, 2005, when Padraig Harrington, one of the country's favourite sporting sons, held aloft a magnificent crystal trophy as winner of the Honda Classic. Their sister company, Wedgwood, has also gained a significant foothold in the game, through the superb trophies for the World Golf Championship events. Indeed Darren Clarke held one of these aloft in February 2000 as winner of the Accenture World Matchplay at La Costa and again in August 2003 as the NEC Invitational champion at Firestone.

Prior to 1975, the company's involvement in golf was limited to sponsorship of the Waterford Glass Tournament at Waterford GC, for which they presented a trophy which would have a current value of about €50,000. In that particular year, however, the BBC happened to launch their Pro-Celebrity golf series on television and were anxious to have suitable, souvenir gifts to give to the contestants. So they approached Waterford Crystal.

Not surprisingly, the company were happy to facilitate the BBC but they had no idea at the time just how valuable an arrangement it would become. Each amateur was to receive a ship's decanter and six glasses while the company also made a suite of crystal and a special trophy for the winning professional.

The event was staged at Gleneagles and the brilliant array of crystal was duly brought over from Ireland and put on display in the foyer of the hotel. Bing Crosby was captain of the

Chapter 5 The Wait

American celebrities, who had as their professional Tom Weiskopf, the 1973 Open champion. Peter Oosterhuis, more familiar these days as a golf commentator on the CBS Network, was the British professional.

As things turned out, Oosterhuis won the crystal award as the leading professional, but as a spin-off, Weiskopf and the BBC became enthusiastic admirers of Waterford Crystal. Even more important was the impact it had on Crosby who, in 1937, launched what was then the first, major pro-am in the history of the game. And the inaugural Crosby Clambake, in which Sam Snead was the leading professional at Rancho Santa Fé in California, moved to its present location on the Monterey Peninsula in 1947.

Incidentally, the Gleneagles tournament was funded by the BBC before a company named Marley became official sponsors. All the while, Waterford Crystal maintained their association with the event and their consequent friendship with the Beeb. The impact of the company's initial involvement can be gauged from this letter which arrived at Waterford Crystal shortly afterwards.

Dated September 16th 1975, it read: "Dear Sirs, I am interested in securing some trophies for a golf tournament I put on in California every year. Something similar to the items that you gave to the participants at the recent Match Play television golf function up at Gleneagles.

"I believe it consisted of a decanter and six glasses. We would have to have some engraving on the decanter, something like 'Bing Crosby National Pro-Am First Prize' and then a depiction of our logo, a copy of which I am sending along.

"Of course I can appreciate the fact that colour would be impossible but maybe it would be just as pretty in the clear crystal. I don't even know whether it can be done, hence this letter.

"I'm also interested in the price of these items. I'd probably want a dozen or so sets in varying sizes, from the Championship down to the lesser players.

"You might want to submit some designs of some other type decanters, because I would like an appreciable difference between the first prize, second prize, third prize and so on down, and rather than do this in size, it might be better to let the difference be determined by quality or some other such measurement.

"Could I hear from you when you have a chance to answer the letter with prices etc, whether or not there'd be any duty bringing them into the States, and how much time you would need to prepare these items.

"The tournament itself takes place the third week in January 1976.

"With very best regards, believe me to be – Sincerely Yours, Bing Crosby (signed)."

Sixteen months after that letter arrived in Waterford, a superb array of crystal prizes were on display in the window of the golf shop at the world famous venue of Pebble Beach. Waterford Crystal had broken into the American golf scene in the showpiece of all pro-am events – the Crosby Tournament. In 1977, Tom Watson won by a stroke from Tony Jacklin and the event was staged over the Pebble Beach, Cypress Point and Monterey Peninsula CC courses. After a year's absence, Spyglass Hill returned in place of Monterey Peninsula in 1978.

"It was a tremendous breakthrough," said Colm O'Connell, the company's production director at that time. "Quite apart from the marvellous field of professionals and amateurs who were being introduced to our product, we received some priceless television exposure. The truth is that we could not have hoped for a better platform for our crystal."

In January 1977, O'Connell received another letter from Crosby. It read: "I did want to get a note off to you to tell you how deeply grateful I and the whole committee connected with the Pebble Beach Tournament are to you and Waterford Company for the beautiful trophies you furnished for the Tournament.

"You may be sure that they caused tremendous conversation and speculation by all the people who saw them, and everyone admired them immensely. I think it's the finest set of trophies that have ever been offered in this country for any type of competition and I'm sure everyone will concur with me in that belief."

Waterford sales executive Kevin Hall, since retired, and Mel Morgan, commercial manager world sports, became acutely aware of the permanence of a tournament trophy, in terms of projecting their company's image. Indeed Morgan referred to the reaction of Ken Venturi after capturing the 1964 US Open at Congressional. While making his victory speech with the winning cheque in one hand, Venturi looked to the US Open trophy in his other hand and famously remarked: "I'll spend the money, but this will last forever". It seemed an admirably sound basis on which to market an internationally-acclaimed product.

In the event, the Crosby Tournament set other wheels in motion. Deane Beman, the then commissioner of the USPGA Tour, approached the company with a view to acquiring a trophy and other crystal for the Tournament Players' Championship (now the Players Championship), which is held each year at Sawgrass. Beman's wife Judy came to Ireland to visit the factory in 1980, by which stage the craftsmen had come to grips with a challenging assignment. They had to produce a crystal replica of the huge, marble trophy which was presented to the winner of the TPC. Since then, Waterford's involvement has grown to the extent that more than one third of all winners on the USPGA Tour receive one of their trophies. And requests have followed from other tournament organisers, including the US Seniors Tour (now the Champions Tour) and the LPGA. Indeed a trophy of which the company is especially proud is for the Solheim Cup, the biennial women'steam event between the US and Europe.

Chapter 5 The Wait

Apart from "home" tournaments such as the Smurfit European Open and the Nissan Irish Open, the crystal's appeal has extended as far away as Australia, with a recent count of 35 trophies for world-class events on all five continents.

Trophy designs vary in accordance with a client's brief, but whatever the requirement, Waterford use a team of more than 10 different designers. For instance, when approached by Nissan to create a distinctive look for their Irish Open sponsorship, the company sought the services of designer Michael Fanning. It then took four months and more than 100 hours of sculpting by staff member Ken McEvoy to deliver the finished product, which stands 22 inches.

Women were captivated by the product, as evidenced by the decision of Barbara Nicklaus to present the wives of competitors and officials with gifts of Waterford glassware at her husband's annual Memorial Tournament. The company also had reason to be pleased with the reaction of Mark O'Meara's wife, Alicia, after he won the Crosby for the first time in 1985.

When a consignment of crystal arrived at their home, Alicia was so overcome by its quality and beauty that she refused to handle any of the pieces until they were insured. And she telexed the company in Waterford to establish the value of the crystal before making the necessary arrangements with her insurance company.

Against that background, involvement in Ireland's staging of the Ryder Cup seemed entirely appropriate from the outset. Bord Bia, on the other hand, came in as the replacement for Aer Lingus in November 2001.

Otherwise known as the Irish Food Board, the company was established by the Government in December 1994 for the market development and promotion of Irish food, drink and horticulture, incorporating the amalgamation of the former Meat and Livestock Board and the food section of the Irish Trade Board. The enactment of An Bord Bia (Amendment) Act 2004 resulted in the amalgamation of the Horticulture Board (An Bord Glas) with Bord Bia, thus creating an extended organisation incorporating responsibility for both amenity and edible horticulture.

The value of Irish food, drink and horticulture exports in 2004 exceeded €7.1 billion and the country's food, drink and horticulture industry represents the largest area of indigenous economic activity and accounts for over 35% of exports from indigenous companies. Output from this sector contributes nine per cent of Gross Domestic Product (GDP) and provides 158,100 direct jobs and nine per cent of total direct employment.

Bord Bia works closely with all sectors of the food and drinks industry to build strong positions in the marketplace through a range of market development, promotion and information services. To that end, it has a network of offices, which comprise the national headquarters in Dublin and offices in Amsterdam, Chicago, Dusseldorf, Madrid, Milan, Moscow, Paris and London.

The company sees its Ryder Cup participation as a "high-impact initiative" which, in an increasingly competitive and global marketplace, can add considerable value and further enhance the concept of Ireland as "The Food Island". As indicated in an earlier chapter, their chairman, Philip Lynch, was approached by Ó hUiginn to fill the gap created by the withdrawal of the national airline. On being presented with the proposal by Lynch, the board viewed the sponsorship as a natural fit for Bord Bia, in terms of targeting key export markets such as the UK and the US. So, in a virtually seamless transition, Ryder Cup sponsorship moved from one Irish semi-state company to another.

Among their objectives for the Ryder Cup is to attract senior trade representatives from key customer accounts to The K Club and to use a premium hospitality opportunity to build goodwill and enhance their relationship with Irish food and drink companies. Principal target markets will be: Ireland and the UK and US, along with France, Holland, Sweden, Germany, Italy and Spain as selected European countries; Eastern European countries and Japan, Korea and China in the Far East.

Of the three main sponsors, Bord Bia were the only ones who knew, when agreeing to the deal, that they would be receiving the unplanned bonus of an additional year's exposure until 2006. Ironically, the opportunity came to them because of the devastating impact which the horror of the Twin Towers had on the fortunes of Aer Lingus.

But whatever the circumstances, all of those touched by 9/11 felt compelled, like Ned Ruffin on the *Delta Queen*, to look forward to a new day.

◆

Chapter 6

The Captains

---◆---

Chapter 6 The Captains

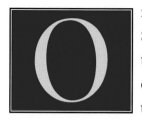n the final day of the Smurfit European Open at The K Club in September 1995, the Ryder Cup was proudly displayed on a table behind the 18th green. As he was about to walk to the clubhouse after completing his final round, Tom Lehman crept mischievously over to the table, picked up the trophy and pretended to sneak away with it.

In that little incident, we had a charming illustration of what Nick Faldo meant when, in the moment of his crucial singles triumph over Curtis Strange at Oak Hill the previous week, he had said: "It's great to have an event that you play from the heart." And Lehman's playfulness gained unimagined relevance in the autumn of 2004, on his appointment as captain of the US Ryder Cup team in Ireland.

Ian Woosnam was also at Oak Hill, which became a highly significant staging for the continued good health of the event. With American wins at Kiawah Island in 1991 and at The Belfry in '93, there were fears that teams from this side of the Atlantic were about to slip back into the bad old times. But the success of Bernard Gallacher's team proved conclusively that the notion of Them against the US, didn't have to include everyone else from the civilised world to ensure a worthy contest.

Though Faldo had delivered a priceless point, it fell ultimately to Philip Walton to secure victory overall. And after being dormie three against Jay Haas, the Malahide man was taken to the 18th where he pushed his final drive into rough on the right. Woosnam, in the role of a concerned colleague, went racing towards the ball as fast as his short legs could carry him. "It's a good lie, perfect for a five wood, if he has a five wood in his bag," said the Welshman.

Earlier on the final afternoon, Woosnam had experienced the bitter disappointment of failing to win his singles match against Fred Couples, after being one up with two to play. The American had squared with a 15-foot birdie putt on the 17th, and amid nerve-racking tension, Woosnam saw a 20-footer for the match slip agonisingly past the 18th cup.

Despite the drama which would later unfold, it remained a bitter blow. "I can't get that putt out of my mind," he said ruefully. "It was so disappointing, not least because it meant I still had to win my first Ryder Cup singles." Defeat by his nemesis, Couples, in what proved to be his last Ryder Cup appearance at Valderrama two years later, meant that Woosnam never got his coveted singles win.

Oak Hill is also remembered as the scene of an amazing match at the top of the singles order, where Lehman was confronted by Seve Ballesteros who, at that stage, would have had great difficulty in driving the ball within the city limits of Rochester, much less the golf hole in play. As the American remembered it the match became a short-game clinic.

"Seve was amazing," he recalled. "When I think of where he was hitting his second shots from, he should have been beaten by 8 and 7 (rather than 4 and 3). I don't think too many guys could have made pars from where he was driving it." When the European team returned in triumph to Dublin, where Walton emerged from Concorde holding aloft the Ryder Cup, Lehman took a different route. In fact I discovered we were on the same Aer Lingus flight when, on going to the back of the plane, I saw him cuddling his then, two-month old son, Thomas Andrew, in his formidable arms.

"I wish we could fast-forward to 1997 and go directly to Valderrama," he said, still smarting from his country's defeat. "We want that trophy back." In the event, he carded admirably steady rounds of 70,72,73,72 at The K Club for a share of ninth place, seven strokes behind the winner, Bernhard Langer. Ten months later, he became Open champion at Royal Lytham, where Paul McGinley tied him for the lead at the halfway stage.

While the Americans had made their decision for 2006, Europe had yet to name their man by the time McGinley met up with Mark O'Meara during the AT&T Pebble Beach National Pro-Am in early February 2005. The Dubliner recalled: "Mark was saying how fortunate we were in Europe that the players chose the captain. We were off to a headstart in that it was not a political decision, like in the US. He felt that having a captain picked by his peers put him on a good footing straight away. I think he had a strong point."

Was O'Meara disappointed to have been overlooked for the captaincy? "I'm sure he was," replied McGinley who, as a member of the European Tour's Tournament Committee, would be involved in the process a few weeks later. "He clearly hoped he would get it but it must be said that, like us, the Americans are very fortunate in having four or five guys waiting in line for the position, every time.

"Tom Lehman will be a very good captain. I know him personally, having played with him in the third round of the Open at Lytham. I have always found him to be a very good man and I'm sure he'll be a worthy leader. He will be very patriotic which I think is great. That's one of the things I admire about the Americans."

In the build-up to Oakland Hills, O'Meara made no secret of his desire to be America's captain at The K Club, not least because of his Irish heritage: his maternal grandmother was an O'Leary and his great-grandfather was an O'Meara from Tipperary. "After playing on five teams, winning 16 tournaments, two majors and being Player of the Year (1998), it would be a great way to finish my career," he said. "I realise other guys are in the running, but I think my record speaks for itself. Golf in the Emerald Isle took on a special appeal for me from the time I competed in the Irish Open at Portmarnock in 1987. My Dad joined me on that trip, making it rather special, and I gave him a little something to cheer about when finishing ninth behind Bernhard Langer."

Chapter 6 The Captains

O'Meara could also have counted on a high approval rating elsewhere in Europe. On the debit side, however, was undoubtedly the controversy which arose over money, prior to the 1999 staging at Brookline. Defending his stand on that particular issue, the player insisted: "We never said we weren't going to play in the Ryder Cup if we didn't get paid. We just wanted to know where the money was going. There was a lot of negative perception in the media, but it's turned into a win-win situation." This latter point was a reference to the nominated charities which have since benefited as a result of that particular rumpus.

It has always been a prerequisite for US captaincy that the successful candidate should have won a major championship. No such requirement applies on this side of the Atlantic, though much was made of the achievements of Woosnam and Faldo in this context, when they were announced as the choices for 2006 and 2008, respectively.

At the outset, there was understandable optimism that an Irishman would get it. Des Smyth, Christy O'Connor Jnr and Eamonn Darcy were seen as genuine candidates. Writing in the *Sunday Independent* Paul Kimmage decided to launch a personal campaign, arising from a trip he made to Baltray for a Links Society Outing on Thursday, December 7th, 2000.

Noting the manner in which Smyth discharged his duties as president of the society, Kimmage wrote three days later: "His words, as ever, are eloquently spoken, and watching, you are reminded of the Ryder Cup at The K Club in 2005 and what an outstanding choice he would make as captain. Has Ireland... No, sorry, let me try that again ..... has Europe ever produced a finer ambassador for the game?" With those words, Kimmage launched the campaign "Des for The K Club 2005." It was a charming thought. No matter that Smyth would be 53 at the time. Wasn't that the age of John Jacobs when he captained Europe at Walton Heath in 1981?

In the context of Ryder Cup history, however, there was an even more persuasive argument. When Sam Torrance led the side at The Belfry in 2002, it meant that 34 teams from this side of the Atlantic had been captained on 20 occasions by an Englishman, seven times by a Scot, six by a Welshman and once by a Spaniard, Seve Ballesteros. Those figures were to acquire an even more distorted look, from an Irish perspective, when a German, Langer, filled the role at Oakland Hills. Not an Irishman in sight, despite the fact that, in 2002, McGinley had become the country's 17th Ryder Cup representative.

Michael Smurfit strongly supported the idea of an Irish captain, especially after I put that particular statistic to him. "In a speech I made at the European Open dinner at Sunningdale (2002), I pointed out that, for the biggest golfing event ever to be staged in Ireland, primarily for an Irish audience, we had better have a very good excuse for not having an Irishman as captain of the Ryder Cup team," he said. "I also made those views known privately to PGA and European Tour officials."

But the democracy which had so impressed O'Meara, worked against the Irish cause. The Tournament Players' Committee determined that the successful candidate would be one of their own in every sense, especially in the context of current tournament activity. And when they announced their decision on March 2nd, 2005, Smyth, O'Connor and Darcy had long since departed the ranks of the regular European Tour and were now competing in senior ranks. In other words, with the possible exception of Ronan Rafferty and Philip Walton, Ireland had nobody who could have been thought of as being in the same mould as Tony Jacklin, Gallacher, Ballesteros, Mark James, Torrance and Langer, in terms of age and current involvement.

Another crucial consideration was highlighted by the announcement itself, which began: "Ian Woosnam and Nick Faldo have accepted invitations from the Tournament Committee ......" When the question of the captaincy in Ireland first arose after Valderrama, it was taken that prospective candidates would formally apply for the position. Which is what Darcy and O'Connor did. Smyth declined to do so, preferring to wait and see how matters developed. As things transpired, he read the situation correctly.

The pendulum began to swing inexorably towards a currently active player and by the autumn of 2002, Colin Montgomerie had emerged as a clear front-runner. Given his enormous contribution to the European Tour, it was felt that if he wanted the position, it was something he simply couldn't be denied. There was also the possibility that ongoing back problems, which had seen him miss the halfway cut in the 2002 USPGA Championship at Hazeltine and then retire the following week after an opening 71 in the NEC at Sahalee, would militate against his future as a Ryder Cup player.

"I don't need to explain how important the Ryder Cup is to me," he said when we met at Mount Juliet in September 2002, a few weeks before the staging at The Belfry. "So I do what I'm told. I've lost 30 pounds since April and with the pressure off the back, I'm now working on the stomach muscles, which is hell. Sit-ups and more sit-ups. But I know I've got to do it, otherwise my career will be finished. And at 39, I don't want it to be finished just yet."

But were his ambitions to captain the 2006 Ryder Cup team not an acceptance of a premature finale? "Not really," he replied. "Seve's career wasn't finished when he captained Europe at Valderrama. So no, my career won't be over then. And I'd love to captain the team at a time when I can still relate to the players and still be winning tournaments. I've already made it clear that I don't accept comparisons between Seve's captaincy in 1997 and the Irish staging in 2006. As I see it, Spain got the Ryder Cup as an acknowledgement of Seve's marvellous contribution to the European game.

"Seve was special, but the 2006 event is intended to honour Ireland, not an individual Irishman. Otherwise, it would be a bit like arguing that when the Ryder Cup went to Brookline

Chapter 6 The Captains

in 1999, the American team should have been captained by a Bostonian.

"Now let's look at the event itself. The 2006 staging at The K Club is going to be a huge, huge occasion for European golf and I'm sure that as staunch Europeans, the Irish will want a home win, even if that happens to be at the expense of an Irish captain. The best man for the job will be somebody who can relate to the younger players coming through.

"By then, the obvious Irish candidates, Des Smyth, Eamonn Darcy and Christy O'Connor Jnr, will be a little bit removed from what's going on. And I believe you can only get close to players if you're still involved at their level." In the light of what Woosnam would be saying in Dubai two and a half years later, Montgomerie then offered a fascinating, Celtic compromise: "There's no reason why one of them couldn't help in the team room." As vice-captain? "Absolutely. That might satisfy the Irish public. I would hate to be seen to be approaching the job with my own, exclusive agenda. My only ambition would be to win the thing, which I believe I could do, with the help of fellow Celts."

As things turned out, Montgomerie effectively played himself out of the job through a magnificent performance at Oakland Hills, where he fully deserved the distinction of sinking the decisive point in what later became a runaway triumph. Three months later, in mid-December, he bowed to the inevitable with an announcement that he had withdrawn his name from the list of candidates for 2006. "My current world ranking is ridiculous and I want to get back into the top 25 next year," he said. "In fact I know I'm a top-10 player really."

Then he added that Langer would be getting his vote at a Tournament Players' Committee meeting to be held a few days later. "It's our job to elect the captain who will win the thing and he would be the Ryder Cup players' choice because nothing frustrated him all week," he said. "If he says he wants to do it again, then there's your captain."

But it wasn't quite that simple. Darren Clarke, who was also a member of the Players' Committee, took the view that Langer should be happy to relinquish the Ryder Cup captaincy and make way for another candidate. Speaking more than two months prior to Montgomerie's announcement, Clarke said: "I have a candidate in mind but I'm not prepared to name names. I simply don't see the point in Bernhard doing it again and changing a system that has worked so well. That would be silly. I don't see any point in that whatsoever.

"He did a fantastic job; indeed there was great work done by the backroom men. We won in America by the biggest margin in our history. It can't get any better than that, so why should Bernhard do it again? If it was me, I'd only be too happy to stand down."

Still, the indications were that Langer would be persuaded to stay on for 2006; Faldo was favourite for the 2008 staging at Oakland Hills and Woosnam would be the obvious candidate for Wales in 2010. In fact, Woosnam had already nailed his colours to the mast, as it were, when he talked in August 2001 of being content to wait for the captaincy until 2009, if Wales were fortunate enough to get the Ryder Cup then:

"The Ryder Cup in Wales is what we want; what we need," he said passionately. "When I go to America and tell people I'm from Wales, they ask: 'What part of Scotland is that?'" A month later, 9/11 happened and as a consequence the Welsh staging went back to 2010. So, it seemed that the little Welshman would have to wait another year.

The most crucial decision in the context of the 2006 captaincy, however, came on February 2nd, 2005, with the announcement that Langer was not prepared to serve a second term. "I wish to end all speculation," said the German. "So I have officially informed the European Tour Tournament Committee, through the chairman, Jamie Spence, that I have every intention of being a playing member of the 2006 European Team.

"Both my wife Vikki and I have the most wonderful memories of the week in Detroit, memories that will never fade, but playing golf remains number one on my priority list. I have made a solid start to this year and I intend to play a full schedule. It was a great honour to be the European team captain, and I am particularly proud of the place that the 2004 team now holds in the record books. But it is the turn of one of my colleagues to take the reins. I look forward to playing on his team in Ireland!"

There it was. At a stroke, Woosnam wouldn't have to wait until 2009 or 2010. The captaincy was going to come to him three years earlier than he had originally anticipated. And there were no begrudging words from Ireland. Rather was it acknowledged that he had been a generous friend to Irish golf, going back to 1983, when he played an exhibition match at Laytown and Bettystown as Darcy's partner against Des Smyth and the local professional, Bobby Browne. And he set a six-under-par professional course record of 65, finishing 2,3,4 – birdie, birdie, birdie.

He and Smyth were firm friends by that stage. In fact, the Drogheda man has been known to refer to a time they roomed together in Nigeria in 1980 when Woosnam, thoroughly dispirited by poor golfing form, pleaded to him: "How am I going to make a living from this game, Des? I can't play." But the man who made three visits to the European Qualifying School, gained many admirers here through his remarkable climb up the competitive ladder during the 1980s and beyond. Especially notable was his achievement in 1987 of becoming the first European to win £1 million in prize money in a single season, by capturing no fewer than eight titles around the world. These involved five in Europe along with the Hong Kong Open, the World Cup individual award and the Sun City Million Dollar Challenge.

Along the way, he seemed to develop a liking for the Irish air. So it was that three weeks after he had won the 1991 US Masters title and when he was in a position to command seriously handsome rewards for a corporate day, he picked up fellow professional Peter Baker in his

Chapter 6 The Captains

private plane and came to Dublin to play in the Chris de Burgh Charity Pro-Am at Hermitage. For nothing. There wasn't even prize money on offer.

During the evening, without prompting, he promised the organiser, Cecil Whelan, that he would be back in Ireland the following month for the Christy O'Connor Charity Pro-Am at Killarney. And there was also a commitment to head a charity fourball at Royal Birkdale, where the Open Championship was being played that year.

His pro-am slot at Killarney was bought at auction for £12,000 by Dermot Desmond, J P McManus and John Magnier, who went on to partner Woosnam to victory. And the Birkdale fourball boosted Links Society funds by a further £25,000. "Woosie has been a super supporter of our activities," said Whelan. "Between signed US Masters and Ryder Cup menus and flags and various other items, he must have earned us more than £100,000 over the years." So, when the little Welshman talked of his affection for this country after being named Ryder Cup captain, it wasn't cheap chat.

"I've had some great times playing golf in Ireland and I suppose the connection started in those early days when I roomed with Des (Smyth) in Nigeria," he said. "Your people are a lot like the Welsh. They love a bit of fun and are always ready to jump at an excuse to let their hair down. I like that."

This fun-loving attitude also created friendships in a nation he will be hell-bent on toppling in the Ryder Cup. "Woosie and I are talking about marriage," remarked John Daly after they had been paired in all four rounds of the Masters. "He says it's the longest relationship I've ever had." And American scribe Steve Hershey wrote: "Wee Woosie is a chatterbox. He makes Lee Trevino look like Marcel Marceau."

Meanwhile, though Faldo could be criticised as a self-absorbed loner, all fair-minded observers felt it was absolutely correct that he should be honoured with the Ryder Cup captaincy. And his peers were clearly aware of this during the meeting in Dubai. As Montgomerie said: "Nick was always a special case, if you will, as Europe's most successful player." Their solution? To take the unprecedented step of naming successive captains in the same announcement. It could be argued that in doing so, they diminished the position, if not the winner of six major championships. But the counter-argument was that as a current pundit with ABC television in the US, Faldo was in the unique position of being able to observe the American scene first-hand, in the build-up to the 2008 staging at Valhalla.

"I can't say how excited I am to be leading the team in the United States," said the player, whose 11th successive appearance in the matches at Valderrama, surpassed the record of 10 by Christy O'Connor Snr, which had stood since 1973. "The Ryder Cup has always been very important to me and I feel honoured to be joining the list of great names who have captained Europe."

As for Woosnam: there was no doubting his delight with the forthcoming challenge. "I felt I would do the captaincy and Ireland was right for me, being the right age and being involved with the players who are on tour now. But I will use the next 18 months to get to know a lot of other players as well and I think it's very important to be on the tour to do that."

On a personal level, he said: "My wife Glen and I are absolutely delighted. The Ryder Cup has been a big part of our lives and it is a huge honour to be named captain of the European team. It makes me feel very proud, especially as Wales has such a great tradition of producing Ryder Cup captains."

One thing is certain: the skipper will be treading familiar terrain. Woosnam has played in all 11 stagings of the Smurfit European Open up to and including 2005; he was one of Darren Clarke's playing partners when the Tyroneman carded a stunning, second-round 60 in 1999, and he was tied second with Padraig Harrington and Thomas Bjorn, when Clarke captured the title in 2001. Woosnam had a second-round 66 to his credit on that occasion and has carded 67 in rounds one, three and four, over the years.

It must also be mentioned that not many visitors could have retained a warm welcome here, given some of the grief which he inflicted on Irish players over the years. One remembers Portmarnock 1989, when he faced and beat local favourite Philip Walton in a play-off for the Irish Open title, which he won for a second successive year. And there was the final of the World Matchplay at Wentworth in 2001, when he overcame Padraig Harrington by 2 and 1 in the final, to capture the coveted title for a third time.

"I like what they've been doing to The K Club in preparation for the Ryder Cup," he said. "If certainly looks as if the change of routing will produce dramatic finishes to matches. My only regret is that we won't be playing the Palmer Course again next year in the European Open, but I can understand they have to get it ready for the big event."

Lehman was predictably generous about his rival. "Of the three Ryder Cup teams in which I've been a member, two of them came when Ian was playing for Europe," he said. "I have great respect for him and his competitive ability. With eight Ryder Cup appearances under his belt, he has all the experience necessary to be a leader and I know his team will reflect his tenacity in the match."

Standing 6ft 2ins with a 13st 8lbs frame, Lehman will be a commanding figure in charge of an American side desperate to rehabilitate themselves after the shambles of Oakland Hills. "When I step on a golf course, I play for the joy of playing, the joy of competing," he once said. It is a philosophy which was strangely absent among the glum faces of the American players in Detroit, even before they got caught up in the heat of battle.

In making their choice, the PGA of America clearly viewed Lehman as a winner, which

Chapter 6 The Captains

meant they had no problem in overlooking his notorious charge onto the 17th green at Brookline, after Justin Leonard had sunk what proved to be the decisive putt. Few of the leading figures from either side came out of that particular event with any credit, including Sam Torrance whose comment, "And Tom Lehman called himself a man of God", may have been politically clever at the time, but was entirely inappropriate in a golfing context.

For his part, Lehman said: "I've never once claimed to be a man of God. I've said I'm a Christian, and the reason why I'm a Christian is that I do a lot of things I need forgiveness for; things that I regret. I know I'm not perfect. The man of God thing is somebody else's words. At Brookline, the Europeans felt the need to make a point and said they were surprised by the way I acted, that it was totally wrong. And the press ran with it."

The fact is that Lehman happens to be a very emotional man. As Cameron Morfit pointed out in *Golf* magazine, he "sobbed after hitting the shot of his life, a laser-like eight iron at the 1990 Q-school that nestled up to the pin and assured him a place to play. He couldn't contain his exuberance before the 1998 British Open, two years after winning the thing, and dislocated his shoulder while attempting a handstand for his kids in a UK kiddie park."

Tiger Woods obviously recognised an admirable balance in his prospective leader when he said: "I've been under different captains with different philosophies and personalities. I think Tom is probably right in the middle. He's not as fiery as Hal Sutton but certainly not as conservative as Tom Kite, though they were both competitive and wanted to win just as much as we all did. I think Tom will be a great captain. He was one of the spearheads at Valderrama and one of the leaders in the locker-room at Brookline."

In a reaction exemplifying his enthusiasm for the job, Lehman said: "I think I will be a good captain. I love being part of a team and I have a huge passion for the Ryder Cup. While my career may not have been as wonderful as other guys, I go back to those five goals that I set for myself and not many guys can say they were number one (in the world, in 1997), or PGA Tour Player of the Year or won the Vardon Trophy.

"Sometimes you can never dream big enough and this is an honour beyond my wildest dreams. I consider the Ryder Cup to be the ultimate golfing experience, even greater than winning the Open. I'm not sure we fully understand how important it is to the European players. I know it's important to us, that the guys are happy to be part of the team and that they get very nervous and uptight, which I think is a problem. My thing from the beginning has been this: the goal is not to be on the Ryder Cup team. The goal is to be on the winning Ryder Cup team."

He then admitted: "My core personality is very emotional and somewhat impulsive and I sometimes tend to fly by the seat of my pants." For that reason, he picked a back-room staff which he felt could offer more considered counsel.

So it was that he named former team-mates Corey Pavin and Loren Roberts as his assistant captains. "They are close friends and contemporaries of mine," Lehman explained. "When the pressure is on, these are the guys I want around me. They have proven to be extremely tough competitors and have risen to the occasion numerous times in their careers."

Pavin was his foursomes partner at Oak Hill in 1995 when Lehman was asked to hit the first shot of the tournament by the US captain, Lanny Wadkins. The drive sailed 30 yards past Colin Montgomerie's ball and the American duo went on to edge out Europe's top pairing of Montgomerie and Faldo by one hole.

He was also given a leading role in the 1999 matches, of which he said: "The wonderful atmosphere at the past two Ryder Cups has shown that what happened at Brookline is a thing of the past. The golf fans in Ireland are the best in the world. They are the most generous and warm-hearted people and they deserve the very best the Ryder Cup has to offer which, above all, is the commitment, passion and excitement it generates. I hate that 'Ole, Ole, Ole' song because the Europeans sing it when they are winning. But I have to admit that without it, the Ryder Cup wouldn't be the same."

With regard to events at Oakland Hills, which he watched on television, Lehman said: "I was living and dying with every shot that was made and every putt that was missed. The European team played better golf that week and there's no doubt we'll be underdogs in 2006, which should be to our advantage."   Since then, a resurgence in his own game has fuelled an ambition to become the first playing captain from either side of the Atlantic, since Arnold Palmer in 1963. "It's a long shot, but I want guys to know how much I want to be on the team. Enthusiasm is contagious."

No one could doubt Lehman's enthusiasm for golf. Unable to gain his card for the 1986 season, he was forced to play in Asia, South Africa and anywhere else there was prize-money on offer. His sponsors deserted him and he was left with only $1,000 in his bank account. "I just didn't feel I belonged in this world," he recalled. Feeling he was on the road to nowhere, it was only the thought of finishing up selling skis in the winter, which stopped him from taking a coaching job.

The launch of the Hogan Tour in 1990 came as a heaven-sent opportunity to him and four years later, the Memorial Tournament gave him his breakthrough victory on the regular US Tour.

"Certain things happen as you go along that help you build confidence, like winning the Hogan Tour player of the year was a big step for me," he added. Lehman's keen competitive instincts came to the fore in the major championships. For instance, after finishing tied third and second in the US Masters in 1993 and 1994, he went on to be third behind Pavin in the 1995 US Open at Shinnecock Hills, where he shared the lead with Greg Norman with a round to play.

Then came 1996 and the US Open at Oakland Hills, where he drove into a bunker on the

Chapter 6 The Captains

final hole to finish tied second behind Steve Jones. Walking down the first fairway that fateful day, he turned to Jones and said: "The Lord wants you to be courageous and strong, for that is the will of God." Though many observers considered it strange, when he spoke of it afterwards, it was no more than an expression of his strong, Christian beliefs.

Either way, his generosity of spirit found handsome rewards in the following months in which he captured the Open at Lytham and won the Tour Championship at Southern Hills to be named US Player of the Year. His last US Tour victory was in the 2000 Phoenix Open.

Since his appointment as captain, he has taken the remarkable step of sending DVDs of the movie *Miracle*, about the American Olympic hockey team beating the Russians, to as many as 142 US Tour players, at a cost to himself of $7 a copy. The objective was to show what passion and pride could accomplish, when a team had a common goal. What he described as the ultimate underdog story.

Against the background of humiliating defeat at Oakland Hills, could such a turnaround be achieved in Ireland? "It wouldn't be a miracle if it did," he replied. "Our problem, I believe, is that deep down inside, the American players believe more in individual achievements. There's a part of us that believes we've always had the stronger team, man against man. Therefore, if you lose, it doesn't change that Tiger Woods is still the best player in the world.

"I've talked to some guys who have said: 'Yeah, maybe there's some truth to that mind-set.' That attitude needs to be changed. Who cares what we're ranked? We need to want to win as badly as they do. It's as simple as that."

As a European Open competitor in 1995, 1996 and 2005, Lehman is familiar with the North Course at The K Club. But other business activities give him a rather special insight into the nature of the layout. By 2004, the Lehman Design Company had 15 projects ongoing or completed. They included the Gallery GC of Tucson, Arizona, which was part of the Chrysler Classic of Tucson Tournament in 2002, and the Troy Burn GC in Hudson, where, close to his native Minnesota, Lehman served as host to the Nationwide Tour's Scholarship America Showdown.

And they also include the TPC of Twin Cities, which was done in collaboration with none other than Arnold Palmer. Which, in the context of Ryder Cup 2006, was an intriguing meeting of minds.

♦

Chapter 7

The Irish

Chapter 7 The Irish

artime rations seemed a world away from the gastronomic delights of the Queen Mary as she cut through the North Atlantic on her journey to New York, like a floating five-star hotel. It was October 1947 and Britain's Ryder Cup team, which included an extremely worthy debutant, were set to engage a familiar golfing foe in the first meeting of the sides for 10 years.

History tells us that the '47 matches might not have happened but for the intervention of a wealthy businessman from the chosen venue of Portland, Oregon. After lean war years, the coffers of the PGA of America were still not sufficiently healthy to finance such a major undertaking. So it was that Robert A Hudson, president of a wholesale grocery complex in Portland, dipped into his pockets to the tune of £10,000 to cover the expenses of both teams. The British PGA gave their players £50 each, the same as they had received in 1929. But on arrival in New York, they were given $100 each by Hudson, who also informed them that they could have a phone call each to their home, on him, after the matches. Among the beneficiaries was Fred Daly, the reigning British Open champion.

When capturing the title at Royal Liverpool GC, Hoylake, Daly joined England's Sam King in the fifth pair to start the final day of the Championship, at 8.40am for the third round and at 1.10 for the last round. He covered the 36 holes in 150 strokes (78,72) to win by a stroke from Red Horne and the American amateur, Frank Stranahan, in a tie for second place. We are informed that the official programme carried the warning: 'Bicycles must not be brought onto the links.'

In his biography, written by the late Eoin McQuillan, Daly recalled the excitement of his first Ryder Cup, especially of sailing on the Queen Mary which, apparently, wasn't always smooth. "It seemed to us landlubbers that it was blowing a gale," he recalled. "I remember I spotted this other liner with all its lights on, going east. I shouted at the fellows to take a look but when they did, it had disappeared."

This prompted some serious ribbing from the other members of the side. "The Irishman's now seeing ghost ships: wouldn't you have expected as much," they chided. But the words had barely been uttered when the liner reappeared and Fred was vindicated. "I'll tell you something," he later mused, "that Atlantic is a wee bit different from Portrush Harbour."

During the voyage, team captain Henry Cotton's analytical mind prompted him to ask Daly: "What do you usually think about when you're addressing the ball on the tee?" "Think about, Henry?" Fred replied blankly. "Sure all I think about is hitting the ball as far and as straight as I can." Simplicity was the key to Daly's success.

On their arrival in New York, the team were entertained at a memorable banquet in the

Waldorf, before an overnight train journey to Chicago. Fred was delighted to discover that among the attendance of about 300, the renowned Silver Scot, Tommy Armour, then 51, had actually heard of him. In the event, it was one of the few high points of a trip in which the American side, led by Ben Hogan, gained a crushing victory by 11-1 on November 1st and 2nd. With a 4 and 3 defeat of Herman Kaiser in the anchor singles, Sam King was the only British winner.

As to the promised phone call after the matches: allowing for the time difference with Portrush, Fred duly booked the call so as to catch his son, Greer, before he left for school in the morning. Then, after talking with his wife and son for what seemed an age, he was saying his goodbyes and about to hang up when the American operator's voice came on the line – "Shucks Mr Daly, don't quit yet. I could listen to that cute Irish brogue all night." So, naturally, Fred kept on talking until there was nothing left to say.

Two years later, Harry Bradshaw was not considered by the British PGA for the matches at Ganton, despite having forced a play-off with Bobby Locke for the 1949 Open at Royal St George's in September of that year. Nor was he a candidate for the team which travelled to Pinehurst in November 1951. The magazine *Irish Golf* reported in August 1949: "The (British) PGA have laid down clearly that they consider professionals from the 26 counties as being overseas members of their Association. It is as overseas players that they take part in the Open itself, and in such tournaments as the *Daily Mail,* they had to qualify in the section allocated to overseas players.

"We have no wish ever to introduce politics into golf but the time does seem ripe when the whole matter of the Ryder Cup was clarified. The Royal and Ancient have ruled that 'Eireanns' as they are termed in England, are eligible for the Walker Cup team. ......We notice that the Rugby Union, who are in a similar position, have anticipated the problem and the team to leave 'these islands' next year, will be known as the British and Irish team. Such a simple change as that should avoid all complications."

The magazine's view became all the more reasonable when one considered that Bradshaw was deemed eligible to travel to South Africa in the winter of 1950-'51 as a member of a four-man British PGA line-up invited by that country's PGA. Perhaps this could be explained by the unavailability of Dai Rees and Charlie Ward for the trip. Either way, The Brad completed a quartet which also included Daly, Ken Bousfield and John Panton.

"During four months in South Africa, Fred and me were never beaten as a partnership, and that included some money matches," recalled The Brad, when I was writing his biography in 1989, the year before he died. "We had a couple of great matches against a fellow called Wilson, who was a scratchman. These involved playing the best ball of himself, a one handi-

Chapter 7 The Irish

capper and a two handicapper. Fred was asked by a friend of his, a chap called George Doak, who had been a member of Balmoral and was now living out there: 'Do you think you can take them?' 'Make no mistake about it; Harry and myself will take them,' came the confident reply.

"We played them for £200 and we won. And when they asked for a re-match, we won that too. And I remember the course had a par five of 675 yards, the longest hole I ever played in my life. But Fred was a huge hitter when he needed it. He always had 50 yards up his sleeve, and you know, he hit that green with two drivers, after about 16 waggles each time."

Bradshaw, invariably a mild-mannered man who never courted controversy, seemed to accept his extraordinary, overseas status which, incidentally, he duly reverted to having done the PGA proud in South Africa. But there was a long-overdue change of heart by the time officials sat down to pick the 1953 line-up. So it was that the side which did battle with the US at Wentworth on October 2nd and 3rd of that year, was, in fact, the first British and Irish Ryder Cup team.

"I remember being delighted to be paired with Fred in my first Ryder Cup," said The Brad. "And we were the only ones to win the foursomes which, of course, were 36-hole matches in those days. I always thought Fred was a fantastic player and I'm proud of our unbeaten record, even in exhibitions against some of the great players from around the world.

"He had a wonderful temperament. Whatever was happening in a match, he would just go along, whistling to himself. And if I put him on the green, he would take out the putter and the whistling would get even louder. I called him Fred but he sometimes called me Harry or Brad, I suppose depending on his mood.

"In the match against Walter Burkemo and Cary Middlecoff (US Open champion in 1949 and 1956 and US Masters champion of 1955) we were three up at lunchtime after a morning round of 70. But things changed when the Americans won the 30th and 31st and we were eventually taken to the final hole, one up. That was where I hit a bad drive into the semi-rough down the left, but Fred hit some two-wood, right up the fairway.

"Twenty-five thousand people were there, hanging out of the beech trees on the right of the green. And the branches cracking under the weight. 'Look out! Look out!', they were shouting, as fellows fell to the ground. I had this shot of 60, maybe 70 yards and as I walked up to it, my two knees were knocking, looking at this crowd. I'd never seen anything like it in my life.

"I said to Fred, 'I don't know whether to play a nine or a 10 up there.' 'Just play what you like,' said Fred, throwing his hands up. And the mere fact of him doing that, gave me a lot of confidence. Whereas most fellows would say 'Now leave this close and I'll hole the putt', it didn't matter to Fred what club I played.

"Anyway, I knocked it in to six feet and Fred holed the putt for a birdie. They (Burkemo and Middlecoff) had missed the green on the right and nearly holed a chip for an eagle. Then, when it was over, there was a mad rush for Fred, and I've often said it to him since that only for the police were there, they'd have knocked him into the hole after the ball."

Two days later, the headline on the *Sunday Express* sports pages read: 'Britain loses Ryder Cup but what a day for two Irishmen!' This salute referred to the singles matches in which the pair of them were again successful: Daly crushed Ted Knoll by 9 and 7, being eight under fours for the 29 holes played, while The Brad was admirably solid in a 3 and 2 win over Fred Haas.

Between them, they had accounted for three points from the home side's total of five and a half over the two days. One report of Harry's match stated that "his steadiness flowered into golfing genius when, over the last 11 holes, he returned figures of four under fours."

Two years later, he and Christy O'Connor were in the side at Thunderbird Golf and Country Club. O'Connor, who was so highly rated that he was picked at number one in the singles, where he lost to Tommy Bolt, would go on to make a record 10 successive Ryder Cup appearances. Meanwhile, for The Brad, there were the makings of further memories for the professional shop at Portmarnock.

"About 30 years after the 1955 Ryder Cup, these Americans came to play at Portmarnock and said they were members of Thunderbird," said The Brad. "I told them their best hole at Thunderbird was the eighth. One of the Americans scratched his head and said 'You're right. It's a helluva par four. And you remember that hole?' 'Yes,' I said. 'And the first is a four and your last is a par five.' Though he tried to catch me out, I knew every one of them. After playing a course once, I can remember each hole more than 20 years later."

Though Thunderbird was not a rewarding venue for the British and Irish line-up, Henry Longhurst wrote: "Harry Bradshaw has proved himself, like his compatriot Joe Carr, to be a wonderful fellow to travel with." The Brad, who lost by 3 and 2 to the 2004 Ryder Cup assistant captain, Jackie Burke, shot an approximate 65 in the morning to be no better than level at the halfway stage.

Lindrick in 1957 is remembered for a remarkable British and Irish triumph and for the ill-tempered reaction of two American players. The fiery exchange between the notoriously volatile Tommy Bolt and Scotland's Eric Brown ranks as an all-time classic. The other exchange involved O'Connor.

In his inimitable way, The Brad took up the story: "That was where Dai Rees and the late Ken Bousfield were the only ones to win the foursomes on the opening day. And Tommy Bolt

Chapter 7 The Irish

and Dick Mayer, the reigning US Open champion, beat Eric Brown and Christy 7 and 5. Christy asked me after the foursomes who I was playing in the singles. And when I told him I was playing an American chap called Mayer, he covered his face and said: 'Oh Brad, I feel sorry for you.' But my reaction was 'I'll knock in putt for putt with him.'

"Father Jack Solon, a two-handicap from Ballinasloe that I used to play a lot with, was there among the Irish supporters. And there was a big American millionaire with a 10-gallon hat, buying drinks for everybody. He was with a group of about 20, sitting there at the lower end of the lounge in the Royal Hotel in Sheffield. And I'm with eight or 10 fellows in the top side of the lounge.

"The chat was all about tomorrow's games. And when they came to mine, the big American millionaire said 'Oh Harry Bradshaw has no chance.' 'Begorrah,' said Fr Solon, 'champion or no champion, he won't get it all his own way. I've played a lot with Harry at Portmarnock and he'll put Dick to the pin of his collar.'

"One word borrowed another and the upshot of it was that the American offered Fr Solon 50/1 again me. Fr Solon immediately put his hand to his back pocket. Fifty to one in a two-horse-race – he thought he'd never get the wallet out fast enough. 'Padraig – the Americans called him Padraig – what would you like to bet.' And Fr Solon said 'I'll have £10 worth of that.' 'Put the wallet away; we have a gentleman's agreement.'

"Well, I won the first and second and I also won the third where I holed a great bunker shot. Going to the fourth tee, Mayer says to me 'You're a great trap player, Harry.' And I replied that I generally holed four or five in a round, as a rule. And he says I hope you don't do it this morning. I was giving him the old one and two, you know.

"He was a helluva nice fellow. Of course we finished all square after I had three-putted the ninth, morning and afternoon. Only for that, I would have had him. I always took the wrong borrow on that green. Anyway, when they met afterwards, the American went to pay Fr Solon on the basis that he had said Mayer would beat me. But Fr Solon wouldn't hear of it. He could have taken the winnings, but didn't."

Bradshaw was playing in the anchor position and, as it happened, O'Connor was in the second-last match, just as Padraig Harrington and Paul McGinley had been in the 2004 matches at Oakland Hills. O'Connor's opponent was Dow Finsterwald, a talented 27-year-old who would gain the distinction of winning the first USPGA Championship played to a strokes format, the following year.

For his part, O'Connor was the only British and Irish player to qualify automatically for the team that year as Matchplay champion. And like Bradshaw against Mayer, he won the first two holes with birdies and at the third, was comfortably on the green in two whereas Finsterwald's approach was wayward. The American then chipped to six feet and O'Connor putted to two feet past the cup. That was when Finsterwald, after missing the hole, stretched out angrily and hooked the ball back while it was still in motion.

It stunned the crowd. "O'Connor three up," said the referee. Finsterwald protested that he hadn't conceded the hole, but the referee insisted: "Pick up your ball; O'Connor is three up."

"I wondered what had happened when I saw Finsterwald cracking the driver off the ground as he walked to the fourth," recalled Bradshaw. "With every Irish doctor in England following Christy and myself, it wasn't long before one of them filled me in. Though Christy went to the pro shop to change his putter instead of joining us for lunch, there was still time for him to give me his version of the story. And I told him: 'Now Christy, you want to knock in everything this afternoon, no matter if you're only two or three inches from the hole. Because this fellow will watch you.'"

As it happened, O'Connor's fortunes on the greens were transformed by the change of putter and he won six of the first eight holes in the afternoon. Then, on the ninth, they both had five or six footers for a half in par. Finsterwald played first, missed and was left with a short one which O'Connor conceded. O'Connor then missed his own effort and with his ball only an inch from the cup, assumed the next was conceded. But when he stepped up on the 10th tee, Finsterwald claimed the honour on the grounds that O'Connor hadn't finished the ninth.

Stung by this, the Irishman went on to hole a chip at the 29th and wrapped up the match by the 30th for a crushing 7 and 6 victory. Finsterwald was so angry at the outcome that he refused to shake hands. "The way he finished off that American, proved to me what a tough competitor Christy could be," said The Brad. "A lot of golfers would have fallen apart when something like that happened."

He concluded: "We were drinking champagne until five in the morning. It was the first win since 1933 and we went absolutely mad."

O f all the honours and distinctions accorded Himself over the years, one stands apart as the product of unique circumstances. Among other things, it was an occasion when some of the world's greatest golfers were involved in a potentially fatal air incident. And it happened en route to the 13th Ryder Cup in which Ireland had what had by then become its accepted two representatives.

For O'Connor, whose compatriot on this occasion was Norman Drew, an enduring memento of the event is a membership card which reads: "J-L (Jolly Lucky) Long Drop Club, 5.30pm October 29th 1959, Los Angeles to Palm Springs. Almost."

Chapter 7 The Irish

Formed on October 30th at the instigation of John Letters of the Letters Golf Company, the club's exclusive membership list included Himself, Rees, Peter Alliss, Brown, Bousfield, Drew, Bernard Hunt, Peter Mills, Dave Thomas and Harry Weetman, all of whom were members of the British and Irish line-up. Doug Ford, a member of the American team, was also on the plane, having hitched a lift.

Barry Nolan of the *Irish Independent,* Frank Pennink of the *Daily Mail* and Ron Heager of the *Daily Express* were among the golfing scribes on board. And Heager's account in the *Daily Express* of October 31st, described how "We were tossed around like a cocktail in a shaker ..... It was like falling in a giant lift when the cable had snapped. Only your stomach stayed on the 10th storey. It was the Big Dipper – without the laughs."

Then, from a distance of 18 years on, he wrote in the 1977 Ryder Cup programme: "The date carved indelibly in our minds was ..... seven days before the team was due on the tee against the United States under Sam Snead. Behind them was a planned acclimatisation after landing in New York (on the SS Queen Elizabeth), golf in Atlantic City, Washington and Atlanta and, that morning, the big hop from Atlanta to Los Angeles.

"Next there were just 140 miles and a brief flight to the air-conditioned comfort of the Desi Arnaz Hotel at Palm Desert. That was what we thought as we filed into the plane.

"The reality proved to be the nightmare none of the 29 passengers would forget. 'Keep your seat-belts fastened; there may be a little rough weather ahead,' our captain warned us. Rough? A little? A few minutes away, as we approached the jagged peaks of the San Jacinto Mountains, the plane began to toss like a cork as we met the storm that lit the vivid, purple skies.

"The bumps were mild at first, but sufficient to turn bronzed golfers ashen. Heads ducked down between knees. Collars were loosened. In the eye of the storm, the jolts increased in frequency and violence. We were trapped in a big lift racing up and down: berserk. And the climax was still to come.

"It arrived with a new dimension of violence. There was a sickening, downward plunge. We were a stone dropped into a well. Anything not strapped down took off and floated to the roof of the plane. Weightless. A grinding, crunching, agonised sound of metal on metal heightened the horror.

"We didn't know it then, but this was the brink of calamity. From that robots' wrestling match of sound, we inched back from the edge of disaster. The metallic judderings of the aircraft were beautiful noises to the grappling pilot. He had regained command of the ship. He had won his battle with the furies of the elements."

In fact the chartered plane had plummeted from 13,000 to 9,000 feet before the pilot's skills eventually triumphed. Whereupon Weetman was moved to remark: "I bloody near messed my pants." Only to get the reply from a colleague: "I've got news for you Harry, I did."

Panton was also a member of the visiting squad for the matches at Eldorado Country Club, but he flew out on his own, having answered an SOS from the PGA, requesting cover for Mills, who had back trouble. As it happened, neither of them got a game.

When the pilot righted the plane, it turned back for Los Angeles with a view to another attempt at completing the trip. But as the players disembarked and several of them had gone down on their knees to kiss the ground, skipper Dai Rees insisted they would resume the journey by Greyhound Bus.

In his autobiography, told to John Redmond, O'Connor talked of how the initial bumps were acceptable. Then he went on: "But as the jolts increased in regularity and violence, collars were being undone. And once the air hostess reached for the sick bag, she started a trend. This was it, I thought to myself. I said a prayer."

At that point, he turned to Brown whom he would deprive spectacularly of the Carrolls International title with an eagle, birdie, eagle finish at Royal Dublin seven years later. "I asked him if he prayed," O'Connor recalled. To which the Scot replied: "No. Will you say one for me?"

Later, on the trip by road, O'Connor recalled helping to ease the tension "with a rendering, though not a good one I might say, of *Galway Bay.*" He added: "As time ticked by, we slowly regained our senses."

The book goes on to outline the conditions of membership of the J-L Long Drop Club: "Being a founder member ... you have a high position to uphold. To avoid the risk of dropping low in the eyes of the other co-founders, you must raise your glass and toast each and every one of them at 5.30pm on 29 October every year you remain alive, which you are jolly lucky to be at the moment."

Sadly, several team members have since gone from us, but according to O'Connor, they met for a number of annual reunions at which they would recount their personal experience of the ordeal. Among them was Drew who had reason to be pleased with his lone Ryder Cup appearance in which he halved with Doug Ford at the top of the singles order.

The American was a formidable opponent, having captured the 1955 USPGA Championship at Meadowbrook, where he beat Middlecoff in the final, and the US Masters two years later, when he edged no less a figure than Snead into second place. In the event, the Ulsterman had a wretched start to the 36-hole match, being four down after nine.

But he fought back to be only one down at lunchtime before going on to produce a fine 69 in the afternoon, finishing eagle, birdie on the 6,823-yard, par-70 course. Acknowledged as the shortest hitter in the British and Irish line-up, he was considered unlikely even to get a match over the two days. So it came as something of a surprise when he won the 522-yard

Chapter 7 The Irish

35th with an eagle three and then out-drove Ford down the 470-yard final hole which was flanked by lakes on both sides.

Drew then hit a glorious fairway wood to 15 feet from the pin and proceeded to hole the putt for a winning birdie and a halved match. Most improbably, he became one of the heroes of a bleak day for the visiting side whose only other singles contributions were a half by Alliss and a win by Brown in the anchor match against Middlecoff.

From a broader perspective, a fascinating aspect of that trip was that it marked the last time a British and Irish team travelled by sea to a Ryder Cup in the US. The future was in the air. It was also the last time that Ryder Cup matches were contested over 36 holes of foursomes and singles. But the really interesting bit is that it produced a partnership which would become one of the most illustrious in the history of the event.

Among the great fascinations of a Peter Alliss television commentary, especially from an Irish standpoint, are the remarks he is liable to make about the daring deeds of "my old pal, Christy O'Connor." The BBC's voice of golf seems to reserve his most glowing tributes for commentaries from Wentworth, which is probably due in no small measure to O'Connor's marvellous achievements there, notably in setting an aggregate record of 274 for the famous West Course, when capturing the Daks Tournament of 1959. There was also the majesty of his play with the big, American ball, when winning the Martini Tournament of 1964 when Alliss, incidentally, finished third.

He and Himself came together for the first time as Ryder Cup foursomes partners for the 1959 matches at Eldorado. I wondered if they had responded in the manner advocated by the celebrated American psychologist, Dr Bob Rotella, who has advised Ryder Cup partners: "Before you start, you've got to turn to the guy you're playing with and say 'Look, I love you; I'm going to support you out there.'"

Alliss permitted himself a quiet smile at the notion of such overt togetherness. "As far as that's concerned," he said, "I remember that on one of our early holes, I hit the ball into bushes and turned to Christy saying 'Oh, I'm so sorry.' To which Christy replied: 'Are you doing your best?' And when I assured him I was, he looked me in the eyes and said: 'Well, never apologise to me again.' And I never did."

Skipper Dai Rees knew he had uncovered some magic when O'Connor and Alliss shot 63 in practice for the '59 matches. And the little Welshman was fully vindicated when the Anglo-Irish partnership beat Doug Ford and the reigning US Masters champion, Art Wall, by 3 and 2 over 36 holes. Henry Longhurst was among those to be greatly impressed with the pairing. Reporting for *The Sunday Times* from Palm Desert on the Saturday of the matches, Longhurst enthused: "Here was a great achievement for a fine and obviously happy combination of England and Eire. O'Connor has been playing magnificently since they arrived and yesterday (in the foursomes) was no exception."

Forty-six years later, Alliss concurred. "It seemed that destiny had decided we were a partnership for the long haul," he said. "They didn't have player-power in those days, so there was no question of the two of us informing the captain that we'd like to play together. You were told what to do and you simply got on with it, despite being terrified of coming up against such American legends as Sam Snead.

"Anyway, who would have thought of pairing chalk with cheese? Because that's what we were. Though we've broken bread together, Christy and I have never dined in each other's homes. We've never done anything that might prompt people to suggest 'Oh they'd make a great partnership; they're like blood brothers.'

"Chalk and bloody cheese. In those days, Christy was what you might describe as a little bit rebellious, a bit of a smoking gun. And I suppose, in a quiet English way, I could have been considered a sort of wayward catapult. Anyway, fate threw us together and I know I always did my very, very best for Christy and, God knows, he did his very best for me.

"I just had the most amazing confidence in him. Neither of us were good putters, yet we holed putts when it mattered. We gave confidence to each other to the extent that we became a very solid partnership. All the while, a wonderful golfing friendship developed over the years. And I love Mary (Christy's wife) to death. I've always thought of her as a great lady."

In successive Ryder Cups from 1959 to 1969, after which Alliss retired from tournament golf, they played 12 matches together, winning five, losing six and halving one. Since then, other notable partnerships from these islands have been Nick Faldo and Ian Woosnam (Played 10, won five, lost three, halved two), and Bernard Gallacher and Brian Barnes (Played 10, won five, lost four, halved one). But in terms of matches played, Alliss and O'Connor reigned supreme, until the so-called Spanish Armada of Seve Ballesteros and Jose-Maria Olazabal was launched at Muirfield Village in 1987. Their record, which is unlikely to be beaten, is: Played 15, won 11, lost two, halved two.

Having started in 36-hole matches, the Anglo-Irish pair remained together when 18 holes became the norm at Royal Lytham two years later, by which stage O'Connor was acknowledged as being at the forefront of European golf. "I would have been among those who considered Christy to be in the genius class as a striker of the ball, despite relaxing his right-hand fingers at the top of the backswing," said Alliss. "He had all the shots except one – the putt.

"He won numerous tournaments with a flicky putting stroke. God knows how many more

Chapter 7 The Irish

he would have won had he the putting skills of even a modest player of today. Anyway, I had been doing some good things myself, when the Americans recognised what a wonderful player Christy was. So we were respected and feared for a variety of reasons.

"Dave Marr (1965 USPGA champion) once said to me that the Americans all wanted to get at me first, because they thought I was a toffy-nosed, if quite an elegant player. A bit snobby, having served my apprenticeship in Ryder Cups going back to 1953 at Wentworth, while my father (Percy) was in the winning team at Southport and Ainsdale, 20 years previously. And, of course, Christy and I were both part of the wonderful, 1957 victory at Lindrick."

Which was their stronger discipline? "It didn't matter to us whether it was foursomes or fourballs, though I suspect we were better at foursomes," Alliss replied. "Better than the record books would suggest. I know I concentrated more on foursomes. You know the thing: if it was my tee-shot I had to get Christy on the fairway, or if it was an approach-iron, I had to get him on the green. And I gave similar care to putting. I concentrated on getting him closer than four feet from the hole, if I could.

"Outside of the Ryder Cup, possibly in the Joy Cup (against the Continental professionals), or in matches against the Walker Cup amateurs, I remember partnering John Panton. He and I were also very different people. And John was a very good putter who never seemed to miss a fairway, which made him a comforting partner. But we never quite hit it off like Christy and myself.

"There was one memorable occasion when we were about 235 yards from the green and Christy was faced with a downhill lie into a left-to-right wind, with out of bounds on the right. And I heard him telling his caddie that he'd take the driver. I have to admit I was terrified by the idea, but as players, it wasn't in our nature to have conversations about such matters.

"We were two up with three to play and our opponents were in trouble. And I wanted to say that the driver was a little bit ambitious, but all that came out was a stammered 'I-I-I ....' Then Christy said casually 'I'll just nick it ...' This prompted a sharp intake of breath from me, which must have sounded like a punctured bellows. Next thing I knew, the ball was going like a bullet for the green, where it landed, naturally. And we won with ease.

"I especially remember Royal Birkdale in 1965, where Christy and I won two games out of four. We played some terrific golf in the foursomes on the opening afternoon (they reached the turn in 31, yet were only one up) when beating Billy Casper and Gene Littler. But the following morning, we got a terrible hammering by 6 and 4 in the fourballs against Arnold (Palmer) and Dave (Marr). That was a very unusual occurrence for us and by way of proving it, we went on to beat the same pair on the 18th in the afternoon. I tell you, over the years O'Connor and I had the ability to surprise the best that America could throw at us."

As with all matters of team selection, their partnership was not thought of as sacrosanct. But the renowned, mellifluous tones acquired a perceptible edge as Alliss recalled how skipper John Fallon had considered it appropriate to split them at East Lake in 1963. That was when Alliss played with compatriot Bernard Hunt and O'Connor partnered Neil Coles.

"They soon put us back together again," he said with obvious satisfaction. "Our last match was in the opening foursomes at Birkdale in 1969, when we halved with Casper and Frank Beard. That was when I decided to retire at the ripe old age of 39.

"Later on, it became obvious that Seve and Ollie were going to beat our record of matches together. And we couldn't have bowed to a more wonderful pair. The interesting thing to me was that Ollie was the strong man in that partnership, which was not generally acknowledged. While Seve produced the flamboyance, Ollie was the anchor. And together, they wrought unbelievable magic. Absolutely majestic.

"Nor does it surprise me that (Bernhard) Langer has had the most partners in Ryder Cup history. (The German's 12 partners were: Manuel Pinero, Faldo, Jose Maria Canizares, Sandy Lyle, Ken Brown, Ronan Rafferty, Mark James, Colin Montgomerie, Woosnam, Barry Lane, Per-Ulrik Johansson and David Gilford). Apart from having the ability to keep the ball in play, there was always a wonderful calmness about him and you knew instinctively he was doing his very best. That's how it was with Christy and me."

There might be the temptation to view such effusiveness with a degree of scepticism, were it not for repeated reminders during golf telecasts on the BBC. Shallow feelings don't stand the test of time. Indeed the warmth of Alliss was palpable, when he concluded: "The day I discovered Christy O'Connor as a partner, was one of the happiest of my golfing life."

hen "Himself" made his 10th successive and farewell appearance in the 1973 matches at Muirfield, he was aged 48 years, eight months and 30 days – the oldest representative from this side of the Atlantic since Ted Ray (50-2-5) in 1927. Inevitably, his departure heralded a changing of the order, where Irish aspirants were concerned. Newcomers arrived in strength for the matches at Laurel Valley in 1975, when the country had an unprecedented three representatives in John O'Leary, Eamonn Darcy and the great man's nephew, Christy O'Connor Jnr.

It was not an especially auspicious occasion for any of the Irishmen. With the visiting side suffering yet another defeat on American soil, a welcome highlight was the performance of Brian Barnes who gained the distinction of beating Jack Nicklaus twice in singles combat in the one day. For Darcy and O'Connor Jnr, however, happier Ryder Cup times lay ahead, while O'Leary would become Irish Open champion in 1982, before going on to give distinguished

Chapter 7 The Irish

service to the Ryder Cup and the European Tour, as a member of their board of directors. Indeed he filled a prominent, ceremonial role at Oakland Hills in 2004.

The emergence of a European line-up in 1979 was also significant for two changes in the match conditions. It marked the introduction of the "envelope", whereby each captain inserted the name of a player in a sealed envelope in the event of either team being reduced to 11 players through injury or illness. The result would be a half-point for each team. This staging at The Greenbrier also made Des Smyth and Peter Oosterhuis the first two wild-card selections in the history of the event.

Smyth was considered an obvious choice after beating Nick Price in the final of the European Matchplay Championship earlier that year. As with other Irish debutants before him, it was not a rewarding exercise. Better was to come two years later, however, when Smyth won a foursomes point with Bernard Gallacher and a fourball point with Jose Maria Canizares against what has since become acknowledged as the strongest-ever American side.

Though American players could be somewhat indifferent about Ryder Cup honours because of the one-sided nature of the matches, the event always held enormous appeal for British and Irish players. And their European brethren became similarly enthused, especially after a marvellous victory at The Belfry in 1985. Claiming a place in the Ryder Cup had now become something really special.

Against that background, it was fascinating to observe Darcy struggle for automatic selection in 1987, when the trophy would be defended at Muirfield Village. By winning a rain-restricted Belgian Open at Royal Waterloo, he moved into ninth position in the qualifying table, where he clung on tenaciously for the following nine weeks.

Even then, there was no let up in Darcy's torment insofar as Mats Lanner, his closest challenger, started the final tournament, the German Open, with a 62. "Still I held on," he later reflected. "And the big pay-off was that I can now look back on it as unquestionably the highlight of my professional career."

It culminated in a typically generous Nicklaus, as the defeated US captain, being moved to talk of "a great effort by a man who had not won a Ryder Cup point in nine previous matches." And by way of emphasis, the Golden Bear suggested that "the putt he holed on the 18th will probably become the most important he will ever hole in his career."

The setting was affectionately known as the "Course that Jack Built". And Nicklaus was right about Darcy: for the remainder of his European Tour career, the Delgany man didn't hole a putt to compare with the one which made such a vital contribution to Europe's first triumph on American soil. It surpassed even a glorious Dunhill Cup triumph at St Andrews a year later, when he captained the Irish trio. "The Ryder Cup stands apart, because of what it meant

Ireland's 17

Fred Daly

Three months after winning the Open Championship at Hoylake in 1947, Fred Daly set sail for the US as the Ryder Cup's first representative from this island. In all, the Portrush native made four successive appearances, playing in eight matches. His status as the Open champion made Daly an automatic choice to lead the singles in Portland, Oregon, but he was soundly beaten, 5 and 4, by the talented Dutch Harrison. He also lost to Lloyd Mangrum in 1949 but went on to halve with Clayton Haefner at Pinehurst in 1951 and produced a storming swansong by crushing Ted Knoll 9 and 7 at Wentworth in 1953.

Sadly, Daly's tournament career was relatively short in that he lost much of his golfing prime to World War II. With nine tournament wins, however, including the supreme prize of the Open, he became a distinguished figure during the post-war years.

Harry Bradshaw

The Brad, as he was affectionately known, became the most notable victim of the Irish Government's decision late in 1948 to declare a Republic. It meant he was treated as an "Overseas Player" by the British PGA, thereby ruling him ineligible for Ryder Cup selection. Commonsense eventually prevailed in 1953, however, when he made his debut at Wentworth, forming a splendid partnership with his great friend, Fred Daly, to beat Walter Burkemo and Cary Middlecoff by one hole. Bradshaw also played at Thunderbird in 1955 and was a member of the victorious British and Irish team at Lindrick, two years later.

Of The Brad's performance in the final singles on that occasion, the distinguished British golf writer, Tom Scott, noted: "We felt sorry for Harry Bradshaw and Dick Mayer, battling it out when nothing mattered." But it ended appropriately in a half.

Christy O'Connor Snr

A remarkable Ryder Cup career ended for "Himself" at Muirfield in 1973, when he was only three months short of his 49th birthday. It was his 10th successive appearance, establishing a record which would remain unbeaten for 24 years until Nick Faldo surpassed it at Valderrama in 1997. Though O'Connor's match statistics may appear rather modest, it should be noted that he was competing as a club professional against the cream of American golf, from the Ben Hogan era into the dominance of Arnold Palmer and Jack Nicklaus.

Along the way, he formed a wonderful partnership with Peter Alliss. His best singles performance was at Lindrick, where he administered a 7 and 6 thrashing to Dow Finsterwald, who would go on to capture the USPGA Championship less than 12 months later.

Norman Drew

By competing in the 1959 matches at Eldorado CC in Palm Springs, Drew gained the distinction of becoming the first player from these islands to gain both Walker Cup and Ryder Cup honours. And a year later, his representative status was further enhanced on being picked for Ireland in the Canada Cup at Portmarnock. At Eldorado, Drew surprised and delighted visiting observers by coming from four down to gain a halved singles against Doug Ford, the 1955 USPGA champion and winner of the US Masters two years later.

Christy O'Connor, who had ten successive Ryder Cup appearances from 1955 to 1973, in his prime.

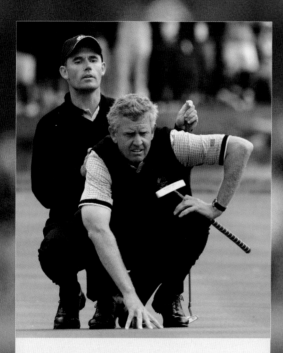

Padraig Harrington

On being asked for his assessment of the teenage skills of Harrington as an international competitor, a GUI official once remarked: "He has an amazing talent for winning matches." This has certainly carried through to Ryder Cup level, where the Stackstown player has won all of his three singles encounters.

Memories remain vivid of a debut win against Mark O'Meara at Brookline, where he hit a glorious pitching wedge of 135 yards to the final green. Then there was a crushing defeat of Mark Calcavecchia at The Belfry in 2002, followed by victory over Jay Haas in a tight, testing match at Oakland Hills.

All of which may explain why good putters in the Harrington mould, are such feared opponents in matchplay. Yet surprisingly, he had to wait until the second day of the 2002 staging to secure his first pairs point, which came in a fourball where he and Colin Montgomerie (above) beat no less a partnership than Phil Mickelson and David Toms.

Padraig Harrington playing to the second green during his match against Davis Love III and Tiger Woods in the second day's foursomes at Oakland Hills. Harrington and partner Paul McGinley went on to win by 4 and 3.

Jimmy Martin

Invariably modest about his considerable tournament achievements, he once carded eight birdies and an eagle in a sparkling 63 at Stoneham in England in the Swallow-Penfold Tournament. A short hitter, even by the standards of the day, Martin was a wonderful putter and captured the Piccadilly Medal Tournament in 1964, followed by the Silent Night Tournament a year later which effectively earned him Ryder Cup selection. As it happened, he played in only one match that year at Royal Birkdale, in a losing foursomes partnership with Jimmy Hitchcock. He won the Carrolls International at Woodbrook in 1968.

Hugh Boyle

In 1966, this native of Omeath, Co Louth, gained the distinction of becoming the first player from these islands to win in Japan. His victory came in the Yomiuri Open and a further success in the Daks Tournament gave him the confidence to earn a place in the Ryder Cup team at Houston in 1967. It turned into a rather unfortunate experience for the visiting players, who were roundly hammered by an American line-up who were famously introduced by skipper, Ben Hogan, at the opening ceremony as "the finest golfers in the world."

Eamonn Darcy

Sporting distinctions are not always as sweet the second or third time around, but Eamonn Darcy became a notable exception to this notion at Muirfield Village in 1987. Having had to settle for only half a fourball point on his debut in 1975, Darcy eventually got a fourth chance of Ryder Cup glory. And he grabbed it with admirable courage. A singles win over Ben Crenshaw became a crucial element of an historic European triumph — their first on American soil.

His prospects against Crenshaw were greatly enhanced when the 1984 US Masters champion broke his putter in anger after three-putting the sixth green.

Yet the level of expectation had also increased, to the extent that there was enormous pressure on Darcy when he stood over a slippery, left-to-right breaking putt for victory on the 18th.

To his eternal credit, the ball found the target.

Eamonn Darcy enjoys a moment of pure satisfaction in beating Ben Crenshaw on the 18th green in his crucial 1987 Ryder Cup singles match at Muirfield Village.

Des Smyth

When Smyth appeared in the Ryder Cup for a second time in 1981, he faced what has since been acknowledged as the strongest American side in the history of the event. He has since outscored most of those players, including Tom Watson, Hale Irwin and Bruce Lietzke, en-route to two tournament victories on the Champions Tour. He and Peter Oosterhuis gained the distinction in 1979 of becoming the first wild-card selections on the newly-formed European line-up. Now he is to be the event's first Irish vice-captain.

The staging at The Greenbrier in 1979 was a disappointment for new Europe, but Smyth had reason to be proud of his two points from the '81 encounter at Walton Heath. The first one came as Bernard Gallacher's foursomes partner in a defeat of Irwin and Raymond Floyd and the second was earned as the foruball partner of Jose Maria Canizares in a 6 and 5 thrashing of Bill Rogers and Lietzke.

Paul McGinley leaps for joy after holing his historic match winning putt against Jim Furyk on the 18th green at the Belfry to seal victory for Europe in the 2002 Ryder Cup.

Paul McGinley

It is always an honour to be given the anchor role in Sunday's Ryder Cup singles. And when McGinley got it at Oakland Hills, one suspected it had much to do with his marvellous, nine-foot winning putt at The Belfry two years previously.

At a function in Dublin two months after that particular achievement, McGinley had his first meeting with the legendary Doug Sanders. And without the slightest hint of rancour, the ill-fated American remarked in a soft, southern drawl: "I've been famous all my life for missing a putt; you're going to be famous for holing one." "Though it's part of my life, I don't want it to be the defining moment of my career," the Dubliner had protested at the time. And by way of ensuring that this would be so, he went on to secure two and a half points out of three at Oakland Hills, including a fine singles win over NEC champion, Stewart Cink. At number 12, naturally.

There is a God: Christy O'Connor Jnr approaches the 18th green following his magnificent two iron shot to four feet at the 1989 staging of the Ryder Cup at The Belfry. **Inset:** Team captain Tony Jacklin congratulates the emotionally charged O'Connor Jnr.

Christy O'Connor Jnr

Great shots have become an integral part of the rich tapestry of golfing achievement, and from recent decades, few have created a greater impact than O'Connor's final shot of the 1989 matches at The Belfry. It was so good that he wasn't even required to putt.

"Hit that on the green and see what happens," urged skipper Tony Jacklin, as the Galwayman stood over a two-iron shot of 229 yards. O'Connor responded by ripping a glorious effort with such accuracy that the ball came to rest on the critical middle tier of the green, only about four feet below the hole.

It delivered such a shock to his opponent, Fred Couples, that the American's approach, with only a nine iron, was pushed ruinously wide of the green from where he failed to reach the putting surface in three. At that point, Couples conceded victory and Europe were on their way to retaining the trophy through a tied match. In the process, Junior and Himself had emulated J C Snead and Sam Snead, along with Jay Haas and Bob Goalby, as nephews and uncles to have gained Ryder Cup honours.

David Feherty

Kiawah Island presented probably the most severe course set-up of recent memory, when the 1991 matches were staged there as its tournament baptism. All of which reflected enormous credit on David Feherty who was approximately level par for the 17 holes he played in beating the reigning US Open champion, Payne Stewart, by 2 and 1.

Not surprisingly, it proved to be the best golf from any player, but it was not sufficient to save Europe from a dispiriting defeat. The so-called War on the Shore was Feherty's only Ryder Cup appearance at a time when he seemed set to become one of the outstanding exponents on this side of the Atlantic. But a television career beckoned, offering him a different tilt at greatness. Main problem for Kiawah competitors was the speed of the exposed greens which, in the view of course-designer Pete Dye, were far too quick for the windy conditions. The upshot was that figures of four or five over par were sufficient to win matches.

And in the final analysis, the Americans made fewer mistakes.

Darren Clarke

Though his Ryder Cup career got off to a slow start at Valderrama in 1997, Clarke gradually matured into a key member of the European side. On the occasion of the Spanish staging, skipper Seve Ballesteros saw fit to choose him in only one match prior to the Sunday singles, but he has played all five matches in three stagings since then.

The benefit of a strict fitness regime was very much in evidence at Oakland Hills where, after winning three of his four pairs matches, he proceeded to gain an impressive half against no less an opponent than Davis Love on the Sunday. Predictably, his earlier wins had been dominated by a partnership with Lee Westwood which had proved to be similarly productive in 2002. We weren't surprised. Skills well-learned during a glittering amateur career had been in evidence in the Accenture World Matchplay at La Costa, where he gained a memorable victory in the final against Tiger Woods in the February of Millennium Year.

Framed against the morning sun, Darren Clarke tees off at the first hole in his second day's fourball match against Tiger Woods and Chris Riley at Oakland Hills, 2004. Clarke and Ian Poulter were to succumb to a 4 and 3 defeat. Inset: Clarke with the Waterford

Philip Walton is hugged by team captain Bernard Gallacher following his decisive victory over Jay Haas at Oak Hill in 1995.

Philip Walton

When Walton birdied the short 15th to go dormie three at Oak Hill in 1995, it seemed that his prospects of delivering a precious point were as secure as anything can be in golf. But strange things began to happen, which would ultimately have Walton exclaiming as he headed for the 18th tee: " Oh Jaysus! I can't believe this. Everything is down to me."

His opponent at number 11 in the order, Jay Haas, holed a bunker shot for a winning birdie on the 16th and then Walton increased the pressure on himself by missing from four feet at the next. Much to the relief of skipper Bernard Gallacher, however, matters finally went Europe's way. With both players feeling the heat, Walton was conceded a short, bogey putt for the match on the final green. As a reward, the Malahide player was given the honour of holding the Ryder Cup trophy aloft at Dublin Airport, as he disembarked from Concorde the following day.

John O'Leary

The gifted Dubliner made his contribution to Ryder Cup history in 1975 at Laurel Valley where himself, Eamonn Darcy and Christy O'Connor Jnr gave Ireland a three-man representation in the event for the first time. As it happened, it was O'Leary's only appearance, though he later won several tournaments, including the 1982 Irish Open at Portmarnock.

He had earlier enjoyed a very productive amateur career which might have culminated in Walker Cup honours. And O'Leary was also noted for his rather flamboyant attire, some of which would make Darren Clarke's current gear appear decidedly sober.

When recurring back problems brought a premature end to his tournament career, he became a highly respected representative of the PGA European Tour and has officiated at successive Ryder Cups, including the 2004 staging at Oakland Hills.

Eddie Polland

Victory in the Penfold-Bournemouth Tournament in 1973, effectively earned Polland a place in the side which played host to the Americans at Muirfield, in the only Scottish staging of the Ryder Cup. It had confirmed the promise of a short-game specialist who had joined the tour five years previously.

Indeed Polland's chipping and putting were so highly regarded by Fred Daly that he compared his skill to that of the great Bobby Locke. Praise indeed. Unfortunately it failed to help his cause at Muirfield where his only matches were in pairings, as a partner for Maurice Bembridge and Clive Clark.

He had several Irish tournament successes and later on in senior ranks, Polland became something of a bionic man, having had reconstructive surgery on a knee and elbow.

Ronan Rafferty

With all the excitement created by Christy O'Connor Jnr at The Belfry in 1989, there was a tendency to overlook the singles achievement of Rafferty, which was significant. He delivered a priceless European point by beating the reigning Open champion, Mark Calcavecchia.

The event came towards the end of Rafferty's finest year on tour, a year in which he led the European Order of Merit. And it was his only Ryder Cup appearance.

After two unsuccessful foursomes matches in partnership with Bernhard Langer and O'Connor Jnr, the Warrenpoint player was named at number four in the singles by skipper Tony Jacklin, who later expressed surprise at how nervous the 25-year-old was on the eve of battle. But everything came good in the end, when Calcavecchia conceded the match, having been twice in water on the 18th.

to European golf," he explained.

It also completed a fascinating, historical link for the Irish player, dating back to 1953. Darcy was only a year-old baby when The Brad was guest of honour at a special function in the Horse and Hound Hotel in Delgany. Now, he stood alongside his celebrated predecessor as a Ryder Cup hero.

Muirfield Village was also where Seve Ballesteros, on hearing that his prospective partner, Jose Maria Olazabal, wanted to stand down because of poor form in practice, had assured skipper Tony Jacklin: "Don't worry. I will play good enough for both of us."

And it was the memorable occasion when Sam Torrance announced his engagement to actress Suzanne Danielle while crossing the Atlantic on Concorde. Such was their closeness on arrival in the US, that in announcing his pairings for the opening foursomes on Friday morning, Jacklin said to the Scot: "Sam, I'm resting you; you're playing."

While predicting heart-stopping Stimpmeter speeds of up to 13 for the Muirfield Village greens, Nicklaus insisted: "I have deliberately removed myself from anything to do with the preparation of the course. Our greens are essentially flat and the idea of making them firm and fast is to place a premium on approach shots."

He then added the telling comment: "This is the way you separate good players from journeymen and I believe Muirfield Village is essentially a second-shot course."

For his part, Jacklin was typically thorough in his preparations. After the opening ceremony, he invited Ken Schofield and other British officials into a bungalow for cocktails. There, they were confronted by the entire European team who spent the next two hours expressing their disappointment with a variety of issues. As a consequence, tension was relieved and the players stiffened their competitive resolve.

As the week progressed, it became clear that Darcy didn't figure in Jacklin's plans for the early foursomes and fourball matches. This prompted the player to insist: "It is important for me to think of myself simply as a member of the European team; I cannot afford to indulge in personal feelings." Meanwhile, with Ballesteros revelling in his regal status in European golf, Jacklin enthused: "Seve's contribution has been incalculable. He is simply a wonderful, wonderful player." Even Nicklaus was moved to comment: "I don't have a Seve on my team at the present time. I think that he and Greg Norman are head and shoulders over the rest of the world right now."

Darcy finally appeared in the fourballs on the Saturday afternoon, but he and Gordon Brand Jnr were no match for the American duo of Payne Stewart and Andy Bean, who won on the 16th.

So to the final day's singles when, facing a five-point deficit, Nicklaus took the remarkable

Chapter 7 The Irish

decision to leave perceived big guns such as Larry Nelson, Curtis Strange, Lanny Wadkins and Sutton at the bottom of the order. Meanwhile Bean, Dan Pohl, Mize and Mark Calcavecchia were expected to achieve a potentially winning momentum, from the top four places.

Ironically, the American collapse came in the last five matches, where Europe claimed three out of five points, including a precious win by Darcy at number eight in the order. He faced Ben Crenshaw, the 1984 Masters champion and winner of 11 other tournaments in the US by that stage, apart from the 1976 Irish Open at Portmarnock.

In an extraordinary act of self-destruction, the world's best putter was so disgusted at three-putting the sixth green – his second putt was from five feet – that he smashed the errant club into the ground in disgust, while walking to the seventh tee. It is now part of Ryder Cup lore how, in the process, he broke the shaft of his beloved "Little Ben" and was forced to putt for the remainder of the match with a one iron or the leading edge of a sand wedge.

When I reminded him of it during a chat we had at Oakland Hills, Crenshaw broke into a warm smile. "Oh Gosh! Muirfield Village....Eamonn and I have had so many chuckles over that match," he recalled. "It was one of the most remarkable things that's ever happened to me in golf. Though I had hit my approach shot very wide of the target, I was still angry not to get down in two.

"As I walked off the green I just....you know there were times when I hit my implements much harder, but on this occasion it just happened to snap." Which, of course, didn't delight his captain. Crenshaw continued to chuckle: "I'll never forget it. A couple of holes later (with Darcy 2 up), we went to a par three and I walked up the steps to the tee, only to be confronted by Jack, who enquired 'How is it going?' And I said quietly, almost under my breath, 'Not so good.' 'What do you mean?' said Jack. And I somehow managed to tell him 'I broke my putter back there on ..'

"Before I could finish the sentence, Jack said 'You did what?' 'I broke my putter, back on number six.' 'Well the way things are going for us,' he said, 'I might be tempted to break a few clubs myself.'

"Eamonn played so well that day. And he killed me off at the end by making a beautiful birdie at 17. Then he got what he needed on 18, getting up and down from a greenside bunker for a winning par after I had driven into water." I suggested that he himself had made a very good bogey on the last. "I did," he replied. "It was all I could do. Eamonn deserved it. He made a beautiful putt coming down the hill. But I'll always remember that match for the way the Europeans, Ian Woosnam, Sandy Lyle, all of them, handled the course so beautifully. They played as if they'd known it all their lives."

Darcy was in no doubt about the importance of his situation, especially when going one down to Crenshaw by losing the short 16th. And to his eternal credit, he found the courage and skill to fight back with a glorious six-iron approach to within three feet of the 17th pin. Then, standing on the 18th tee, he looked at Crenshaw and thought: "Your Masters and all your other titles are no good to you now. Your insides are churning just like mine. It's man to man and I'm going to win."

Crenshaw pulled his drive into water and after their approaches, both players were in the same greenside bunker – Crenshaw in three, Darcy in two. Then, their recoveries left Crenshaw six feet below the hole while Darcy had the most slippery putt on the green, five feet downhill and breaking left to right.

When Crenshaw holed for a five, Darcy seemed to take an age surveying his effort. Then, his mind made up that it would break from the left lip, he stood over it and hit the putt almost straight away. Twenty thousand star-spangled banners had been handed to American supporters coming through the gates that morning. Not one was visible as Darcy's putt ran unerringly into the middle of the 18th cup. But if vision was curtailed, there were resounding cheers – from the delighted European contingent gathered around the green.

"When old Darce sank that putt ...... well, what can you say?" was all Jacklin could muster before being overcome by emotion. And after the winning point had been secured by Ballesteros – who else! – the skipper added: "This is a dream come true for us – a victory that could change the entire course of world golf."

Darcy had never been happier. "I was nervous playing the bunker shot at 18, but my hands were rock steady," he said. "I kept telling myself I could get the ball close to the pin. Mind you, that was the toughest putt I ever faced."

It was some time later before he revealed what was really racing through his mind, as he stood over that fateful putt. "Don't fucking miss," he had thought. And he didn't.

A year later, as a postscript to Darcy's achievement, a venerable fellow countyman visited Muirfield Village, which is located in Dublin, a suburb of Columbus, Ohio, as the envoy of the Lord Mayor of Dublin, Ireland. And remarkably, it was the first time that Harry Bradshaw had met Jack Nicklaus.

"I met him on the steps of the clubhouse and told him 'I never shook your hand before'," recalled The Brad. "And Nicklaus looked at me and replied, 'surely not, Harry.' And I said 'Yes, it's true.'" He went on: "When I said I wanted to see where Eamonn Darcy had holed that famous putt, two committee men brought me to the 18th. This putt he holed was some putt. Television didn't give you a true picture of the slope. The green was so fast, that had he missed that putt, he'd a went (sic) eight or nine feet past. But he didn't. It must have been the best putt of his lifetime."

Chapter 7 The Irish

At the annual dance of the Delgany Artisans' Golfing Society in 1953, The Brad was congratulated by the Society's secretary, Charles Byrne, on his victories in the Ryder Cup matches and the Dunlop Masters that year. Replying to the toast, he said: "I look forward to the time when some other Delgany golfer will bring much greater honours to the area than I ever could."

Listed among the organising committee for what proved to be a memorable function was the name C. Darcy. Thirty-four years later, on October 31st 1987, Christy Darcy's son, Eamonn, was honoured with life membership by Delgany GC for the distinction he had brought his country, and former club at Muirfield Village the previous month.

Harry, too, was honoured with life membership at the same function, in recognition of his past achievements. Delgany is that sort of place.

By this stage Jacklin was being universally acknowledged as an exceptional leader. And having achieved an historic win on American soil, he set his sights on a third successive European triumph at The Belfry in 1989. Looking towards the prospect of further Irish involvement, he said: "Though I dislike the format of the Dunhill Cup, which I consider rather contrived with every match going to the 18th, I thought the Irish victory (in 1988) was sensational. I have never seen three happier guys on a golf course than Eamonn Darcy, Des Smyth and Ronan Rafferty.

"Ronan appears to have mellowed a lot in the last three or four years. He always seems to be there or thereabouts in tournaments, but I believe he will have to step up a gear if he is to make the Ryder Cup team. He must find that extra bit of drive if he is to be strongly placed in the top-10 next season.

"Eamonn has been playing well since Muirfield Village and who's to say that he won't be capable of making the team again. Ireland has always produced some very fine players, but there have been disappointments. Two years ago (1986), when David Feherty won the Scottish Open and the Italian Open, I felt he might go right to the top, but he has been heading backwards since then." Ironically, Jacklin would not be around when Feherty proved that players could change, and very much for the better.

Meanwhile, the shock of the 1989 team, which was announced in Germany on Sunday, August 27th, was the naming of 41-year-old O'Connor Jnr as a wild-card choice. "I went for Christy's experience, his steady, consistent play which is reflected in his stroke average, and the fact that he has won a tournament this season – the Jersey Open," explained the skipper. "Philip Walton was very much in my thoughts, but these are difficult decisions which I have to live with. Walton has a great opportunity of going into future teams. He's a young player of tremendous promise."

In the wake of the actual matches, when a tie meant that the trophy was retained, Jacklin expressed particular pleasure that a much-publicised rift with O'Connor Jnr, going back to 1985, had been healed. In fact, he took obvious delight in the Galwayman's memorable singles victory over Fred Couples the previous day. "I know that many Irish people, especially Christy, were hurt and angry by the fact that I left him out of the 1985 team," said the skipper. "But I remain convinced that I did the right thing at the time, just as I believed that he was the correct choice this time around.

"When I consider players for the Ryder Cup team, I'm not concerned with nationalities. Professional golfers are essentially the same the world over and the unifying factor which I have attempted to instil into my teams, has simply been an over-riding desire to beat the Americans. I am absolutely delighted for Christy's sake that he played so well. When I joined the match with Couples on the 18th, I knew he could win. I knew he could do a job for me. Christy and I chatted during the past week and sorted out a lot of misunderstandings."

For his part, O'Connor was deeply appreciative of Jacklin's support in the climactic moments of Sunday's singles. "It was great to have Tony close by in those anxious moments," he said. "He's a wonderful captain."

Jacklin was also rich in praise of Rafferty's performance in beating the reigning Open champion, Mark Calcavecchia. "I knew Ronan was unhappy with his foursomes effort (he lost two matches in partnership with Langer and O'Connor Jnr) and I said to him on Sunday morning: 'You're too good a player to come through these matches without a point.' It was really wonderful to see the way he responded. One can easily forget that he is only 25 and that, by his own admission, he encountered the greatest pressure of his young career, greater even than facing the 18th green in the Open Championship."

O'Connor's match against Couples is now the stuff of legend. Level with the American and facing a treacherous approach of 229 yards over water to the 18th green, he heard Jacklin whisper in his ear: "Put this on the green and see what happens." The two-iron was struck beautifully; it had to be to achieve the required distance. Amid tumultuous cheering the ball sailed straight and true and came to rest within four feet of the hole, situated on the middle tier.

Just as Jacklin had anticipated, Couples was so shocked by the majesty of the shot that he himself missed the green with only a nine-iron approach. And after duffing a chip, he conceded victory. O'Connor didn't have to putt.

Those wins in '89 by Rafferty and O'Connor meant that Irish players had now won three singles points over two successive Ryder Cup stagings. And the sequence was extended at Kiawah Island in 1991, when Feherty did himself proud with a 2 and 1 win over Stewart, the reigning US Open champion. Victory was secured with a three on the fearsome, short 17th, by which stage Feherty was level-par, which was the best golf of the three days on a wickedly difficult course.

While these Irish performances must be acknowledged as important and of an admirably high quality, none was actually decisive in turning the tide in Europe's favour. Which is why Walton's performance of 1995 at Oak Hill, stands apart.

Nick Faldo's displays of emotion have been rare in a golfing context. We think of his Open win at Muirfield in 1992 and his US Masters triumph over the hapless Greg Norman in 1996. And we think of his Ryder Cup singles win over Curtis Strange in 1995. "You can see what it does to you," he said with tears welling in his eyes, as the full impact of what had been achieved, eventually sank in. One down with three to play, Faldo had crushed an old adversary into submission as the American, who finished with three bogeys, was ultimately undone by a marvellous, four-foot par putt from the Englishman on the 18th.

So, three days of intense competition hinged ultimately on Walton, playing at number 11 in the singles against the experienced Jay Haas. Dormie three and with a two-footer for par at the 16th where his opponent was in a greenside bunker, the Dubliner was convinced it was all over. But in an instant, everything changed. With a bunker recovery which seemed likely to overshoot the green, the American's ball hit the flag and dropped in for a winning birdie. "Oh God!" thought an anguished Walton. "This is all I need."

He had another chance to seal the match on the 17th, this time with a four-foot putt. But the stroke with his trusty broomhandle lacked the necessary conviction and the ball slipped past the target. Now he realised the worst. "Oh Jaysus," he thought, "everything is down to me."

Still, salvation was at hand, in the shape of a badly-hooked drive from Haas on the 18th. Ultimately, it meant that Walton had two putts from 12 feet to secure victory. And when he eased the first one to within a foot of the target, the American conceded. A famous European win had been secured. A win more dramatic than in 1987, because of the huge importance the Ryder Cup had acquired in the intervening years.

On Monday September 25th, Concorde landed in Dublin Airport for the first time and when the door opened, Walton stood there, proudly holding the Ryder Cup aloft. Local wits considered it appropriate that the victorious team should have been ushered into the North Terminal, which was little used at the time except for pilgrimage flights to Lourdes. Hadn't these players produced something akin to a golfing miracle through their exploits in upstate New York? The landing had been made for the convenience of players competing in the first staging at The K Club of the European Open under the Smurfit banner. "Though Philip obviously played a special role, this was essentially a great team effort," insisted skipper

Bernard Gallacher. "It was, perhaps, more of a team effort than any previous occasion, because every player won a point and could feel they had really contributed to the win."

Though the visit to Dublin was a short one, there was still sufficient time to lower some of the black stuff in between holding the Ryder Cup aloft. Two years later, the trophy was retained at Valderrama where Darren Clarke became the 15th Irishman to gain Ryder Cup honours. And as a further endorsement of significant investment in the amateur game by the Golfing Union of Ireland, another new Ryder Cup representative came on the scene at Brookline in 1999.

Having emerged from amateur ranks with probably not as many titles as he should have secured, Padraig Harrington still had an outstanding record in team golf. Now, only four years into a professional career, he was being asked to perform at an unbelievably higher level. And at one stage during a torrid Sunday afternoon, he seemed to be cast in the role of potential European hero – the player on whose shoulders would fall the weight of having to produce the winning point, as Walton had done in 1995.

Only 15 minutes, in fact, elapsed between Harrington hitting a 135-yard wedge onto the 18th to set up a singles win over Mark O'Meara, and Justin Leonard delivering an extraordinary, American coup de grace. After storming heaven in quest of successful putting, the home side were positively sated by Sunday's mastery on the greens, not least by a 45-foot birdie putt on the 17th by Leonard to cap a remarkable comeback against Jose Maria Olazabal and secure a most improbable victory.

Inevitably, every local angle was exploited in the various comments, written and spoken. Particularly memorable, from an Irish standpoint, was the remark by NBC commentator Dick Enberg as Harrington walked the 90 yards to the 17th green before hitting his second shot. In Enberg's view, Harrington's preparation for the shot gave "new meaning to the Boston Marathon." Yet the Dubliner could take justifiable pride in becoming the first Irishman since David Feherty to take one and a half points from a Ryder Cup staging.

Three years later, after the horrors of 9/11 had caused a rescheduling of the 2001 matches, with a knock-on effect on subsequent stagings, Irish players made their biggest contribution to a Ryder Cup so far. Not only did the country have three representatives in the side in Harrington, Clarke and Paul McGinley: all three of them made crucial contributions to the overall winning effort.

Indeed memories remain vivid of a classic Harrington half at the eighth, en route to a 5 and 4 thrashing of Calcavecchia. When the American saw his opponent drive into water down the left of this treacherous hole, he could have reasonably expected to do some damage. After dropping back under penalty, however, Harrington recovered to a greenside trap from where he got up and down for a most improbable half in bogey.

But McGinley quite properly stole a major share of the limelight as singles combat reached a breathtaking climax. His halved point against Jim Furyk was sufficient to give Europe a winning edge, so bringing the trophy back to this side of the Atlantic.

In December of that year, at a sports function in the Burlington Hotel in Dublin, a legendary figure of American golf turned to a player very much wealthier than himself, though almost half his age. There wasn't the slightest hint of rancour in the soft, southern drawl of Doug Sanders as he said with a warm smile to McGinley: "I've been famous all my life for missing a putt; you're going to be famous for holing one."

When the 69-year-old met Ireland's latest Ryder Cup hero, it was almost inevitable that a gaping wound would be probed once more. Nothing in sport is more painful than failure at the last gasp, yet Sanders has stubbornly refused to be crushed by his pain. Nor did he think of inventing a noise from the gallery nor the click of a camera as an excuse for missing a three-foot putt, which would have given him the 1970 Open Championship at St Andrews.

Instead, he bared his soul to the world and let us all make of it what we would. "I made a mistake by not letting Trevino (Lee Trevino, his playing partner) putt first," he admitted. "I made the mistake of thinking which section of the crowd I was going to bow to. It was all my fault. There was only one person to blame – Doug Sanders."

McGinley saw the video of the incident when it was re-run for the umpteenth time by the Golf Channel in the US. He observed how, after bending down to pick up an imagined speck on the line of the putt, Sanders made the fatal error of failing to mark the ball so that he could step away from it and compose himself.

The Dubliner then noted how, in his anxiety to finish out, the so-called Peacock of the Fairways opened the blade disastrously to send the left-to-right breaking three-footer, slipping past the right lip. And he heard the eerie silence being broken by the immortal words of the commentator, Henry Longhurst, as he said: "Oh dear! There but for the grace of God ...."

Such images provided a stark contrast to the glory of The Belfry in late September of 2002. McGinley's challenge in attempting to achieve a trophy-winning half, also involved a left-to-right breaking putt on the final green, though his effort was from the considerably longer distance of nine feet. And instead of strictly personal gain, he was carrying the hopes of an entire Continent.

Yet the player later argued that his most valuable contribution that weekend was not on Sunday afternoon, but 24 hours previously. The scene was the final fourball in which he and Clarke were one down to Scott Hoch and Furyk playing the 18th. From the four drives, McGinley was longest and should have been last to hit, whereas Clarke, in a bunker, should have been first. But Bernhard Langer saw things differently. He urged European skipper, Sam Torrance, to instruct McGinley to hit first, with a view to pressurising the Americans. The Scot agreed and an exemplary four iron of 211 yards from the Dubliner, achieved the objective. The hole was won for a halved match, leaving the teams dead level going into Sunday's singles.

"Though you will often see players hit fairway shots out of turn in amateur fourballs, it very rarely happens in the Ryder Cup," said McGinley. "On the green, yes. But not from the fairway. That four-iron shot was huge, probably bigger than Sunday's putt. And Langer read the situation perfectly. That's one of the things which convinced me he would be an outstanding captain at Oakland Hills. He certainly wasn't going to be outsmarted.

"Nowadays, it is vital that a captain treats the 12 players differently rather than the same. Standing at the head of a room with a 'Now listen here lads...' kind of speech, won't work. We're all at the peak of our profession and we all have big egos which have to be treated in different ways. The principles are the same, whatever the sport, be it golf, soccer or Gaelic Football. Managers must be part-psychologists. There is no longer any room for dictators."

Sanders didn't have such guidance at St Andrews in 1970. But McGinley wanted to hear him talk about a situation in which he couldn't have asked for a more astute leader. It was the 1967 Ryder Cup at the Champions in Houston, Texas, where Ben Hogan, as American skipper, famously introduced his line-up as "the finest golfers in the world".

Recalling how his captain had made it clear to each individual player that he didn't want to be associated with failure, Sanders said:"Standing there, tapping the ash off a cigarette and with those cold, grey eyes boring into me, he said: 'Doug, you will win today, won't you?' I took it as an order. There wasn't a mention of country allegiance: I was playing for Hogan."

"It has only dawned on me in recent years, how much better I play in team events," added McGinley. "I can't really explain it except that I seem to be more relaxed. It's certainly more enjoyable for me to be bouncing things off a partner."

As the witching-hour slipped past at that Dublin function, Sanders pondered once more the miss which cost him a fortune. "I had waited for that moment," he said. "I had done all the other things except win a major. Now I was ready. But I missed it." For McGinley, the chance of a lifetime didn't slip away. Under the most extreme pressure a professional golfer could face, he found a way of getting the job done.

Sanders was honest enough to admit that he hadn't seen it. "I can't watch those things any more," he said. And who could blame him.

♦

Chapter 8

Testing The Waters

Chapter 8 Testing The Waters

t was 1.30am and a long day of golf, food and wine at The K Club had eased into the wee, small hours. In the normal way of things, people had broken into little groups when my attention was caught by a distinguished threesome whose various achievements included a combined 19 Ryder Cup appearances.

There was "Himself", Christy O'Connor Snr, resplendent in dinner wear, swishing his outstretched hands in a simulation of the golf swing, full shoulder turn and all. Even more fascinating was the look of rapt attention on the faces of Ian Woosnam and Peter Baker.

In the background, former Irish international Noel Fogarty, who has known O'Connor as a friend and golfing colleague for close on 45 years, took it all in with a quiet smile. "Christy learned his swing from old Bob Wallace in Galway and it has never changed in all these years," he remarked.

The next development in this O'Connor masterclass had Woosnam moving centre-stage. Himself looked, then shook his head disapprovingly. Words weren't necessary. Not that way, this way, he indicated while raising the little Welshman's hands noticeably at address.

Then it was the turn of Baker, who, among other competitive achievements, had been one of the outstanding European players in the Ryder Cup defeat of 1993 at The Belfry, where he took three points out of four, including two fourball victories with Woosnam. This time O'Connor was more demonstrative, slapping him repeatedly on the outside of his left thigh.

"Isn't golf a wonderful game," mused Fogarty. "There you have players from different generations, totally absorbed in the wonder of it all. And you know, Christy is a terrific teacher; a far better teacher than most people imagine."

When I met up with Baker a few days later down at Ballybunion for the Irish Open, he agreed wholeheartedly. "Christy got chatting with Woosie and told him he had seen something wrong with his swing, from watching him on television," he said. "And since I was in the company, I wasn't about to turn down the chance of a chat with Himself.

"I have a tendency to tilt, which becomes a reverse pivot and Christy told me that it couldn't happen if I kept my left knee inside when starting the backswing. That's why he kept slapping me. I have been fortunate to see him play on a few occasions and he still has a wonderful swing. He must have been a fantastic player in his prime."

Earlier on that Monday night in June 2000, auctioneer Arthur French had given a rather more devious encouragement to the Welshman, lauding his status as a former US Masters champion and world number one. The best French could extract, however, was a bid of £70,000 from Woosnam for a Roderick O'Connor portrait which was ultimately knocked down to Dr Michael Smurfit for £100,000.

And when O'Connor came on the scene, it could be said that artist followed art.

Thoughts of that meeting of Woosnam and Baker with the one-time record-holder of 10 successive Ryder Cup appearances, were brought to mind on Wednesday June 29th, 2005 at The K Club, where some crucial announcements regarding Ryder Cup 2006, were made. "I suppose you're all waiting to hear Woosie confirm Des Smyth as one of his vice-captains," said Tom Lehman with a mischievous grin, as he passed a group of us scribes having lunch in the clubhouse.

Back on March 2nd, at the time of his own appointment in Dubai, Woosnam had made it clear that he would be choosing an Irish vice-captain, a move which Colin Montgomerie described as "very, very astute". Then Bernard Gallacher, three-times a Ryder Cup captain, suggested: "It wouldn't surprise me if Ian picked Des Smyth. Des played on the European Tour right up until he was 50; he has Ryder Cup experience (Gallacher played foursomes with him in 1981) and knows The K Club well." Meanwhile, as an Irish member of the Tour's Tournament Committee, Paul McGinley took the more democratic view that there were three strong candidates – Smyth, Eamonn Darcy and Christy O'Connor Jnr – while Philip Walton and Ronan Rafferty also had to be considered.

Almost four months later, here we were on Smurfit European Open Pro-Am day and in the first of two shotgun starts, Lehman was rather pleased to discover he had led in the winning team from the morning session, with a fine score of 14 under par. And his sense of achievement wasn't diluted even by a potentially deflating experience as he and his pro-am partners headed for the clubhouse chased by eager autograph-hunters. "Who's your man with Keith Wood?" asked one of them, who was clearly a lot more familiar with the former Irish rugby captain than with the current skipper of the US Ryder Cup team.

In fact, it had been a decidedly interesting morning for Lehman. As he headed towards the 18th green, having started on the 10th, his son Thomas, who was a few weeks short of his 10th birthday at the time, edged up to him and began whispering anxiously. After a couple of efforts at making himself heard, the youngster eventually delivered the message: "Don't move your head when you putt."

On the next hole, the long 10th, Lehman remembered his son's advice and holed a testing effort for a birdie. Young Thomas was at his father's side once more. "That was better," he declared sagely, before breaking into a proud smile. And a few hours later, his satisfaction was complete on learning that dad had led in the winning team.

Thomas wouldn't remember anything of his first trip to The K Club in September 1995, when he was an infant of only two months, but it turned out to be a memorable visit for the Lehman family. "Though I had fished quite a bit, my wife, Melissa, had never thrown a fly rod

Chapter 8 Testing The Waters

before her arrival here," Tom explained. "So you can imagine our delight when, just a stone's throw from the hotel, she caught this beautiful four-pound brown trout which we cooked for dinner. With her first cast she caught a fish and I remember her saying 'That's it; I'm done.'"

After finishing ninth that year, Lehman returned to the European Open in 1996 having won the Open Championship at Royal Lytham. Now, nine years later, he was back as captain of the US team, and I suggested that things hadn't changed much in the intervening time, given that he was still desperate to get the Ryder Cup trophy back in US hands.

There was a thin smile. "You're right," he acknowledged. "Things haven't changed much, have they?" Then, gently changing the subject, he continued: "I don't believe much in coincidence. I believe in fate, no question. When I played here in 1996, I spent some time with a couple of European Ryder Cup committee guys. It was a time when we all knew Ireland were pushing pretty hard for the Ryder Cup. And these guys told me I would be coming back to Ireland for the Ryder Cup in 2005. As the American captain. And I remember saying to them: 'I certainly hope you're right.'"

Lehman would discover later in the week that the course had been altered significantly since his visits of 1995 and '96. Indeed it had also changed markedly from a rather special Saturday of bright, beguiling sunshine on the August Bank Holiday weekend in 1999. The occasion was the second round of the 1999 Smurfit European Open and in starting on what has become regarded as the members' 10th tee but is now the established first hole for tournament play, Darren Clarke was about to gain a unique place in the history of the professional game on this side of the Atlantic.

With the customary two-tee starts in operation, Clarke set off from the old 10th. But unlike the routing which will be followed in matchplay against the Americans, when the old ninth will follow the old 17th, and the 18th will retain its position on the card, his finishing hole would be the ninth.

Now that you are suitably confused, we will go back to events on a unique occasion when the tournament happened to finish on a Monday. And as if decreed by the golfing gods, Clarke's playing companion and marker was none other than Woosnam, who was about to gain a rare insight, both as player and observer, into Ireland's future Ryder Cup battleground.

Swept along by the highly-charged emotion of the situation, Woosnam felt that a touch of levity was appropriate at the end of it all. So it was that he handed Clarke a scorecard in the recorder's room, on which the nines added up to 30 and 29 – a combined 59. Let it be emphasised that the scores on the individual holes were correct; only the total was fanciful.

"Thanks very much Woosie," said the Irishman, forcing a smile. "But I had a 60, not a 59." His marker, all too aware of the tantalising, near-miss, quietly acknowledged the deliberate error. As the ball sailed towards the final, ninth green minutes earlier, Woosnam had urged: "Get up there! Go!" But despite his urging, it still came to rest 24 feet short of the flag from where Clarke had to settle for a two-putt par.

Despite his understandable disappointment, it has become acknowledged as arguably the finest scoring round to have been played in the history of the European Tour. Though eight previous 60s had been carded, including the Monte Carlo effort by Clarke himself, only two were on par-72 courses and none compared in length with the then 7,179 yards of The K Club. Since then, Fredrik Jacobson also shot a 12-under-par 60 at Gut Larchenhof in the Linde German Masters in 2003, but only the opening round of 60 (12 under par) by Ernie Els in February 2002 in the Heineken Classic on a Royal Melbourne course measuring 6,981 yards, bears serious comparison. Miguel Angel Martin, who shot a magical 59 in the 1987 South Argentine Open, could imagine how the Irishman felt. "The last putt I made was longer than Darren's, about 30 feet," he recalled.

One fewer putt and Clarke would have broken three European Tour targets. He needed one birdie from his last two holes to do it, but the pressure increased when, after a nine iron to 10 feet at the eighth (his 17th), the right to left breaking birdie putt didn't move as much as he expected towards the River Liffey and slipped past the right edge of the hole.

Huge crowds flanked the ninth fairway (his 18th) and surrounded the green in anticipation of an historic breakthrough of the 60 barrier. The drive was perfect but as he hit his wedge approach, Clarke sensed he had been cheated by a gust of wind, a fear shared by Woosnam. The ball came to rest little more than three feet into the green and, with the pin placed at nine yards, he had 24 feet remaining. On a right-to-left line, the putt was bold, so bold in fact that when it missed the target, the ball went a full five feet past, leaving Clarke with an unenviable return effort for his 60. But he made no mistake.

So, he had to be content with setting two records and equalling two others. In carding 12 birdies, of which eight were successive, he matched two previous targets, but became the first player to do so in the same round. And there was the satisfaction of being the first player to shoot two rounds of 60 on the European Tour. The first such effort led him to purchase the number-plate DC 60. "It would be nice to have had to change it," he said with a wry smile. "In fact, I'm very disappointed. This was the best I have ever played and opportunities to break that number don't come along too often." His figures for a round which he started on the 10th were:

Par (from 10th):	4 4 3	5 4 4	4 3 5 = 36
Clarke:	**3 3 3**	**4 4 4**	**3 3 4 = 31**
Par (from 1st):	5 4 3	4 3 4	5 4 4 = 36
Clarke:	**4 3 2**	**3 2 3**	**4 4 4 = 29**

Chapter 8 Testing The Waters

"Not many people have done it and it would have meant an awful lot to achieve it at home here in Ireland," he went on. By way of compensation, he beat the existing course record by four strokes, while putting himself in line for a second tournament victory of the year, having captured the English Open two months previously. In the event, further disappointment awaited him on the Monday, when his friend, Lee Westwood, swept past him to take the title. Still, a coveted triumph at The K Club eventually came to Clarke in 2001.

In terms of spectacular scoring in this country, Clarke's exploit of 1999 rivalled the eagle-birdie-eagle finish which Christy O'Connor Snr produced to win the Carrolls International at Royal Dublin in 1966. The Tyroneman's longest, successful birdie putt was a 30-footer at the 10th, his opening hole. Otherwise, everything was inside eight feet, reflecting the purity of his approach irons. Indeed he two-putted from eight feet at the short 12th, from 10 feet at the long 18th and from 10 feet at the eighth. All the while, he achieved 92.9 per cent accuracy off the tee with drives averaging 284 yards and had a total of only 25 putts, 11 of them singles.

Friends, rivals and admirers gathered around him afterwards, expressing genuine regret that a benevolent course hadn't yielded him just one more stroke. But such is golf. Meanwhile, as is so often the case at tournament level, Clarke's figures were largely the product of hard work and confidence. The work came in a 90-minute session on the putting green on the previous evening after the blade had repeatedly failed him in an opening 73. The confidence stemmed from being reunited with his then favourite Scotty Cameron putter.

Former tournament player John McHenry, who is now Director of Golf and Head Professional at The K Club, was set to start his second round that day, as Clarke was about to finish. "I think Darren's 60 was as good as the 59s that have been achieved on the US tour," he said. "I really do. You would need to have competed in the European Open on this golf course to get a proper appreciation of just how good that score was.

"I remember everybody being simply gobsmacked by what he had done. The general view was that if somebody played really well, a 64 was probably achievable. But to go out and shoot 60, with opportunities on the last two greens to shoot a 59, put the achievement into perspective.

"Indeed it is a testimony to the quality of the round that nobody has come near to matching that score since then. And I have no hesitation in predicting that it will never be repeated, especially in view of the way the course has been toughened up as part of the preparation for the Ryder Cup.

"Having said that, I don't think the changes are all that significant from a scoring perspective. Essentially, through strategic and fairly extensive tree-planting, we have significantly changed the angles off certain tees and for some of the approach shots. For instance, anybody now attempting to fly certain corners, will discover that there are two or possibly three additional trees still to be negotiated. So they must be sure to make the carry. Then there is the fact that, four or five years ago, there were some loose gatherings of trees where the ball might fly through and bounce out. These have been eliminated."

McHenry went on to describe how the new angles off certain teeing areas will demand greater levels of concentration from competitors, even though the overall length of those holes will not have changed. Additional bunkers have also been created, partially for definition and partially to protect some areas of the greens. And in specific circumstances, it was considered appropriate to change the greens themselves, especially the 12th (members' third) on the tournament course, which was a very benign par three. It is now a much tougher prospect, causing players to think more about club selection and shape of shot.

"I don't subscribe to the idea of making a player feel uncomfortable on a tee, but I believe a player should be made to consider his options," McHenry continued. "Rather than seeing them walk onto a tee with a pre-set strategy, I would prefer they had to ask themselves what they were trying to achieve. And if they chose the tiger line on a particular hole, that they would be aware of the penalties associated with getting it wrong."

Though handicap players would roundly disagree, McHenry does not consider the Palmer Course to be a long layout. In fact, it plays relatively short for professionals in firm, summer conditions. And the fairways are comparatively generous by tournament standards.

"Looking towards the Ryder Cup, it is the individual's approach to matchplay, rather than the nature of the course, which changes things. Essentially I would view matchplay as a gambler's game where contestants feel a freedom to throw caution to the wind, in appropriate circumstances. They will take on a shot in the knowledge that getting it wrong could mean only a loss of a hole in singles, while they can look to the back-up of a fourball partner or an inspired recovery from a foursomes partner. In that respect, a good venue becomes all the more exciting.

"Over at The Belfry in 2002, I saw players make difficult holes look very easy, simply because they were gambling with their shots. When those shots came off, it made for a marvellous spectacle but when they ended in disaster, onlookers simply shrugged their shoulders and waited for the next match through to provide the fireworks. One poor shot didn't really matter. That's the essence of exciting matchplay.

"I don't think you can talk about a matchplay golf course as such. As has been proved in the US Open, you can set up a golf course to make good scoring nigh impossible, but it must be remembered that the Palmer Course was designed to test players of all levels, including those of 15 or 16 handicap, who will represent the majority of its patrons. Ideally, it has to be an enjoyable as well as a challenging experience.

Chapter 8 Testing The Waters

"We would certainly like to think that this applies to elite players such as tournament professionals. And the indications are that it does, given the pedigree of the winners we've had here in the European Open. That, in my view, is an endorsement of the quality of the design work by the Palmer Organisation."

McHenry further explained that the change to the routing for the Ryder Cup was done primarily to facilitate access by the general public. As we indicated earlier, instead of the traditional members' routing of one to 18, the course will now start on the 10th, go on to the short 17th, then have the outward journey completed on the ninth. The homeward journey begins on the members' first and continues to the eighth, before competitors move to the 18th as their finishing hole. As he explained: "With all the water areas around the members' 15th, 16th and 17th holes, it would be very difficult to control spectators, while suitable television structures would be almost impossible.

"On the other hand, by finishing with the members' seventh, eighth and 18th, we achieve far greater ease of crowd control with the considerable bonus of creating a dynamic spectacle. We would envisage greatly enhanced television images, with the background of the hotel and the River Liffey. We imagine this will be especially true of the second or third shot over the water to the members' long seventh, when it's played as the gamble 16th. And the change of routing won't be a problem to either team insofar as our players will be well used to it through the European Open while the Americans won't know any difference, anyway."

As for the greens: Woosnam has requested that they be a reasonable pace on the Friday and Saturday and slow on Sunday. This is essentially because he believes the Americans won't like slow greens in singles combat.

"If you cast your mind back to The Belfry in 2002, Curtis Strange (US captain) had obviously instructed his players to hit an iron off the 10th tee (a comfortably reachable par four)," said McHenry. "I don't think you should do that in matchplay. I think the player has to respond to situations as they arise in the heat of battle. Woosie, by his nature, will advocate well thought out shots and an overall game plan. But he will offer advice rather than instruction. Like Bernhard Langer did at Oakland Hills and Seve Ballesteros didn't in Valderrama. That was where we remember Seve, in exasperation, threatening to hit the shot himself, if his player wasn't prepared to do as he was told.

"Psychology is huge in matchplay, especially if you're the underdog, which has generally been the European position. As Mark O'Meara remarked to me on one occasion, the Americans play not to lose whereas the Europeans play to win. That's why we have been so successful." Meanwhile, back in the Media Centre on the eve of the 2005 Smurfit European Open, Woosnam duly confirmed what everybody had suspected: Smyth and Baker would be his vice-captains for 2006. And again to nobody's surprise, Sandy Lyle and David J Russell would also be part of the backroom team as Woosnam's personal assistants. "We have in Des and Peter two very experienced guys," he said. "Like me, they are not only overjoyed but also very proud to be involved in the next Ryder Cup. And I know that Des's wife, Vicki, and Peter's wife, Helen, will be as committed to the cause as my wife Glen. We're all looking forward to the qualifying process getting under way at the Omega European Masters in September."

Woosnam had delivered on his promise of an Irish vice-captain and his choice seemed to gain national approval. "All of Ireland and particularly his home town of Drogheda, will be delighted that Des is representing the country as vice-captain," said John O'Donoghue, Minister for Arts, Sport and Tourism. "As one of our true golfing legends, he will be bringing a wealth of experience to support the European team."

Another attribute which Smyth will bring to the European cause, is an ability to keep a secret. In the preceding months, enquiries as to whether he had received any interesting phone calls from a Welsh winner of the US Masters, were met with a coy "'Fraid not" followed by an innocent smile. But of course he knew, quite some time before the news was made public.

When the announcement eventually came, it received a ringing endorsement from Padraig Harrington, who is certain to be filling a crucial role once more in Europe's attempt to retain the trophy. "Des is an ideal choice; a real gentleman," he said. "In the Ryder Cup you have got to be very trusting of the guys you put out there in front. They've got to be diplomatic and Des can always be relied upon to say the right thing."

Then there was the matter of competitive values. In this context, Smyth's credentials couldn't be faulted either, given some truly remarkable tournament performances in recent years. A long, enriching Indian summer began for him on the St Patrick's weekend of 2001, when victory in the Madeira Island Open brought the distinction of becoming the oldest winner on the European Tour. At 48 years and 34 days, the Drogheda man proved that if you're good enough you're young enough, when beating the previous record set by Neil Coles, who was 48 years and 12 days when capturing the 1982 Sanyo Open, his last "regular tour" win.

O'Connor Snr was six months short of his 48th birthday on the occasion of his last European Tour triumph, in the Carrolls International at Woodbrook in 1972. And Smyth also became the first Irish golfer to win top-grade tournaments in four successive decades, having achieved his breakthrough in the European Matchplay Championship of 1979.

As for family reaction to his Madeira triumph: wives have a way of getting to the nub of things. "Obviously I'm thrilled for him, especially since it means he can now spend more time at home this year," said his wife Vicki, who couldn't have imagined the success which lay in wait for him on the US Champions Tour. Nor the extended time away from home which this would entail. But she clearly knew her man. "Des remains very ambitious about his golf and I fully support him," added this daughter of former Curtis Cup player, Clarrie Reddan, and sister of former Irish amateur international, Barry.

From a matchplay perspective, Smyth can look back to a Ryder Cup appearance in 1979 as recognition of his status as the reigning European Matchplay champion, having beaten Nick Price in the final. And he was honoured again in 1981 at Walton Heath, where he earned two points against what is widely acknowledged as the strongest team ever to represent the US. Then there was the medal-matchplay Dunhill Cup triumph of 1988 and the Irish Matchplay success of 1995, when he beat Paul McGinley in the final at Seapoint, a course which Smyth had co-designed with Declan Branigan.

In describing his method, Peter Alliss once said: "Smyth sets the angle early in his backswing and gets through to an exceptionally full inverted C position on the follow through. Possibly because of the early setting, he has been one of the best mid-iron players on the European Tour, though less secure with woods."

The confidence gained in Madeira carried through to the Open Championship at Royal Lytham that year, when he finished in a highly creditable share of 13th place behind David Duval, having come through final qualifying with a course-record 64 at St Anne's Old Links on the Monday. "Where's Laytown and Bettystown?" observers enquired about Smyth's home course, when he returned to the top of the leaderboard for a spell after a second-round 65 on the Friday afternoon. "Why does the place have two names?" Like a Kerryman answering a question with a question, one could just as easily have asked why Lytham St Annes had two names. Or Southport and Ainsdale.

As it happens, the golf club which represents the adjoining seaside villages of Laytown and Bettystown can claim a very rare and possibly a unique distinction in the game, in that two of its Captain's Prize winners, Smyth and Philip Walton, went on to become Ryder Cup players.

Still, Smyth had fallen some way short of the Open target for an Irish 48-year-old. Almost predictably, this was set by O'Connor at Troon in 1973 when, five months before his 49th birthday, he finished seventh behind Tom Weiskopf. As an interesting aside, Lytham brought Des together with his current caddie, Ray Latchford, for the first time. "It was 1973 and the occasion was the Men's Amateur Home International Championship," recalled Latchford. "I was on a week's holiday at the time, and I came over just to look at the golf and finished up working for Des." They have been together now for 11 years.

Soon, senior golf beckoned, and Smyth made a stunning entry into the Champions Tour by winning the Qualifying School at World Woods GC in Crystal River, Florida, in November 2002. There, late on the Friday afternoon in the shade of a towering oak, he and Latchford loaded the last pieces of golf gear into a 4 x 4 after what had been a truly memorable final day.

The job had been done with absolute conviction. While a place in the top-eight of final qualifying would have been enough, there was the considerable bonus of $42,000 as a reward for leading the field – handy spending money for a family holiday in the West Indies, the following week.

Smyth had entered the final round four strokes behind Seiji Ebihara who had won successive AIB Irish Seniors Open titles in 2001 and 2002. Gradually the lead was whittled away until it had totally disappeared by the time the pair reached the 72nd tee. Then, in a dramatic, closing surge, Smyth holed an eight-footer to outstrip his rival by one stroke and claim top spot with a 13-under-par total of 275.

Among the reactions back in Ireland to this splendid achievement were his adoption as a hero, a role model by every corpulent, sedentary middle-aged golfer, whose only honest identification with the slim, fit Louthman, could have been the aches and pains of the odd, non-golfing injury, as when Smyth damaged his back while taking a nap in a hired car.

As for thought processes: Smyth claimed that his levels of concentration on the golf course were better at 50 than they had been as a 30-year-old. "I never feel tired when I'm competing," he said, with absolute conviction. All the while, it was clear he had maintained the respect of his peers, even at the highest level. Like after the third round of the Senior British Open in July 2003 at Turnberry, where he had carded a sparkling 66.

Suddenly, his attention was drawn to the television screen and the sight of Jack Nicklaus standing over a 12-foot putt for a birdie at the 14th. The game's greatest competitor was on a roll at six under, with the prospect of shooting his age, a magical 63. But the putt slipped past the target. And when Smyth saw an apparently good tee-shot break right of the green for a bogey at the short 15th, he knew the chance had gone. So, off he went to meet Vicki and son Gregory, who were with him at the event.

"About an hour and a quarter later, we were driving out of the car-park when I saw Nicklaus walking towards us," he recalled. "And when I lowered the car window to ask how he had finished, he leaned in, said 'hello' to Vicki and then started to talk. For the next 20 minutes, arms resting against the car, he passionately told me every shot he had hit from the 14th, leading eventually to a disappointing 67.

"He was absolutely gutted, because he knew he had had the makings of a terrific round, with the chance of shooting his age. And as he talked, I couldn't help thinking that here was the greatest golfer the game has ever seen – unless Tiger outstrips him – baring his soul to a fellow pro; devastated that he didn't shoot the number he wanted.

"Finally he said 'It would have meant so much to me.' Then, before leaving us, he added:

Chapter 8 Testing The Waters

'Maybe tomorrow. Though the worry is that those chances don't come around too often these days.'"

A few weeks later, Smyth recounted this story to new-found American colleagues. "Their reaction was that people tend to forget how much the game has meant to Jack, especially when he's playing well and the competitive juices start flowing," he said. In the process, Smyth realised, not for the first time, that the same could be said of himself and the vast majority of golf's so-called pensioners.

In a wickedly funny aside while commentating for the ABC Network, Peter Alliss reacted to a camera shot of Chris DiMarco's putting action by informing his US television audience: "I haven't seen a grip like that since they closed the gentleman's lavatory at Charing Cross Station." Since then, heaven forbid, he could have made the same observation about Smyth, who in December 2004, abandoned the long putter and adopted a variation of the so-called claw or saw grip, which made DiMarco one of the best putters on the USPGA Tour.

Explaining the change, Smyth said: "I used a long putter for seven years and won twice with it, but since joining the Champions Tour, I felt I hadn't been making enough putts. So I thought I'd go back to the short putter and try this claw grip which seems to have helped a lot of people."

Tony Lema, winner of the Open Championship at St Andrews in 1964, could have been speaking for the generation of golfers which was to follow him, when he said: "You don't necessarily have to be a good golfer to be a good putter, but you have to be a good putter to be a good golfer."

The upshot of it was that Smyth made his breakthrough on the Champions Tour in the SBC Classic in California in March 2005. And it happened on the same St Patrick's weekend on which Harrington made a USPGA Tour breakthrough by winning the Honda Classic. And little more than a month later, Smyth won again, this time in the highly prestigious Legends Tournament in Savannah.

His reaction? As Don Corleone might have suggested, it was all about respect. "That is what I have wanted from my peers," he explained. "If you're going to march the fairways with guys who have won US Opens and Masters and the like, you want them to know you feel capable of turning them over. Big things were expected of me when I led the Qualifying School (November 2002) after playing so well in Europe.

"I was supposed to make a big difference over here. And I didn't. Which meant that apart from disappointing even myself, I went totally off the Richter Scale as far as the big guns were concerned. Let's be honest, if you're going to have the respect of your peers as a professional golfer, you have to win. You can be second until you're blue in the face and it makes not a whit of difference."

Bruce Lietzke, who was a member of that illustrious US Ryder Cup team at Walton Heath, knew what he meant. "I'm not surprised that Des has won, because he's a player with probably no weakness in his game," said Lietzke in Savannah. "But I'm surprised by the fact that as a player who used the long putter, he switched over to a short putter and had success. That surprises me." Was the notoriously lazy American tempted to go down the same route and abandon his own trusty broomhandle? "I don't think so," Lietzke replied. "I'm kind of a low maintenance guy and if I switched putters I'd have to practise. That wouldn't suit me. I've got better things to do." With seven senior wins to his credit at that time since 2001, who was to say he was wrong?

Indeed Lietzke's surprise at Smyth's putter preferences seemed to be validated by events in the Senior British Open at Royal Aberdeen in late July 2005. That was when Smyth reverted to his trusty old broomhandle and proceeded to battle into a play-off for the title against Tom Watson, only to lose at the third tie hole. This renewed challenge with Watson for a major title came 23 years after they had clashed at Troon for the Open Championship of 1982. That was when the American won the fourth of his five Open titles, with Smyth producing his best-ever performance for a share of fourth place. The critical hole for the Drogheda man was the short 14th where he took a bogey on the way to a final nine holes of 37, compared with 35 from the winner.

As it happened, he was joined as a leading challenger in both the Senior British Open and the US Senior Open in 2005 by Loren Roberts, who celebrated his 50th birthday on June 24th. Apart from sharing with Smyth the distinction of being a former Ryder Cup player (as a member of the beaten US team in 1995), Roberts was also a current Ryder Cup vice-captain, or a captain's assistant, as the Americans prefer. Which meant they would have similar involvements in the build-up to 2006.

Meanwhile, the week in Savannah in late April was one of the occasions when, partly out of a sense of duty and partly because I imagined Smyth would have expected me to, I asked if he had heard anything from Woosnam. And, as usual, he smiled and indicated that he hadn't.

So, it was clearly a relief when the entire matter eventually came out into the open. "Ian spoke to me and asked me to say very little, to keep it under wraps," he said after the official announcement. "Apparently he always had me in mind and it's a relief to be able to talk about it now. I'm absolutely thrilled to be part of the Ryder Cup.

"Though I was hoping for it, of course, you don't want to count your chickens. He obviously wants guys he's familiar with and he and I go back a long way. We've been friends right from the start, when both of us were trying to make a living from the game. We could never have imagined what was going to happen in our sport, which has really exploded in recent years. Our only concern was to try and make a decent living.

"Anyway, he called me a couple of months ago and I have to say it was a very big deal for me. Long before I played in the Ryder Cup, I viewed it that way, so getting on the team was like fulfilling a dream. There have been huge changes, however, over the last 20 years, especially in the media interest. It has become a tremendous TV success which, in turn, has boosted spectator appeal. But the nerve-racking pressures on the players remain essentially the same.

"Woosie and I have exchanged phone and fax numbers, though I am not yet sure what he wants me to do. He knows I'm playing in America and the captain seems to bear the brunt of the work, anyway. But when the time comes, I expect to be busy as vice-captain. The important thing is that the players should be able to focus totally on playing golf. I have been with players when they get distracted and I've seen them suffer.

"I will be keeping pace with all the tournament news through the Golf Channel, which I watch in the morning in the US. I think it goes without saying that there will be difficulties at the time of selection, but I'm still confident we will have the strongest possible side.

"Having an Irishman as a vice captain was obviously part of the politics of the thing. I'm just glad to be that Irishman. I think Ian will be a terrific captain. After all, we're talking about a guy who was number one in the world; you don't have to say any more than that. He is a great character who enjoys a bit of fun but I've also seen the serious side of him. He knows this is a very serious business and, believe me, that's the way he'll treat it."

Peter Baker was the reigning English Amateur Open Strokeplay champion and still two months short of his 18th birthday, when he played in the Walker Cup at Pine Valley in August 1985. The skipper, Charlie Green, seemed to be somewhat protective of his young charge, in that he omitted him from the first day's singles, despite the fact that Baker and Peter McEvoy had a resounding, 6 and 5 foursomes win in the morning.

Anyway, the gifted teenager grabbed his chance on the afternoon of the second day and proceeded to hand a 5 and 4 thrashing to Randy Sonnier, who had been a member of America's Eisenhower Trophy team the previous year. So, he could feel pleased to have contributed two points from his three matches, even if the British and Irish side lost overall by 13-11.

In 1986, Baker made his anticipated move into professional ranks and his winning breakthrough was nothing short of remarkable. Having learned his craft from Alex Lyle, Sandy's father, he became Rookie of the Year in 1987. Then, in the Benson and Hedges International at Fulford GC in York, almost exactly three years after the Walker Cup, he became a tournament winner.

After he and Nick Faldo had carded identical rounds of 68,68 and 66, Baker did the unthinkable by sinking an eagle putt of 15 feet on the 72nd hole to match his rival's closing 69. Then, in sudden-death, he eagled the hole again, this time from about 18 feet, to take the top prize of £41,660. "He's the guy we've been looking for – the best young professional in Britain," enthused the 1987 Open champion.

Baker recalled: "It was the stuff of dreams to win like that against one of the best players in the world. The secret was that I traded in my old putter after the Open the previous month, plus a fiver, for a ladies 'La Femme' putter at the local golf shop at Wolverhampton. It was a couple of inches shorter than standard and worked wonders for me."

Five years later, there were three outstanding European players in the Ryder Cup at The Belfry, albeit in a losing side – Woosnam, Colin Montgomerie and Baker. In fact, Woosnam was the star, with four and a half points out of a possible five, the only glitch on his record being a halved singles point with Fred Couples, who would inflict the same disappointment on him at Oak Hill two years later.

But Baker was a revelation, displaying remarkable courage and maturity as Woosnam's fourball partner on the afternoon of the opening day. In this, his Ryder Cup baptism, he holed for a winning birdie at the short 14th against Jim Gallagher and reigning US Open champion Lee Janzen, to take a one-hole lead at that stage. And he also won the notorious 18th with a four-iron approach followed by a 25-foot putt for his fifth birdie of the match. Not surprisingly, skipper Bernard Gallacher left them together for the second series of fourballs, having paired Woosnam and Bernhard Langer in the foursomes.

This time, Baker and Woosnam faced the formidable partnership of Couples and Paul Azinger. Again, Baker sparkled, with putts ranging from 10 to 35 feet finding the target for a total of six birdies in 13 holes en route to a 6 and 5 triumph. And the putter worked magic for him once more in the number four singles match against no less an opponent than Corey Pavin, whom he beat by two holes.

Against that background, it seems sad that Baker was never again to challenge for Ryder Cup honours as a player. But he was understandably gratified to be back in the fold as a vice captain. "Ian and I have been good friends ever since I joined the Tour," he said. "And I've never forgotten that experience with him in the '93 Ryder Cup. I'm so delighted to be part of the 'team' at The K Club and it will be a great thrill for Helen (his wife) and I to be helping with plans for the matches over the next year."

Later on that memorable day, Lehman was back at the on-site hotel, where his eye followed the crescent-shaped line of the elegant structure which would be home to the respective teams and officials during a momentous week, nearly 15 months ahead. "Our rooms will be down there," he said, pointing to the new West Wing. "The Europeans will be at the other end."

He went on to suggest that separation was an integral element of team sports, especially at the highest competitive level. "When I was here for the American Express (at Mount Juliet) in 2002, I went down to Temple Bar (in Dublin) and watched the Armagh fans celebrate their win over Kerry," he said. "I'll bet those players didn't sleep in adjoining rooms the night before the match."

The fact that he retained such a vivid recollection of that particular All-Ireland Gaelic football final, reflected his determination to acquire a full understanding of what the Ryder Cup represents. "In a way, it's like brother against brother," he suggested. "Look at the huge number of people in the States with Irish and British heritage and you also have countless people who can claim backgrounds elsewhere in Europe, like Italy, Germany and Spain.

"I see great passion in the Irish about their sport. In 2002, I played with Padraig Harrington in the first two rounds of the US Open at Bethpage Black. I remember the weather got really nasty on one of the days – rain, wind and cold. Nearly all the fans just disappeared. In fact, it seemed there was nobody on the golf course except for about 300 Irishmen following Harrington. They cheered everything he was doing, and while he was hitting it pretty good, he was also getting it up and down from a garbage can, making some incredible saves. And the Irish fans just got more into it, especially when he was second behind Tiger at the halfway stage."

Though he claimed there was a consensus that his ill-fated predecessor, Hal Sutton, had done "a pretty good job", Lehman was clearly formulating a grand plan of his own, to turn US fortunes around. "Oh yeah," he acknowledged. "Obviously I'm not going to tell you, but I have done a lot of thinking about this. I've spent hours and hours and hours thinking about the Ryder Cup and our team and our players. Getting people's ideas from guys who played last.

"The best motivation is internal – pride in being on the team. This is what I tried to produce when I played. (He won both singles matches at number one in 1995 and 1999 and also won in the anchor position at Valderrama in 1997). Before my match in 1999, our captain, Ben Crenshaw, said something to me which is going to remain between us. But it had to do with him expecting something special. So, when I got the captaincy, my thinking was that the goal is not simply to be on the Ryder Cup team; the goal is to be on the winning Ryder Cup team."

As for the venue, he considered it to be vastly improved on when he first experienced it 10 years previously. "I love the course," he said. "The changes are amazing. I think it's great." Would he still love it in a Ryder Cup context? "Yes I will." Should we be concerned about that? "I would say that if my team loves it as much as I do, you have reason to be very concerned."

Then, walking down the driveway from the hotel, he looked across the road at the short-game practice area. "I've told officials I'd like that chipping green over there to be usable during the Ryder Cup," he said. "I could imagine our guys going over there in the evenings, to chip and hit bunker shots and have some fun."

But what if the Europeans happened to get there first? "We'd invite them to have a match," said Lehman, with a broad smile. And he continued to stand and stare, thinking, no doubt, of thrilling times ahead.

Soon, it was time to test the waters in tournament competition on the Palmer Course, in a manner of speaking. With all the distractions of Wednesday, it was entirely understandable that Woosnam should miss the cut with rounds of 78 and 72. But Lehman survived, only to run up a third-round 79 on the Saturday when, in his own words, he committed an unforgivable sin by being late on the tee for the first time in his tournament career, so incurring a two-stroke penalty.

When the tournament swept towards its climax, testing the waters took on a ruinously literal meaning for Thomas Bjorn, who had led by four strokes entering the last round. Indeed the Dane was still joint leader with two holes to play when he had the horrific experience of running up an 11 on the treacherous, par-four 17th, where three tee-shots found a watery grave, in the Liffey. "If you play golf long enough, that sort of thing happens," said the Dane, attempting to be philosophical about his torment, while Kenneth Ferrie collected the winner's cheque. Only 12 months previously, in the same tournament on the adjoining Smurfit Course, Bjorn felt obliged to quit after only six holes, because of what he described as his "demons." Now, there was further evidence that his collapse in the Open Championship at Royal St George's in 2003, when he led by three strokes with four to play, only to card bogey, double-bogey, bogey and lose by one to Ben Curtis, had left enduring scars. Jean Van de Velde, who had been down that Open road in even more dramatic circumstances at Carnoustie, offered the advice: "Thomas has to say to himself 'I'm going to try and put myself up there as many times as possible and not let it affect me.'"

It was McGinley, in his capacity as the tournament professional attached to The K Club, who was largely responsible for the increased difficulty of the 17th hole. By moving the tee back significantly, he brought the Liffey far more into play. As he explained: "Prior to that, it was a two-iron, wedge hole. Now, because of the additional length, you're forced to hit three wood and probably driver, when facing a south-west wind. I had been advocating the change for two years and the response came when Darren (Clarke) shot 60 in the second round in 1999. Then it was done."

What was crushing for Bjorn clearly augured well for spectator excitement during the Ryder

Chapter 8 Testing The Waters

Cup. Indeed a general toughening of the course was clearly reflected in Ferrie's three-under-par winning aggregate of 285 which was the highest winning total since the tournament was launched in 1995. Indeed it was a full 11 strokes higher than Philip Price's winning aggregate in 2003.

Meanwhile, there would be nothing new about 17th-hole disasters for Smyth, especially after his Dunhill Cup experiences on the Old Course at St Andrews. In the vast majority of cases, he had come out on the right side, given his record of seven wins, one halved match and only one defeat in nine Dunhill clashes over four years, from 1985 to 1988. Along the way, there were individual wins over Ryder Cup representatives Paul Way, Jose Maria Olazabal, Gordon Brand Jnr and, most notably, against Faldo.

That victory over Faldo came in the 1988 semi-finals in which, famously, play was suspended because of heavy fog on Saturday evening, when the Englishman declined to play his second to the 18th. Then, in the final against Australia, the title hinged on Smyth's match in which his opponent, Rodger Davis, drove out of bounds at the 17th to run up a triple-bogey seven and effectively hand Ireland victory.

It was a triumph which provided Smyth with his finest moment in team golf, a form of competition very dear to his heart. "What memories!" he enthused of the success he shared with Rafferty and Darcy. "We were rank outsiders and we had to beat all the top teams to secure the trophy. It was as if we were destined to win it against all the odds."

Success in his view, could be attributed to the special feelings generated by what he described as "the Irish thing." Now, in a line-up which will be firm favourites rather than rank outsiders, those feelings are set to adopt a European dimension. And Smyth cannot wait for battle to be joined.

As he put it: "It's time to create new team memories."

♦

Chapter 9

Starting Over

Chapter 9 Starting Over

now-capped Alpine peaks glistened in early morning sunshine at Crans-sur-Sierre. It was Thursday, September 1st 2005 and with a drive on the long first, high into rarefied air, Sweden's Fredrik Henge hit the opening shot in the Omega European Masters, the first qualifying tournament for the 2006 Ryder Cup. And skipper, Ian Woosnam, was among those who delighted in glorious, summer temperatures.

Indeed it developed into a golfing weekend with a distinct Ryder Cup flavour. While K Club aspirants were in action in Switzerland, Sam Torrance, Mark James and Neil Coles were prominent among heroes of the past, competing at Woburn in the Bovis Lend Lease European Senior Masters, where Ireland's Eamonn Darcy and Eddie Polland were also in action.

Coles, the oldest of these distinguished practitioners by some years, represented Britain and Ireland in eight Ryder Cups, achieving the highly creditable record of 12 wins and seven halves from 40 matches. Another competitor, Antonio Garrido, had the distinction in 1979 of joining fellow Spaniard Seve Ballesteros as the first Continental players to compete in a European side. And, of course, Woburn was where James recorded a victory in the 1990 British Masters. And James was to win there again, this time in a play-off with Torrance, who, of course, succeeded him as Ryder Cup captain for 2002.

But Switzerland, understandably, held the main focus, not only from a competitive perspective but for promotional purposes, where Failte Ireland and The K Club were concerned. And there was an inescapable sense of relief that the attention was largely on golf, insofar as it would have been daunting to try and sell Irish scenery against the spectacular beauty of Crans. Golf cannot have a more magnificent setting than this extraordinary plateau, almost 5,000 feet above sea level. As Luke Donald, a dab hand with brush and palette, observed: "It's a beautiful place to play golf: something you don't see anywhere else. You never get bored with the views, looking around here."

Remarkably, the Royal and Ancient game has been there since 1905 when Arnold Lunn, owner of the Palace Hotel, commissioned two Englishmen named Freemantle and Gedge to lay out a golf course. So it was that the original nine holes were opened in 1906, followed by an extension to 18, two years later. With the outbreak of World War I in 1914, the British left the so-called Haut-Plateau and in 1924, the Crans-sur-Sierre Golf Club was founded.

Ballesteros, a three-time tournament winner at Crans, was commissioned in 1997 to remodel and up-grade the main course, while the adjoining nine-hole stretch, which had been there since 1951, was totally transformed in 1988 to a design by Jack Nicklaus.

An indication of the progressive nature of the Crans club is that there are plans to extend the Nicklaus course to 18, making the complex a 36-hole facility. During the European Masters, the tented village, down by the 18th fairway, included an Irish stand decked out with appropriate images, from the iconic photograph from Oakland Hills of Darren Clarke, Paul McGinley and Padraig Harrington draped in the Tricolor, to the backdrop of a scene from the host venue under the strapline "Welcome to the home of the Ryder Cup 2006." There was also a poster on the left, incorporating images of the Kildare Hotel.

Damian Ryan, Failte Ireland's director of golf, was there, along with colleagues Tracey Coughlan from East Coast & Midlands Tourism and Caragh Curran from Cork/Kerry Tourism. And The K Club was represented by Bernadine Grogan of the marketing staff, who spoke of a first-hand awareness among numerous Swiss enthusiasts of everything the Straffan venue had to offer. All four were involved in a special "Ireland 2006" reception on the Saturday night, to mark the official Ryder Cup countdown.

Malcolm Connolly, Failte Ireland's Director of Research and Development, and Keelin O'Rourke, a member of his Ryder Cup staff, flew in for the occasion and Connolly addressed the proceedings in French, as did Scott Kelly, Group Marketing Director of the European Tour. Their audience, which included the great and the good of Swiss golf, seemed to approve heartily of their remarks.

Prior to the reception, the so-called "Ryder Cup Challenge" was held after the end of play in the third round. With Woosnam acting in the role of a not-too-critical analyst, it involved Sergio Garcia, Miguel Angel Jimenez, Paul Casey and the European Masters defending champion, Donald, in what was essentially a fun exhibition on the 18th. Significantly it was prefaced by memorable moments from Oakland Hills on a video lasting three minutes and 20 seconds and compiled by Jeff Harvey of European Tour Productions.

Created by the Tour as a promotional vehicle for the benefit of Failte Ireland and shown on a huge screen beside the 18th green, it contained familiar images of Irish Ryder Cup heroes, whose influence was highlighted by McGinley. And it finished with the message: "Ryder Cup 2006 at The K Club in Co Kildare, Ireland on September 22-24." The impact was immense.

Garcia, Jimenez, Casey and Donald were the only Oakland Hills survivors in the tournament field. But Woosnam headed a special list who had made distinguished contributions to the Ryder Cup through the years. There was Sandy Lyle, who had Ballesteros and Garrido as colleagues in the inaugural European team of '79, and Paul Broadhurst, whose sparkling contribution at Kiawah Island in 1991 comprised a fourball win with Woosnam and a 3 and 1 singles victory over Mark O'Meara. Then there was Peter Baker, an admirable partner for the Welshman in the 1993 matches and now one of his vice-captains.

Chapter 9 Starting Over

Philip Walton, who secured the winning European point at Oak Hill in 1995, revealed for the first time a fascinating detail of the scene when Concorde landed in Dublin and the triumphant team were about to disembark. "I was embarrassed at the idea of standing there with the cup, so I refused," he said. "It was only when Prince Andrew grabbed me by the arm and insisted I did it, that I finally agreed."

Also at Crans was Costantino Rocca, another hero of recent years, who will be remembered for his hole-in-one at Oak Hill and for a 4 and 2 victory over no less an opponent than Tiger Woods at Valderrama two years later. Then, of course, there were the sterling contributions of Woosnam, himself, over eight successive stagings from 1983 to 1997.

An increasing awareness of the demands of the captaincy had Woosnam reflecting on the critical years when Tony Jacklin guided European fortunes, from 1983 to 1989. "What Jacklin did was brilliant, and I see it as my duty to carry on the great tradition he established," he said. "As a captain, he made us feel important and confident in our ability, asking how we felt and who we wanted to play with. Everybody felt involved and with a great bunch of guys, we gradually began to strike fear into the Americans.

"From the major championships, Nick Faldo, Sandy Lyle, myself, Bernhard Langer and Seve knew we were capable of matching their best, provided we played well, and gradually they became more afraid of us than we were of them. That was the big turnaround. Now, we no longer have to depend on five players. Guys who are just as confident as we ever were, believe they can beat any opponent on the day. My job is to mould them into one, big happy family, just like Jacklin did."

Lyle, who will be a member of Woosnam's back-room team at The K Club, shared this view as he, too, was caught up in the excitement of the launch. "Jacklin insisted that everything was first-class all the way, from Concorde to cashmeres," he said. "That made a huge difference to morale. And he was easy to talk to; a sort of father-figure who was greatly respected because of what he himself had achieved in the game. You took note of what he said. In my mind, if you have a captain who's been through the mill at the highest level, you've got to respect his decisions. As a major winner, I hope I can now make a contribution in that way.

"There's a good depth now, which is what we were trying to achieve for so long, so that we wouldn't be looking to the leading five guys to play their boots off. The last Ryder Cup showed that the middle-order guys in the singles had the confidence to dig their heels in against American pressure."

While Woosnam was planning essentially for a leadership challenge spanning 12 months, the focus of his US counterpart, Tom Lehman, on the other side of the Atlantic, was more immediate.

He was eagerly awaiting the President's Cup matches later in September in the hope they would enlighten his thinking on pairings for The K Club. He was also reflecting on the experience of three summer weeks in Britain and Ireland, playing the Smurfit European Open, the Scottish Open and the Open Championship at St Andrews.

"A typical conversation at the British Open would be 'Hey, nice birdie on 15. Who's going to win the Ryder Cup?'" he said. "Then there would be a comment such as 'I hope we beat you again like at Oakland Hills.' That would be an average conversation with a golf fan. And there were hundreds if not thousands of fans with that kind of enthusiasm. They get it from the media and I really believe that understanding this Ryder Cup mentality is essential for us. As far as the European players are concerned, there's no bigger thing than being part of a winning Ryder Cup team. It has made me realise that you need to have exactly the same mentality, if not better, in order to beat them."

Qualification for the European Team is a dual process. The first involves the leading five players on the Ryder Cup World Ranking List compiled from September 1st 2005 to September 3rd 2006: in the event of a tie, placings will be decided by the higher ranking on the Official World Golf Rankings as of Monday August 28th, 2006. The second five, not qualified through the first list, will come from the Ryder Cup World Points List as of Sunday, September 3rd 2005. In the event of a tie, placings will be decided by the higher ranking on the European Order of Merit as of Sunday September 3rd 2006. Then there are two captain's picks.

Unlike the European system, which is based over 12 months, selection for the US team for 2006 is assessed on points earned on their tour from August 22nd 2004 to the completion of the USPGA Championship at Medinah on August 20th 2006. The top-10 in the US team standings at the end of that period qualify automatically and a further two selections are then made by the captain, as in Europe. Points are awarded on this basis: 2004 and 2005 Regular Tour events – 75, 45, 40, 35, 30, 25, 20, 15, 10, 5; 2005 Major Championships – 450, 225, 200, 175, 150, 125, 100, 75, 50, 25; 2006 Regular Tour events – 375, 180, 160, 140, 120, 100, 80, 60, 40, 20; 2006 Major Championships – 675, 360, 320, 280, 240, 200, 160, 120, 80, 40.

In this context, Woosnam and Lehman had intriguing observations about the make-up of the US Tour. "I think there are now 78 full-time international players, which is a great thing in that it makes it the most competitive tour in the world," said the American. "But the down side of it is that there is less opportunity for our young players, kids coming out of college or just starting out as professionals. Let's face it, when you have the best players from South Africa and Australia and everywhere else coming here to play, you need to be doggone good to get a spot away from them. So it's taking longer for our young guys to get on tour. Still, at

Chapter 9 Starting Over

the end of the day, I think that our American players have proved themselves to be great players."

Woosnam was also concerned about the number of non-American players on the US Tour – because they happen to include some key Europeans. "It's great that Justin Rose has re-joined the European Tour (albeit as an associate member), but it is a problem that others have chosen not to. Luke Donald came and made the effort last time and although he didn't quite make the team automatically, he got a wild card. The opportunities are there and hopefully these guys will come back to our Tour and play here."

George O'Grady, executive director of the European Tour, shared that view. "There are currently 13 European-born members of the European Tour in the top-50 of the World Ranking, which is an all-time record," he said. "The ones who have chosen to leave the European Tour and join the (US) PGA Tour are much lower in the ranking. If you're a top-50 ranked player, dual membership is not difficult. All you've got to find is another four events each year. We share Ian's desire to see players like Justin Rose, Alex Cejka and Greg Owen all back in the world's top-50 and as European Tour members.

"The Ryder Cup is about Europe versus America, not the European Tour against the PGA Tour. The fact of the matter is that if we didn't have a really strong European Tour and we didn't have a tour in place to create really strong players, then the Ryder Cup wouldn't be what it is today. Certainly the players who are now choosing to play on the PGA Tour, wouldn't have got to this stage of their career without a strong European Tour on which to hone their skills."

Garcia, a Ryder Cup veteran at 25, played with Woosnam over the opening two rounds at Crans, insisting all the while on referring to the older man by the affectionate title of Cappie. And the player who seems to be capable of infuriating American Ryder Cup fans more than any other, expressed a determination to play his way into the side for a fourth successive time. "I would change my schedule if it looked as if I mightn't make the team by myself," he said. "No matter who you are and what you have done, you might not get picked. Anyway, I would rather Woosie used one of the spots (captain's picks) for someone else rather than me. It would make me happier, and probably him, too." Such considerations seemed a world away, however, when the irrepressible Spaniard, who happens to have a home at Crans, went on to capture the European Masters title by a stroke from Sweden's Peter Gustavson. "I am first on the Ryder Cup table which is definitely a great start, but there is a long way to go," he said, after dedicating his victory to a close friend, Maria Garcia Estrada, who had died the previous week after battling lung cancer.

We can assume that when viewed on their own Golf Channel, Garcia's victory surge would have revived unwelcome images in American consciousness of his boyish histrionics after making various, crucial contributions to the Ryder Cup. Indeed these could also have been in Lehman's mind when he said: "You talk to any American player right now and they'll tell you they're sick and tired of losing. They're sick and tired of hearing all the negatives like they're not together as a team and that they don't get along. Which is why I think you'll see a very committed group of guys in Ireland."

No amount of Alpine beauty could soften the raw intensity of those words, when Woosnam contemplated the challenge ahead. "Sure, Tom Lehman will be looking for blood," he said. "But we've got to be ready. And at this stage, I can confidently predict that we'll have the right players to do the job."

The American poet, Walt Whitman, had Abraham Lincoln in mind when he penned the evocative lines:

O Captain! my Captain! our fearful trip is done,

The ship has weathered every rack, the prize we sought is won....!

One can only imagine the storms and trials which lie in wait for Woosnam and Lehman, before the good ship Ryder Cup is steered once more towards what we hope will be a familiar, blue haven.

♦

Chapter 10

Shaping The Legend

Chapter 10 Shaping The Legend

vents on the 17th green at Brookline in 1999 provoked such a storm of controversy that one would have imagined nothing comparable had ever happened in the history of the Ryder Cup. Not so. A gross breach of etiquette was the worst the Americans could have been accused of for their efforts at replicating *Riverdance,* whereas charges of flouting the actual rules of the game had previously been levelled against teams from both sides of the Atlantic.

The fact is that controversy and the Ryder Cup have been regular bedfellows through the years. Indeed the event has also thrown up remarkable happenings, somewhat removed from the playing of the game. The first of these occurred in 1931 in only the third staging of the biennial tournament. As the British team prepared to defend the trophy at the Scioto CC, Columbus, Ohio, there were three notable absentees from their line-up.

Percy Alliss was not chosen because he was living in Germany at the time and Aubrey Boomer, who was based in Paris, was also missing. Though both players were members of the victorious 1929 team when Alliss didn't play, the PGA decided that only players working and resident in Britain were eligible under the terms of Samuel Ryder's Trust Deed.

This came on the heels of a major rift between the PGA and Henry Cotton, whom the association had always treated with suspicion, because of the public school education which, in terms of social graces, raised him a cut above his colleagues. In the event, Cotton declined an invitation to play, on the grounds that he wished to remain on in the US.

For their part, the PGA insisted that he would have to return to Britain with the remainder of the team. In justifying his action, which was based on the need for further tournament experience aimed at one day winning the Open, Cotton contributed a lengthy article to *Golf Illustrated.*

There was rich irony in the fact that he happened to be playing-captain of the British team when the next controversy erupted on the eve of the matches in Portland, Oregon, in November 1947. That was when the bold Henry demanded an inspection of the American clubs.

While no official reason was given, the suspicion was that the Americans had grooves which were imparting more than normal spin and were thereby illegal. Ben Hogan, Cotton's US counterpart, agreed to an inspection and the upshot was that nothing untoward was discovered about the clubs on either team.

Meanwhile, an angry Hogan bided his time in getting even with Cotton. The Hawk's opportunity came at the 1949 matches at Ganton, where he was non-playing captain due to horrific injuries sustained in a car crash earlier that year. On the eve of battle he demanded an examination of the home team's clubs.

As a consequence, several British players had to file down club-faces, so as to make grooves shallower and thereby reduce backspin. Hogan had exacted revenge, and his players rubbed salt in the wound by coming from behind to win the matches 7-5.

Incidentally, the Ganton staging was also notable for the mouth-watering supplies which the Americans took with them to post-war Britain. Aware of continued shortages of foodstuffs, they travelled with rations of 600 steaks, 12 sides of rib for roasting, a dozen hams and 12 boxes of bacon. Some observers felt they had insulted their hosts by implying that British food would be somehow inadequate, but such considerations would have been of no concern to Hogan.

These undercurrents were as nothing, however, compared with the open warfare which erupted during the 1957 matches at Lindrick, where a home team which included Christy O'Connor and Harry Bradshaw recorded a memorable triumph. It was perhaps not surprising that the main focus of the ill-temper was the match between Scotland's Eric Brown and the notoriously volatile Tommy Bolt, he of club-throwing fame and known to his colleagues as Thunder (Bolt).

Brown crushed Bolt by 4 and 3 in the top singles. Later, in the locker-room, the American snapped ungraciously: "I guess you won but I didn't enjoy it a bit." There are two versions of Brown's reply. The sanitised one is: "Nor would I have done, after the licking I've just given you." But the version which includes one or two choice expletives seems more in character with the abrasive Scot.

Some years later, another defeated player was prompted to remark: "Losing the Ryder Cup did not bother me as much as the behaviour of the galleries. All that cheering when we missed putts. I've never known anything like it before." A European comment after Brookline in 1999? Not so. This was the reaction of America's Peter Jacobsen to the defeat at The Belfry in 1985.

But there have been other interesting happenings where temper was not a factor. Like in the 1933 matches at Southport and Ainsdale where J H Taylor, the British captain, was determined to impress upon his players that the Ryder Cup was "no picnic." So, he employed the services of a physical training instructor who took the team out on Southport beach at 6.30am for a pre-breakfast run.

By way of contrast, there have also been wonderful memories for both the players and spectators. Like when Dai Rees complimented Jimmy Demaret on his bunker play during their match at Pinehurst in 1951. Handing his opponent the sand iron, Demaret said: "Keep it, Dai, as a gift. The one you've got has too sharp an edge and you'll never have any finesse with it."

Chapter 10 Shaping The Legend

Years later, Rees recalled: "I took the club to Britain and had it copied for my own set. So, although I lost the match, I came away with a profit."

Then there was the gesture by Jack Nicklaus at Royal Birkdale in 1969, which has since led to a joint venture with his British rival in a course development in Florida, appropriately called The Concession. As Tony Jacklin stood over a two-foot putt on the 18th, Nicklaus knew that if he missed, the American team would gain overall victory.

At that moment, the Golden Bear stepped forward, picked up Jacklin's marker and said: "I'm sure you would have holed, but I was not prepared to see you miss." With the overall result a tie, it seemed in that precious moment that the sporting rivalry conceived by Samuel Ryder had received its finest endorsement.

It was April 1998 and with the decision by the European Tour still nine months away, it seemed somewhat premature to be linking the 2005 Ryder Cup with a specific venue. Yet the golfing public had their own ideas about where it should go, while those interested in a bet could recognise an attractive gamble when they saw one. Like the possibility of it being landed by The K Club.

This was the basis of a fascinating charity auction during the Audi Chris de Burgh Classic at Straffan, where Dr Michael Smurfit invited bids for three nights' accommodation, gratis, at the Kildare Hotel during the Ryder Cup – assuming of course, that it was staged there.

"I'm offering a simple gamble," he said at the time. And it had undoubted appeal, judging from an immediate bid of £25,000 (punts). And as quickly as you could say "serious loot", the prize was knocked down to businessman Brian Lynam for £28,000.

"If the Ryder Cup comes here, that accommodation will be priceless," said Dr Smurfit, who indicated that all other rooms in the hotel would be allocated. And if it didn't? The successful bidder had paid a rather inflated price for a two-bedroom suite which cost £2,100 for three nights at that time: breakfast and trimmings extra.

Royal Lytham in 1977 marked a watershed in the history of the biennial event. And almost inevitably, Jack Nicklaus was a central figure in a decision which not only saved the Ryder Cup, but caused it to prosper out of all recognition, over the following 10 years. Events at Lytham also led to the adopting of a format which has remained unchanged since 1979.

From the inaugural matches until 1959, the then two-day Ryder Cup format comprised four 36-hole foursomes matches on the opening day and eight 36-hole singles matches on the second day. Then came a change in 1961, ironically at Lytham, where all matches were

The Archive

V

Seve Ballesteros and Howard Clarke captured on the big screen at the opening ceremony of the 1995 Ryder Cup at Oak Hill Country Club. Europe were to come out on top by 14½ to 13½.

Seve Ballesteros poised to strike on the 7th tee of Oak Hill Country Club during the 1995 Ryder Cup.

Far left: Third time lucky for Europe's captain, Bernard Gallacher, at Oak Hill. As captain, Gallacher endured near misses in 1991 and 1993 but pulled off a one point victory over the United States at Oak Hill in 1995. Left: Ian Woosnam fails to convert on the 18th green in his singles match against Fred Couples which was halved. Below left: Nick Faldo sees the line while (below right) Philip Walton comes out of a bunker. Bottom left: Brad Faxon under cover during his fourball encounter with Peter Jacobsen against David Gilford and Seve Ballesteros which Europe won 4 and 3. Bottom right: Bernhard Langer who partnered David Gilford to a 4 and 3 victory over Corey Pavin and Tom Lehman in the second day's foursomes.

Far left: An ecstatic Tom Lehman following a holed chip at the 1997 Ryder Cup at Valderrama which saw Tiger Woods **(above left)** make his first of appearance in US colours. It was to be the start of a less than successful relationship with the Ryder Cup. Woods managed only 1½ points out of a possible 5 in his 1997 outing. **Top right:** Lee Westwood from behind one of Valderrama's famous cork trees. **Left:** Team captain Seve Ballesteros with his hands on the prize which Europe won 14½ to 13½. **Above:** Mark O'Meara in action on the opening day's fourball matches. He and partner Woods defeated Bernhard Langer and Colin Montgomerie 3 and 2.

The infamous invasion of the 17th green at The Country Club, Brookline, during the 1999 Ryder Cup. Justin Leonard (above) holed a 45-foot miracle putt in his singles match against Jose Maria Olazabal prompting wild celebrations from Leonard, team mates led by Tom Lehman, wives and supporters who ran onto the green to celebrate what they believed was a winning effort for the US. But Olazabal still had a putt to prolong the match and had to wait until the green was cleared some minutes later. Meanwhile the Spaniard, having been forced to watch uncomfortably as his line was being trampled on, missed – and it was indeed all over. The incident became the focus of major controversy with the Americans protesting that it was an entirely impromptu and innocent outburst. Europeans thought otherwise.

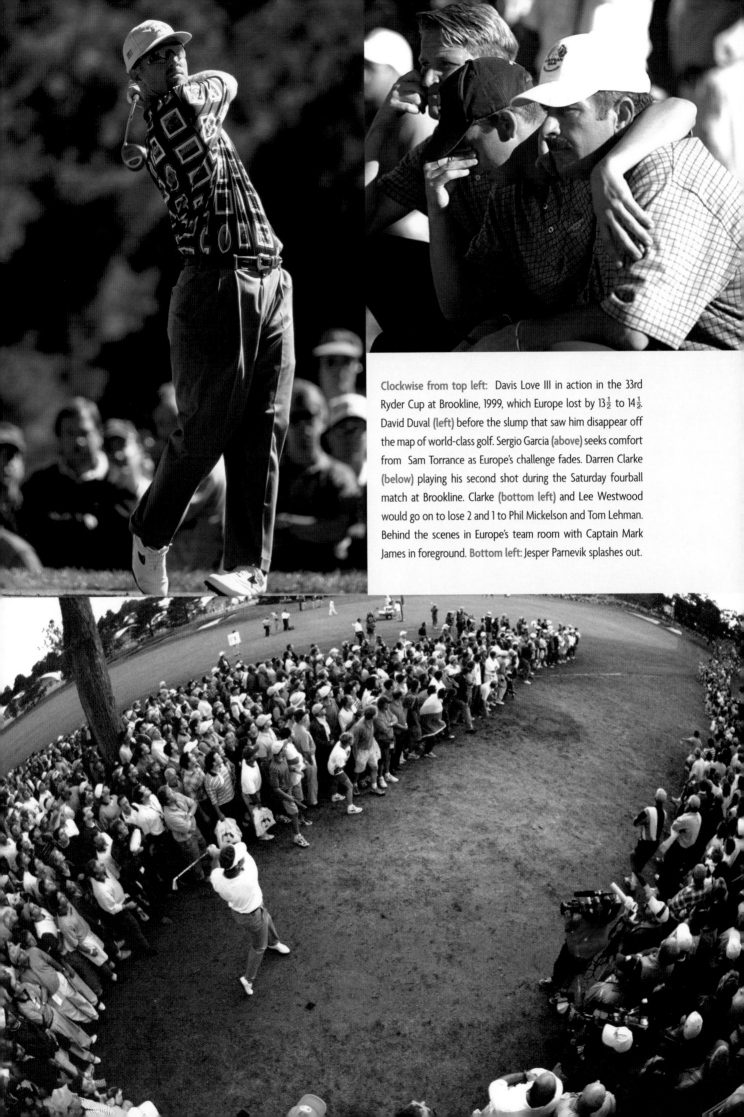

Clockwise from top left: Davis Love III in action in the 33rd Ryder Cup at Brookline, 1999, which Europe lost by 13½ to 14½. David Duval (left) before the slump that saw him disappear off the map of world-class golf. Sergio Garcia (above) seeks comfort from Sam Torrance as Europe's challenge fades. Darren Clarke (below) playing his second shot during the Saturday fourball match at Brookline. Clarke (bottom left) and Lee Westwood would go on to lose 2 and 1 to Phil Mickelson and Tom Lehman. Behind the scenes in Europe's team room with Captain Mark James in foreground. Bottom left: Jesper Parnevik splashes out.

RYDER CUP 1927 2001

MATCH No		EUROPE 15½	RESULT	12½ USA
1	MONTGOMERIE	V HOCH	5 & 4	
2	GARCIA	V TOMS	1 HOLE	
3	CLARKE	V DUVAL	HALVED	
4	LANGER	V SUTTON	4 & 3	
5	HARRINGTON	V CALCAVECCHIA	5 & 4	
6	BJORN	V CINK	2 & 1	
7	WESTWOOD	V VERPLANK	2 & 1	
8	FASTH	V AZINGER	HALVED	
9	McGINLEY	V FURYK	HALVED	
10	FULKE	V LOVE III	HALVED	
11	PRICE	V MICKELSON	3 & 2	
12	PARNEVIK	V WOODS	HALVED	

Clockwise from top left: Padraig Harrington in his second appearance in the Ryder Cup at The Belfry in 2002. Harrington had a stunning victory 5 and 4 victory over Mark Calcavecchia (below left) in Sunday's singles and partnered Colin Montgomerie to a 2 and 1 victory (top right) over Phil Mickelson and David Toms in Saturday's fourballs. Above: The final tally from The Belfry 2002. Below left: Jesper Parnevik just missing for birdie at the 18th with Davis Love III (far left) checking the line during the first of his four outings in 2002.

Paul McGinley memorably celebrating Europe's victory at The Belfry in 2002. His putt at the 18th sealed his place in Ryder Cup history.

reduced to 18 holes, with four foursomes morning and afternoon on the opening day and eight singles, morning and afternoon on day two, making 24 matches in all.

In 1963, fourball matches were added for the first time, increasing the number of matches to 32. But in a dramatic change, which proved to be an unmitigated flop, the number of matches in 1977 was reduced to 20 over three days – five foursomes on day one, followed by five fourballs on day two and culminating in 10 singles on the third day.

So as to spread the matches, largely for the benefit of television, there was a gap of 45 minutes between each. Among other things, it meant a three-hour time span between the first and last foursome going off the tee on the opening day. As Michael Williams pointed out in his splendid, 1989 book, *The Official History of the Ryder Cup*, the essential spirit of the event was lost, with play dragging along at such a snail's pace that not even television was happy.

The upshot was that when the 1979 matches at The Greenbrier were being planned, the format was revised, with four fourballs and four foursomes on each of the opening two days, followed by 12 singles on day three. As it happened, the opening series of matches changed to foursomes in 1981, and the format was retained up to and including 1995. As skipper of the 1997 team, however, Seve Ballesteros advised a change back to fourballs on the grounds that it would work more to Europe's advantage. Somewhat bemused by this, his US counter-part, Tom Kite, acquiesced, believing it to be a matter of no consequence. In the event, the opening series of fourballs at Valderrama ended 2-2.

The major change at Lytham, however, led to a broadening of the selection base on this side of the Atlantic to include players from Continental Europe. As Michael Williams wrote: "..... And if credit for the move has to go to one man more than any other: it was Nicklaus – still, of course, a player but in all other respects an elder statesman – whose counsel was sought on all aspects of golf. It was he who approached Lord Derby, President of the British PGA at Lytham, saying in effect that the fixture could not go on like this or it would surely die. Later, he was to back up his words with a letter in which he stressed that it is vital to widen the selection procedures if the Ryder Cup is to continue to enjoy its past prestige.'"

We are informed that arising from Nicklaus's advice, Ken Schofield was summoned to Lord Derby's home at Knowsley. Whatever the feelings of some of his lordship's colleagues, change would be embraced and it was arranged for Brian Huggett, the 1977 captain, and Peter Butler of the Ryder Cup committee, to complete the formalities during the 1978 US Masters at Augusta National.

It so happened that a pictorial biography, *Jack Nicklaus On and Off the Fairway,* was about to be published at the time. It included the passage: "I've played in all five Ryder Cup matches since I became eligible for the US team in 1969, and I have greatly enjoyed both the

Chapter 10 Shaping The Legend

camaraderie of the event and the relationships and goodwill that it promotes. However, I also happen to feel as a golf contest pure and simple, it badly needs a change of format. As far as the American players are concerned, everyone wants and enjoys the honour of making the team but many find it difficult to get charged up for the matches themselves. By saying this, I'm not trying to put down my British friends, but the fact must be faced that British professional golf in recent years simply hasn't developed sufficient depth of good players to make a true contest of the event. Nor, from what I see, does there appear to be much likelihood of that situation changing in the foreseeable future.

"I know national pride is involved, but at some point reality must prevail if the event isn't to decline into little more than an exhibition bout – and especially if it is to remain a vital part of the US golfing calendar. When you consider that the golfing population of the United States is roughly equivalent to that of the rest of the world, maybe a World versus the United States format would make the most sense. If that's too presumptuous, then the United States versus the English-speaking countries or even the United States versus Europe would seem viable formats." Not for the first time, Nicklaus was right on the money.

The European idea had obvious appeal at a time when a young conquistador named Seve Ballesteros was taking golf by storm. In only his second appearance in the World Cup in 1976, he partnered Manuel Pinero to a Spanish victory at Mission Hills, Palm Springs. And with Antonio Garrido as his partner, Ballesteros inspired another Spanish win the following year in Manila. There was also huge significance in the fact that at the time of the 1977 Ryder Cup, he was on his way to retaining his position as the leading money winner in European tournament golf.

For their part, the PGA of America has acknowledged that the development of European golf, "with its varying types of golf courses, climates, food, language and customs, was to produce players of unprecedented durability. They possessed the technique and confidence to deal with all course situations and make the Ryder Cup Matches ever more of a quality event."

So, despite the reluctance of the British PGA, change became inevitable, not least because of the enthusiastic response of influential players from both sides of the Atlantic. It meant what when the Americans were defending the trophy at The Greenbrier in September 1979, they faced a 12-man side which included five Englishmen, four Scots, an Irishman (Des Smyth) and Spaniards Ballesteros and Garrido. A thrilling new day had dawned, which would be inspirational to players who experienced a new sense of pride in a much-loved team event.

But progress was not without its problems. With increasing numbers of European players opting to join the USPGA Tour, change became inevitable in a selection system which was formulated for the 1979 matches, when Des Smyth and Peter Oosterhuis were Europe's first wild-card choices. For the record, neither side chose wild-cards in 1983 and the US didn't adopt this system until 1989, when skipper Raymond Floyd completed his 12 for The Belfry with the formidable duo of Tom Watson and Lanny Wadkins.

So it was that in the wake of the 2002 matches, Ken Schofield advocated a total overhaul of the European selection system with five places in the side coming off the world rankings. Bernhard Langer, one of the heroes of that particular staging and a future captain at Oakland Hills, was of similar mind.

"Given that I now live in America, a different selection system is probably the only way I could get into a future team as a player," said the German. "To get the 12 best players, we need to go off the world rankings. As things stand, a player who picked up money in, say, 35 tournaments, would get into the team if he won 100 Euro more than a player competing in 12 tournaments. But who is the better player? The one who played 12 or 35? That's what I'm saying is wrong with the system."

As things turned out, the proposal met with general approval on this side of the Atlantic, with the result that Padraig Harrington, Sergio Garcia, Darren Clarke, Miguel Angel Jimenez and Lee Westwood made the team for Oakland Hills, on the basis of their world ranking.

"For the President's Cup, our guys went halfway around the world to Australia to play a bunch of guys from Orlando. Enough said." Lanny Wadkins, the 1995 captain at Oak Hill, highlighting the difference between the President's Cup and the Ryder Cup.

The staging at The Belfry in 1989, when Christy O'Connor Jnr hit his famous two-iron shot to the 18th en route to victory over Fred Couples, was the golden jubilee of the Ryder Cup that never was. And the occasion would have been noted with decidedly mixed feelings by the members of the Ponte Vedra Inn and Club in North Florida. For it was there that the 1939 matches were scheduled to take place in November, only for the outbreak of World War II causing a late, unprecedented cancellation.

The venue was chosen after a magazine article had described it as "one of the hardest" in the US and comparable with such celebrated locations as Pebble Beach and Oakmont. In 1998, Ponte Vedra earned glowing praise following a $3.7 million tee-to-green facelift. In the course of the upgrading, architect Bobby Weed introduced features such as angled teeing areas, undulating fairways, pot bunkers and roll-lipped bunkers.

Among other things, the 1939 cancellation meant that the US, through their victory in 1937, retained the trophy throughout the war period. It also led to a challenge by the overlooked Gene Sarazen, to put up a team capable of beating the chosen one. The match took place in 1940 at Oakland Hills and Sarazen's line-up included such luminaries as Ben Hogan, Jimmy Demaret and Craig Wood.

For their part, the British PGA had selected eight players under skipper Henry Cotton before hostilities scuppered their plans. Those eight were: Jimmy Adams, Dick Burton, Sam King, Alf Padgham, Dai Rees, Charles Whitcombe and Reg Whitcombe. The remaining two places were never filled.

Despite the direct involvement of the US in World War II after the bombing of Pearl Harbour on December 7th 1941, they continued to select annual Ryder Cup teams up to and including 1943. The idea was to raise funds for the America's United Service Organisation (USO), which was done most successfully. Walter Hagen captained the 1940 and '41 teams at Oakland Hills and Detroit GC, and Wood, the 1941 US Open champion, captained the team in 1942 at Oakland Hills and 1943 at Plum Hollow CC.

The American Ryder Cup team won four out of the five challenge matches, but the most interesting of these was at Detroit GC on August 23rd and 24th 1941, when Hagen's "official" team faced the so-called Bobby Jones Challengers. The partnership of Jones and Sarazen was crushed 8 and 6 by Byron Nelson and Harold "Jug" McSpaden on the opening day. In singles combat, however, the game's greatest amateur proved that he retained much of the skill which had secured him the Impregnable Quadrilateral 11 years previously. With a 2 and 1 singles win over 1938 Masters champion, Henry Picard, Jones inspired his players to victory by 8½ to 6½ before an attendance of 18,000. This was the only time a "challenging" line-up beat the official selection.

The most lucrative fund-raiser during that period, however, was the brainchild of John Kelly, a champion sculler and father of movie star, Grace Kelly, later Princess Grace of Monaco. The 1942 Hale America National Open in Chicago raised $25,000 and was won by Hogan.

Samuel Ryder lived to see only two British stagings of the event he created. While on holiday with his family in London, he died of a massive brain haemorrhage on January 2nd 1936, aged 77. His favourite golf club, a mashie (five iron), was sent by his eldest daughter, Mrs Marjorie Claisen, to be placed in his coffin. Another daughter, Mrs Thomas Scarfe, who didn't share her father's love of golf, took over the family business.

Yet another daughter, Joan, was old Sam's constant companion at the golf events he attended and she retained her passion for the game long after he died. In fact she attended successive Ryder Cup matches staged in Britain up to 1985. On the occasion of the Walton

Heath clash of 1981, she met the Duke of Kent to whom she expressed her father's surprise at the success of the matches.

"He had the idea that when the Americans came over for a match, he would give a 'small, friendly lunch party' to both teams," she said. The Duke observed the teeming crowds around the 18th green and said: "I wonder what your father would think of this little lunch!"

Her only appearance at an American staging was in 1983 at Palm Beach Gardens, which marked the development of the European team into a highly competitive unit under the captaincy of Tony Jacklin. And it seemed highly appropriate that her final event was at The Belfry in 1985, when Europe broke through for a memorable victory. In the view of Joan Ryder, this was "the most exciting ever". She died at her home in Sussex later that year, aged 81.

Recalling the challenge he faced as the newly-appointed skipper of the European Team in 1983, Tony Jacklin observed: "We were on some sort of British Airways charter not knowing who was buying the drinks or who was paying for the dry cleaning. It was all sort of done on a shoestring back then."

Now a US resident, Jacklin went on: "I tried to put my players on the first tee not feeling they were two down before the match started. We were dressed in whatever anybody would give us, whereas the Americans were always decked out in the finest. Until we got that straightened out, we were always in the back of the bus."

Jacklin, who captained Europe from 1983 to 1989, concluded: "When I started out, it was very much them and us and trying to figure out a way we could win the thing. Once we achieved the breakthrough (1985), the attention of the American press, media and public was caught up. I like to think that the players will all come out with their integrity intact, that the matches will be close and the event itself will continue to be successful."

The 1997 staging at Valderrama was especially memorable for the pre-tournament rumpus over Miguel Angel Martin, who became a non-playing 13th man in the European line-up, the histrionics of skipper Seve Ballesteros .... and a cry for help from Tiger Woods which went unanswered.

Only five months after he had won his first US Masters by a record, 12-stroke margin, Woods experienced serious putting problems on the Saturday at Valderrama. That was when he sent a putt across the green on the long 17th ruinously into the water in fourball partnership with Mark O'Meara and they lost by 2 and 1 to Nick Faldo and Lee Westwood. In normal circumstances he would have gone straight to his father for help, but Earl Woods

Chapter 10 Shaping The Legend

wasn't there. Woods senior had declined to travel to the Ryder Cup because the PGA of America refused to include him in the official party. And when Tiger phoned him on that Saturday at his home in Cypress, California, Earl was out playing golf with friends. His wife, Kultida, left a message that he was to phone their son urgently, but because of the nine-hour time difference, it was the middle of the night in Spain when the call came.

The Spanish operator in San Roque refused to put the call through on the grounds that the player was sleeping and shouldn't be disturbed. When Earl rang a second time, at 7.00am Spanish time, the players had already left for Valderrama.

The upshot of it was that father and son never made contact and after a shock, 4 and 2 singles defeat by Costantino Rocca on the Sunday, an emotional Tiger was reduced to tears as Europe retained the trophy.

"It was my fault," Earl Woods later claimed. "I should have been there to support Tiger when he needed me. I won't let it happen again. Tiger was having problems with his putting and he doesn't trust anyone with it except me."

David Leadbetter took the view that the American skipper should have rested Woods on the Saturday, given that the player had been struggling in every session of matches. "You have to wonder whether Tom Kite was afraid to leave him out because of the public pressure," said the Florida-based coach.

As a consequence Woods delivered only one and a half points to the American cause, in an event he was expected to dominate.

L ooking back on seriously lopsided matches prior to the emergence of a European line-up, it may be difficult for current enthusiasts to imagine the attraction of the Ryder Cup as a golfing spectacle. The answer was provided by the inimitable Pat Ward-Thomas in his regular pieces for the magazine *Country Life*.

When previewing the 1961 staging at Royal Lytham, he wrote: "The great benefit of the Ryder Cup match to the British watcher is the opportunity, rare these days, of studying some of the finest players in the world. *(These were times when golf was a rarity on television: D.G.)*. Several are in this American side. It is headed by the formidable and delightful (Arnold) Palmer and thousands will welcome the opportunity of seeing him again so soon after his (Open) triumph at Birkdale. Of the rest, only four have competed in Britain previously. (Dow) Finsterwald, (Doug) Ford and (Art) Wall alone remain of the Lindrick side and (Mike) Souchak played in the Open at Hoylake five years ago, finishing eight strokes behind (Peter) Thomson."

In the wake of a 14½ to 9½ win by the Americans, he wrote: "There may be those who claim that the difference between the sides was less than five points, especially as five games were lost by the British on the last green of all, but this would be false reasoning. On the highest level of competitive golf, the margin of quality is slight indeed, and by no means is it always technical. More often than not, it depends upon competitive ability alone and in this, as every thinking observer knows, the Americans have an advantage. They play infinitely more competitive golf, for far greater rewards, than the British and it stands to reason that, when the plot thickens and the pressure mounts, they are less likely to weaken."

Ward-Thomas then highlighted a splendid singles battle which dominated the morning of the second day when, for the first time, two series of 18-hole singles matches were played rather than the previous 36-hole encounters. "Down the years, men will talk of the match that (Peter) Alliss played against the mighty Palmer," he wrote.

"Here was the very essence of golfing conflict, stern in its resolve, admirable in its mood and compelling in its strength. For Alliss, it was the severest test of matchplay imaginable, because beyond any question, Palmer is the world's supreme golfer. Aside altogether from his formidable strength, there is the instinct of genius for improvisation of flight, the sensitivity of touch and control in all the short shots, a truly remarkable competitive nature, and withal a flair for the game such as few other men have possessed. Against these things, Alliss stood erect, assured and strong and played superbly in the face of brutal thrusts from Palmer."

In the matter of the captaincy, Ward-Thomas went on: "It is almost a quarter of a century since (Dai) Rees played his first match against the Americans and beat Byron Nelson, and here he was, the only British player to win three points. His unquenchable spirit knows no bounds; it burns ever brighter and never more so than on the great occasions. No one in the match hit the ball with finer control or more consistent accuracy than (Neil) Coles, who has taken his place in the highest company with a rare modesty and poise, and has proved beyond question that he has the competitive temper for any affair. Did he not almost beat Littler, the American Open champion, and then hours later undo Finsterwald?

"There was some criticism of Rees for not leaving out (Bernard) Hunt and (John) Panton after they had lost their morning foursome, but to be a playing captain in this match was no enviable task. In spite of starting before the sun's rim had appeared over the clinging early mists, the players had only a few minutes for lunch.

"Thus Rees had no time for deliberate enquiry. He could not leave himself out without weakening the side as Barber (the US skipper) was able to do, and indeed might have done with advantage on the last afternoon. Barber was the weakest American player, yet chose to play in place of Casper or Hebert."

Though describing the result as "honourable," he concluded that the "the playing of 18-

Chapter 10 Shaping The Legend

hole matches has turned out as I feared. Had the old order (36-hole encounters) been retained, the contest would not have lost its light at lunch. Nevertheless, the Ryder Cup is in a sense an exhibition, and as such it did not fail."

W hatever his views, Tom Humphries could never be accused of lacking an appreciation of sport in all its forms. Indeed with typical eloquence, he referred in *The Irish Times* of September 29th, 1997 to the beauty of golf being its pace, "its lonely agonies, its eternal symmetry."

Yet in the same article, he damned those who would turn it "into a raucous team sport .... squeezing the delicacy out of it." Against that background, you will have gathered that this prince among sportswriters, does not approve of the Ryder Cup.

"I don't understand the Ryder Cup," wrote Humphries. "I don't see the point. I don't get the attraction. I just don't watch it. As I write, I am in a state of shock. I am apparently the only person in the world who doesn't understand or like the Ryder Cup. Around me, the population at large is experiencing the sort of bizarrely-disproportionate communal hysteria generally reserved for deceased royals. Come on Europe! Now I'm no bigot. Just because the sport is elitist and sexually discriminatory doesn't mean I'll bear an eternal grudge against the Knights of the Diamond Pattern Sweater. I'll wear my Pringle and swing my Big Bertha with the best of them.

"The Ryder Cup is a hoax, the last kick of a dying European Tour, a televisual concoction which was lucky to survive the 1970s but is now being milked as a cash-cow. It was cooked up to show that American professionals were as fit as Brits to be full-time pros in their local clubs. When it got to the stage where the Brits couldn't beat the Yanks at all, it should have been laid to rest. Instead, we Paddies were dragged into it. To no avail. Then the rest of Europe was trawled and deemed fit to wear the blazer. Europe started winning matches before it became necessary for us to annex Asia......There is so much about the Ryder Cup that is squalid, contrived and commerce-driven."

There was more, much more, in the incomparable Humphries style, which regularly bears testimony to the Alexander Pope observation that "True ease in writing comes from art, not chance, as those move easiest who have learned to dance." But the reason his Ryder Cup rant still appeals to me has much to do with its timing. It was written in the wake of Ireland being awarded the event for 2005, when the country was beside itself in celebrating a great sporting coup. And Humphries had the courage to be a dissenting voice.

Mind you, I disagreed profoundly with his views at the time. And I still do. Sure, the Ryder Cup is commerce-driven. That is the nature of professional sport, especially at the highest level. But is it not to the credit of the participating players that they do it without pay – and let's not muddy the waters with arguments about endorsements? And as Padraig Harrington, Darren Clarke and Paul McGinley excelled themselves at Oakland Hills, those Irish supporters fortunate enough to have shared that stunning spectacle would have had extreme difficulty in categorising the Ryder Cup as a hoax. In fact they would have scoffed at the notion.

As to Tom's difficulty in grasping the "Europe" concept: in my view, it is a lot less contrived than, say, a Manchester United team who would be more accurately described as a European XI than genuine representatives of the City of Manchester. And on Monday February 14th 2005, the Highbury faithful found themselves in the extraordinary situation of applauding an Arsenal team which contained not even one Englishman. Which left the *Express and Star* from the West Midlands mystified that the cheers continued to ring out for what could be seen as "an assortment of mercenaries...." It went on to ask: "Where does their loyalty come from? To non-fans it is all a mystery. Sometimes the beautiful game is a bewildering game."

In the Ryder Cup, players from this side of the Atlantic see themselves as representatives of the European Tour, of which they are justifiably proud. And there have been others among them, notably Seve Ballesteros, who gained huge, additional motivation simply from the prospect of beating Americans.

No doubt, the country's most highly-regarded sportswriter will have further, pungent views to air on the actual 2006 staging of his least-favourite tournament. And as always, I will read them with interest.

I n 1931, when Charles Whitcombe was set to captain the British team, a Ryder Cup trial was held at Royal Lytham prior to the departure to the US for the matches at Scioto, Columbus, where Walter Hagen would captain the American team. As an experiment at Lytham, it was decided to use what was then the new, larger-sized American ball.

Faced with a strong, easterly wind, however, even the longest hitters had trouble getting the ball to travel 200 yards. Which would explain why it was that at the end of the experiment, everyone concluded that the 1.68 inch pill would never catch on in these islands.

By a remarkable coincidence, Lytham was again the venue of choice when the Royal and Ancient took the contrary view on this touchy issue. For the Open Championship of 1974 on the Lancashire links, the bigger, American ball became compulsory. And, of course, the Ryder Cup followed suit, bringing ball uniformity to the matches for the first time.

Chapter 10 Shaping The Legend

Colleagues from the 1955 team met during the week of the 2002 Ryder Cup. And at 74, John Jacobs, who gained the distinction of beating the reigning US Masters champion, Cary Middlecoff, on that occasion, could hardly credit that Christy O'Connor, three years his senior, was still swinging the club so well.

They met at Kilworth GC, about 40 miles south-east of The Belfry, where a number of Ryder Cup old boys had come together for a charity pro-am. "One of the great joys of the occasion, for me, was seeing Christy, *the* Christy," said Jacobs. "I'm almost afraid to describe him as the best natural hitter of a golf ball I've ever seen, knowing the way he protests about the amount of practice he did. But it's true just the same."

The man they describe as "Dr Golf" because of his status as one of the leading tutors on this side of the Atlantic, went on: "I could watch Christy hit golf balls forever. People often criticised him for letting the club go at the top of the backswing, but it would have killed Christy to hang onto the club with the last three fingers.

"Happily, the Lord took over and what we saw from there on, was absolute perfection. Not only does his swing look right to me, it remains correct in every key, technical sense. Which is truly remarkable for a man of 77."

Meanwhile, given Jacobs' position as captain of the first European Ryder Cup teams in 1979 and 1981, by which latter stage he was 53, I wondered how he felt about the captaincy for The K Club staging in 2006. "It doesn't necessarily follow that because the event is in Ireland, it should be an Irish captain," he replied. "But given their Ryder Cup experience, I believe that Des Smyth, Christy O'Connor Jnr and Eamonn Darcy are all worthy candidates."

Though the incomparable conquistador was missing, the Ballesteros family still had a proud representative at The Belfry in 2002. In the absence of his illustrious father, 12-year-old Baldomero, better known as Javier, was there with some friends from the private boarding school he was attending in England.

Apparently the entrance tickets to the matches were supplied, on request, by the Ryder Cup committee. But with respect to the youngster, everybody there would have much preferred to have seen his illustrious father. "We made many attempts in recent weeks to try and contact Seve about the Ryder Cup but he could not be contacted," said a member of the Spanish media at the time. So, the only former Spanish Ryder Cup players in attendance were Antonio Garrido and Manuel Pinero.

Even at that point, only five months after he had beaten Colin Montgomerie in the Seve Trophy at Druids Glen, Ballesteros had already become something of a recluse, because of the dramatic decline in his golfing fortunes. As another Spanish observer put it: "Seve is hiding himself away because he can't accept that he'll never be a great player again." Which was profoundly sad, especially for those of us who had thrilled to his amazing exploits in the Ryder Cup.

For all its faults, the Ryder Cup has shown us that there is more to golfing success than large pay-cheques or the gratification of contributing to a triumphant team effort. The most meaningful rewards are personal and far more enduring, as former European captain, Sam Torrance, was to discover.

It will be recalled how Torrance wept unashamedly while securing the winning point for Europe in his famous triumph at The Belfry in 1985. But it was only later that he revealed the full extent of the emotion he felt in that unforgettable moment of victory over America's Andy North.

Roddy Carr had known the same feeling at St Andrews 14 years previously, after holing a 30-foot putt on the 18th to gain a priceless win over Jim Simons in the Walker Cup. "As I stood over that putt, I bowed my head, said a *Hail Mary* and beseeched the Almighty to guide the ball into the hole," he recalled. And when it dropped, he was rewarded with the biggest prize of all – a hug from his father, Joe.

"It was the first time in my life that I could remember him hugging me," he said. "Years later, when Sam Torrance secured the winning point in the 1985 Ryder Cup, his father, Bob, hugged him for the first time. And I was fascinated to discover that Sam felt the same way about it as I had done.

"Both men were from the same, conservative school which apparently ordained that you didn't show your emotions. As Sam said, the hug he got from Bob was better than the Ryder Cup win. And I felt the same way." Which was why, on those occasions of unparalleled joy, both players walked away from the 18th green in tears.

Music was in the air, during Ryder Cup week at Brookline in 1999. "I think Padraig would like to sing with Celine Dion," said European colleague Jean Van de Velde. "He told me that earlier on." The Frenchman was replying to a question as to what he and Harrington would like to have done outside of golf that week, given the chance. And Diva Dion had given a special Ryder Cup concert in Boston the previous night.

Arnold Palmer, however, experienced the real thing while at Brookline, in that he was honoured through a concert in the Symphony Hall, where the noted composer, John Williams, conducted the Boston Pops Orchestra for the occasion. And as a further accolade to the last player-captain in the Ryder Cup, in 1963, Williams chose the music.

Chapter 10 Shaping The Legend

"I'm not particularly good at golf but I do love the game," said the musician, who had become the so-called laureate conductor of the Boston Pops at that time. He added: "I've always admired Palmer, particularly as a person of great character and appeal to the public. He's an icon, a marvellous figure."

During the course of the musical evening, former US President George Bush Snr, made a presentation to Palmer who was serenaded by legendary crooner Tony Bennett, among others. Proceeds from the event were in aid of the Deacon Palmer Scholarship Fund, established in memory of Arnie's father, the long time professional and greenkeeper at Latrobe, Pennsylvania.

Meanwhile, security officers at Boston's Four Seasons Hotel could have been forgiven any confusion at arrangements for resident dignitaries during that week. Apart from concerns over the security of the respective teams, there were the visiting police from Cambridge – that's Cambridge, England not Cambridge Massachusetts – who had responsibility for Prince Andrew. Then there was the Spanish security for King Juan Carlos and Queen Sophia.

Dignitaries seemed to be arriving daily. Among other things, it meant that US secret service men and state police from Texas and Florida got there in advance of former US President George Bush and his wife Barbara; the then Texas Governor and US presidential candidate, George W Bush and his brother, Jeb, the Governor of Florida.

And the hotel's reaction? "Everybody's so nice; there's none of the negativity you hear about," said general manager Robin Brown. "Everyone we've dealt with has been great. You can feel the pride the players have in being a part of this."

The cartoon in the *Boston Globe* had two cigar-smoking businessmen enjoying lavish corporate hospitality at the Ryder Cup. Suit One: "In truth, I don't know a foursome from a fourball from a ball four." Suit Two: "The important thing is to remember it's all tax deductible."

From the outset, money had become a key element of what would be the biggest sporting event in Boston's history, bigger even than the 100th staging of the Boston Marathon in 1996. All of which represented an astonishing turnaround from the situation only 10 years previously.

When Christy O'Connor Jnr, among others, spiked US hopes of regaining the trophy at The Belfry in 1989, none of the major American networks was prepared to pay for the transmission rights which eventually went to the USA Network for a giveaway $200,000.

The NBC Network, however, were only too delighted to pay $13 million for the rights in 1999, an increase of 189 per cent on the fee for the Oak Hill staging in 1995. They re-sold the rights to the Friday broadcast to the USA Network but still provided nearly 17 hours of coverage on Saturday and Sunday.

Even more significant was the fact that eight advertisers each paid $2 million to sponsor the broadcast. Which contrasted sharply with NBC's miserable experience at Kiawah Island in 1991 when, having paid nearly $2 million for the rights, their two major sponsors, IBM and General Motors, pulled out. And no replacements were forthcoming. "We took a pretty significant bath," an NBC executive later recalled.

The American view is that the Ryder Cup was transformed by the missed six-foot putt by Bernhard Langer against Hale Irwin in a highly-charged atmosphere on Kiawah's 18th green. Had it gone in, the teams would have been level; Europe would have retained the trophy once more and American interest would have waned.

Instead, Langer's miss resulted in American acceptance of the Ryder Cup as golf's ultimate cash cow.

Richard Hills, Director of the Ryder Cup, has the experience of being involved in every European staging of the event, dating back to 1981 at Walton Heath, where he had charge of the media centre. "In 1985, I was a car-park attendant at The Belfry," he said self-deprecatingly. "That was when I learned that if your traffic system isn't working at 6.0am, you're in for a difficult day."

On that occasion, he recalled that difficulties duly arose when "we had a bit of a run-in with the local constabulary who changed the plan on us only 24 hours before the event. The result was that by 6.15am, traffic was beginning to stack up and by 8.30, queues were pretty much back to the M6. So we put a contingency plan into operation. This entailed getting the greenkeepers' JCB and making a hole in a fence so that cars could park in a nearby field.

"We had gradually begun to release the dam when this chap, looking for all the world like Mr Magoo, drove up in a Hillman Imp and wound down the driver's window. I instantly decided a PR approach might be appropriate. 'Terribly sorry, sir. The police changed the plan. But I've got news on the radio that we're up in three and level in one. You'll be able to catch the matches at the ninth hole.' To which Mr Magoo responded in the broadest Brummie accent: 'I didn't want to come here. I was going to do my mum's shopping in Sutton Coldfield. How do I get out?'"

 hortly after the selection of The K Club had been officially announced in January 1999, one of its members received a fascinating phone call. The caller from Dallas was quite clear as to the nature and value of his requirements. "100,000,"

Chapter 10 Shaping The Legend

he said. "Is that Sterling or punts?" enquired Bill Cullen. "I live in the States," came the terse reply. Either way, there wasn't a chance that the chairman and chief executive of Renault Ireland would, as he put it, turf himself out of his own home.

With the event still more than six-and-a-half years (later to become seven-and-a-half) away, the Ryder Cup at The K Club was already generating major interest internationally. Hence the call from the Texas tour operator seeking to rent Osberstown House, which happens to be close by The K Club, during Ryder Cup week.

The former Osberstown House Hotel was bought by Cullen as a home and is clearly not short on accommodation. "We have 10 bedrooms and a ballroom, so it would be ideal for entertaining," he said at the time. "But it's not for sale, rent or lease. In fact if we're all alive and well in 2005 (2006), I'll be the host at whatever celebration we have."

Which would be nothing new to him. As a K Club member, he holds the distinction of having been on the winning team of the Smurfit European Open pro-am for three successive years – with Padraig Harrington in 1996, Ian Woosnam in 1997 and Darren Clarke in 1998. "We have a party on the Saturday night of the tournament," he said. "Maybe that's how the word got out.

Meanwhile, there were wiseacres who were prepared to look back to an auction in April of the previous year and claim there was no real gamble involved. But as the five-figure bidding rose impressively, not even Dr Smurfit could have been sure of landing the game's major team event.

So, it took courage for Dublin builder, Brian Lynam, to make the winning bid of £28,000. Now, the gamble had been landed and it was confirmed that all available rooms would be occupied by players, officials and special guests of the owners. Then there was the matter of inflation...... which made Lynam's investment something of a snip.

♦

Record
Book

1927-2004

The Ryder Cup
European Players' Record

Player		Years played	Years	Matches played	Record W/L/H	Singles W/L/H	Foursomes W/L/H	Fourball W/L/H	Total Points won	Points %
Jimmy	Adams	1947-49-51-53	4	7	2-5-0	1-2-0	1-3-0	0-0-0	2.0	0.27
Percy	Alliss	1929-33-35-37	4	6	3-2-1	2-1-0	1-1-1	0-0-0	3.5	0.58
Peter	Alliss	1953-57-59-61-63-65-67-69	8	30	10-15-5	5-4-3	4-6-1	1-5-1	12.5	0.40
Peter	Baker	1993	1	4	3-1-0	1-0-0	0-1-0	2-0-0	3.0	0.75
Seve	Ballesteros	1979-83-85-87-89-91-93-95	8	37	20-12-5	2-4-2	10-3-1	8-5-2	22.5	0.59
Harry	Bannerman	1971	1	5	2-2-1	1-0-1	1-0-0	0-2-0	2.5	0.50
Brian	Barnes	1969-71-73-75-77-79	6	25	10-14-1	5-5-0	2-4-0	3-5-1	10.5	0.42
Maurice	Bembridge	1969-71-73-75	4	17	6-8-3	1-3-1	3-5-0	2-0-2	7.5	0.44
Thomas	Bjorn	1997-2002	2	6	3-2-1	1-0-1	0-2-0	2-0-0	3.5	0.58
Aubrey	Boomer	1927-29	2	4	2-2-0	1-1-0	1-1-0	0-0-0	2.0	0.50
Ken	Bousfield	1949-51-55-57-59-61	6	10	5-5-0	2-2-0	3-3-0	0-0-0	5.0	0.50
Hugh	Boyle	1967	1	3	0-3-0	0-1-0	0-1-0	0-1-0	0.0	0.00
Harry	Bradshaw	1953-55-57	3	5	2-2-1	1-1-1	1-1-0	0-0-0	2.5	0.50
Gordon	Brand Jr.	1987-89	2	7	2-4-1	0-1-1	0-2-0	2-1-0	2.5	0.34
Gordon	Brand Sr.	1983	1	1	0-1-0	0-1-0	0-0-0	0-0-0	0.0	0.00
Paul	Broadhurst	1991	1	2	2-0-0	1-0-0	0-0-0	1-0-0	2.0	1.00
Eric	Brown	1953-55-57-59	4	8	4-4-0	4-0-0	0-4-0	0-0-0	4.0	0.50
Ken	Brown	1977-79-83-85-87	5	13	4-9-0	2-2-0	1-4-0	1-3-0	4.0	0.29
Richard	Burton	1935-37-49	3	5	2-3-0	0-3-0	2-0-0	0-0-0	2.0	0.40
Jack	Busson	1935	1	2	0-2-0	0-1-0	0-1-0	0-0-0	0.0	0.00
Peter	Butler	1965-69-71-73	4	14	3-9-2	2-3-0	1-4-0	0-2-2	4.0	0.27
J.M.	Canizares	1981-83-85-89	4	11	5-4-2	2-1-1	2-1-0	1-2-1	6.0	0.53
Paul	Casey	2004	1	2	1-1-0	0-1-0	0-0-0	1-0-0	1.0	0.50
Alex	Caygill	1969	1	1	0-0-1	0-0-0	0-0-0	0-0-1	0.5	0.50
Clive	Clark	1973	1	1	0-1-0	0-0-0	0-0-0	0-1-0	0.0	0.00
Howard	Clark	1977-81-85-87-89-95	6	15	7-7-1	4-2-0	0-4-0	3-1-1	7.5	0.50
Darren	Clarke	1997-99-2002-04	4	17	7-7-3	0-2-2	3-3-0	4-2-1	8.5	0.50
Neil	Coles	1961-63-65-67-69-71-73-77	8	40	12-21-7	5-6-4	4-8-1	3-7-2	15.5	0.37
Andrew	Coltart	1999	1	1	0-1-0	0-1-0	0-0-0	0-0-0	0.0	0.00
Archie	Compston	1927-29-31	3	6	1-4-1	1-2-0	0-2-1	0-0-0	1.5	0.25
Henry	Cotton	1929-37-47	3	6	2-4-0	2-1-0	0-3-0	0-0-0	2.0	0.33
Bill	Cox	1935-37	2	3	0-2-1	0-0-1	0-2-0	0-0-0	0.5	0.15
Fred	Daly	1947-49-51-53	4	8	3-4-1	1-2-1	2-2-0	0-0-0	3.5	0.42
Eamonn	Darcy	1975-77-81-87	4	11	1-8-2	1-3-0	0-1-1	0-4-1	2.0	0.18
William	Davis	1931-33	2	4	2-2-0	1-1-0	1-1-0	0-0-0	2.0	0.50
Peter	Dawson	1977	1	3	1-2-0	1-0-0	0-1-0	0-1-0	1.0	0.33
Luke	Donald	2004	1	4	2-1-1	0-1-0	2-0-0	0-0-1	2.5	0.61
Norman	Drew	1959	1	1	0-0-1	0-0-1	0-0-0	0-0-0	0.5	0.50
George	Duncan	1927-29-31	3	5	2-3-0	2-0-0	0-3-0	0-0-0	2.0	0.40
Syd	Easterbrook	1931-33	2	3	2-1-0	1-0-0	1-1-0	0-0-0	2.0	0.65
Nick	Faldo	1977-79-81-83-85-87-89-91-93-95-97	11	46	23-19-4	6-4-1	10-6-2	7-9-1	25.0	0.54
John	Fallon	1955	1	1	1-0-0	0-0-0	1-0-0	0-0-0	1.0	1.00
Niclas	Fasth	2002	1	3	0-2-1	0-0-1	0-0-0	0-2-0	0.5	0.15
Max	Faulkner	1947-49-51-53-57	5	8	1-7-0	0-4-0	1-3-0	0-0-0	1.0	0.11
David	Feherty	1991	1	3	1-1-1	1-0-0	0-1-0	0-0-1	1.5	0.50
Pierre	Fulke	2002	1	2	0-1-1	0-0-1	0-1-0	0-0-0	0.5	0.25
Bernard	Gallacher	1969-71-73-75-77-79-81-83	8	31	13-13-5	4-3-4	5-6-0	4-4-1	15.5	0.50
Sergio	Garcia	1999-2002-04	3	15	10-3-2	1-2-0	6-0-0	3-1-2	11.0	0.73
John	Garner	1971-73	2	1	0-1-0	0-0-0	0-0-0	0-1-0	0.0	0.00
Antonio	Garrido	1979	1	5	1-4-0	0-1-0	1-1-0	0-2-0	1.0	0.20
Ignacio	Garrido	1997	1	4	0-1-3	0-1-0	0-0-2	0-0-1	1.5	0.36
David	Gilford	1991-95	2	7	3-3-1	1-0-1	1-2-0	1-1-0	3.5	0.50
Malcolm	Gregson	1967	1	4	0-4-0	0-2-0	0-1-0	0-1-0	0.0	0.00

The Ryder Cup
European Players' Record

Player		Years played	Years	Matches played	Record W/L/H	Singles W/L/H	Foursomes W/L/H	Fourball W/L/H	Total Points won	Points %
Joakim	Haeggman	1993	1	2	1-1-0	1-0-0	0-0-0	0-1-0	1.0	0.50
Tom	Haliburton	1961-63	2	6	0-6-0	0-2-0	0-3-0	0-1-0	0.0	0.00
Padraig	Harrington	1999-2002-04	3	12	7-4-1	3-0-0	2-2-1	2-2-0	7.5	0.61
Arthur	Havers	1927-31-33	3	6	3-3-0	2-1-0	1-2-0	0-0-0	3.0	0.50
Jimmy	Hitchcock	1965	1	3	0-3-0	0-2-0	0-1-0	0-0-0	0.0	0.00
Bert	Hodson	1931	1	1	0-1-0	0-1-0	0-0-0	0-0-0	0.0	0.00
Tommy	Horton	1975-77	2	8	1-6-1	1-1-1	0-2-0	0-3-0	1.5	0.17
David	Howell	2004	1	2	1-1-0	0-1-0	0-0-0	1-0-0	1.0	0.50
Brian	Hugget	1963-67-69-71-73-75	6	24	8-10-6	3-3-1	5-3-2	0-4-3	11.0	0.44
Bernard	Hunt	1953-57-59-61-63-65-67-69	8	28	6-16-6	4-3-3	1-9-1	1-4-2	9.0	0.32
Geoffrey	Hunt	1963	1	3	0-3-0	0-1-0	0-1-0	0-1-0	0.0	0.00
Guy	Hunt	1975	1	3	0-2-1	0-1-0	0-1-0	0-0-1	0.5	0.15
Tony	Jacklin	1967-69-71-73-75-77-79	7	35	13-14-8	2-8-1	8-1-4	3-5-3	17.0	0.47
John	Jacobs	1955	1	2	2-0-0	1-0-0	1-0-0	0-0-0	2.0	1.00
Mark	James	1977-79-81-89-91-93-95	7	24	8-15-1	2-4-1	1-7-0	5-4-0	8.5	0.35
Edward	Jarman	1935	1	1	0-1-0	0-0-0	0-1-0	0-0-0	0.0	0.00
Miguel A.	Jimenez	1999-2004	2	9	2-5-2	0-2-0	0-2-1	2-1-1	3.0	0.33
Per-Ulrik	Johansson	1995-97	2	5	3-2-0	1-1-0	1-0-0	1-1-0	3.0	0.60
Herbert	Jolly	1927	1	2	0-2-0	0-1-0	0-1-0	0-0-0	0.0	0.00
Michael	King	1979	1	1	0-1-0	0-1-0	0-0-0	0-0-0	0.0	0.00
Sam	King	1937-47-49	3	5	1-3-1	1-1-1	0-2-0	0-0-0	1.5	0.30
Arthur	Lacey	1933-37	2	3	0-3-0	0-2-0	0-1-0	0-0-0	0.0	0.00
Barry	Lane	1993	1	3	0-3-0	0-1-0	0-1-0	0-1-0	0.0	0.00
Bernhard	Langer	1981-83-85-87-89-91-93-95-97-02	10	42	21-15-6	4-3-3	11-6-1	6-6-2	24.0	0.57
Paul	Lawrie	1999	1	5	3-1-1	1-0-0	1-1-0	1-0-1	3.5	0.70
Arthur	Lees	1947-49-51-55	4	9	4-5-0	2-3-0	2-2-0	0-0-0	4.0	0.44
Thomas	Levet	2004	1	3	1-2-0	1-0-0	0-2-0	0-0-0	1.0	0.33
Sandy	Lyle	1979-81-83-85-87	5	18	7-9-2	1-4-0	3-3-1	3-2-1	8.0	0.44
Jimmy	Martin	1965	1	1	0-1-0	0-0-0	0-1-0	0-0-0	0.0	0.00
Paul	McGinley	2002-04	2	6	2-1-3	1-0-1	1-1-0	0-0-2	3.5	0.58
Peter	Mills	1957	1	1	1-0-0	1-0-0	0-0-0	0-0-0	1.0	1.00
Abe	Mitchell	1929-31-33	3	6	4-2-0	1-2-0	3-0-0	0-0-0	4.0	0.65
Ralph	Moffitt	1961	1	1	0-1-0	0-1-0	0-0-0	0-0-0	0.0	0.00
Colin	Montgomerie	1991-93-95-97-99-2002-04	7	32	19-8-5	5-0-2	8-3-1	6-5-2	21.5	0.67
Christy	O'Connor Jr	1975-89	2	4	1-3-0	1-0-0	0-2-0	0-1-0	1.0	0.25
Christy	O'Connor Sr	1955-57-59-61-63-65-67-69-71-73	10	36	11-21-4	2-10-2	6-6-1	3-5-1	13.0	0.36
Jose M.	Olazabal	1987-89-91-93-97-99	6	28	15-8-5	1-4-1	7-2-1	7-2-3	17.5	0.61
John	O'Leary	1975	1	4	0-4-0	0-1-0	0-2-0	0-1-0	0.0	0.00
Peter	Oosterhuis	1971-73-75-77-79-81	6	28	14-11-3	6-2-1	3-6-1	5-3-1	15.5	0.55
Alf	Padgham	1933-35-37	3	7	0-7-0	0-4-0	0-3-0	0-0-0	0.0	0.00
John	Panton	1951-53-61	3	5	0-5-0	0-1-0	0-4-0	0-0-0	0.0	0.00
Jesper	Parnevik	1997-99-2002	3	11	4-3-4	0-2-1	2-0-2	2-1-1	6.0	0.53
Alf	Perry	1933-35-37	3	3	0-2-1	0-0-1	0-2-0	0-0-0	0.5	0.15
Manuel	Pinero	1981-85	2	9	6-3-0	2-0-0	2-2-0	2-1-0	6.0	0.65
Lionel	Platts	1965	1	5	1-2-2	1-1-0	0-1-0	0-0-2	2.0	0.40
Eddie	Polland	1973	1	2	0-2-0	0-0-0	0-1-0	0-1-0	0.0	0.00
Ian	Poulter	2004	1	2	1-1-0	1-0-0	0-0-0	0-1-0	1.0	0.50
Phillip	Price	2002	1	2	1-1-0	1-0-0	0-1-0	0-0-0	1.0	0.50
Ronan	Rafferty	1989	1	3	1-2-0	1-0-0	0-2-0	0-0-0	1.0	0.33
Ted	Ray	1927	1	2	0-2-0	0-1-0	0-1-0	0-0-0	0.0	0.00
Dai	Rees	1937-47-49-51-53-55-57-59-61	9	17	7-9-1	5-4-0	2-5-1	0-0-0	7.5	0.44
Steven	Richardson	1991	1	4	2-2-0	0-1-0	0-1-0	2-0-0	2.0	0.50

The Ryder Cup
European Players' Record

Player		Years played	Years	Matches played	Record W/L/H	Singles W/L/H	Foursomes W/L/H	Fourball W/L/H	Total Points won	Points %
Jose	Rivero	1985-87	2	5	2-3-0	0-2-0	1-1-0	1-0-0	2.0	0.40
Fred	Robson	1927-29-31	3	6	2-4-0	0-3-0	2-1-0	0-0-0	2.0	0.33
Costantino	Rocca	1993-95-97	3	11	6-5-0	1-2-0	3-1-0	2-2-0	6.0	0.53
Jarmo	Sandelin	1999	1	1	0-1-0	0-1-0	0-0-0	0-0-0	0.0	0.00
Syd	Scott	1955	1	2	0-2-0	0-1-0	0-1-0	0-0-0	0.0	0.00
Des	Smyth	1979-81	2	7	2-5-0	0-2-0	1-2-0	1-1-0	2.0	0.27
Dave	Thomas	1959-63-65-67	4	18	3-10-5	0-4-1	3-2-2	0-4-2	5.5	0.29
Sam	Torrance	1981-83-85-87-89-91-93-95	8	28	7-15-6	2-3-3	3-7-0	2-5-3	10.0	0.34
Peter	Townsend	1969-71	2	11	3-8-0	0-3-0	2-2-0	1-3-0	3.0	0.27
Jean	Van de Velde	1999	1	1	0-1-0	0-1-0	0-0-0	0-0-0	0.0	0.00
Brian	Waites	1983	1	4	1-3-0	0-1-0	0-1-0	1-1-0	1.0	0.25
Philip	Walton	1995	1	2	1-1-0	1-0-0	0-1-0	0-0-0	1.0	0.50
Charles	Ward	1947-49-51	3	6	1-5-0	0-3-0	1-2-0	0-0-0	1.0	0.15
Paul	Way	1983-85	2	9	6-2-1	2-0-0	1-2-0	3-0-1	6.5	0.72
Harry	Weetman	1951-53-55-57-59-61-63	7	15	2-11-2	2-6-0	0-4-2	0-1-0	3.0	0.20
Lee	Westwood	1997-99-2002-04	4	20	11-8-1	1-3-0	6-2-0	4-3-1	11.5	0.56
Charles	Whitcombe	1927-29-31-33-35-37	6	9	3-2-4	1-2-1	2-0-3	0-0-0	5.0	0.54
Ernest	Whitcombe	1929-31-35	3	6	1-4-1	0-2-1	1-2-0	0-0-0	1.5	0.25
Reg	Whitcombe	1935	1	1	0-1-0	0-1-0	0-0-0	0-0-0	0.0	0.00
George	Will	1963-65-67	3	15	2-11-2	0-3-1	2-3-1	0-5-0	3.0	0.20
Norman	Wood	1975	1	3	1-2-0	1-0-0	0-1-0	0-1-0	1.0	0.33
Ian	Woosnam	1983-85-87-89-91-93-95-97	8	31	14-12-5	0-6-2	4-3-2	10-3-1	16.5	0.53

Playing Records of Ireland's 17 Representatives

Player		Years played	Years	Matches played	Record W/L/H	Singles W/L/H	Foursomes W/L/H	Fourball W/L/H	Total Points won	Points %
Hugh	Boyle	1967	1	3	0-3-0	0-1-0	0-1-0	0-1-0	0.0	0.00
Harry	Bradshaw	1953-55-57	3	5	2-2-1	1-1-1	1-1-0	0-0-0	2.5	0.50
Darren	Clarke	1997-99-2002-04	4	17	7-7-3	0-2-2	3-3-0	4-2-1	8.5	0.50
Fred	Daly	1947-49-51-53	4	8	3-4-1	1-2-1	2-2-0	0-0-0	3.5	0.42
Eamonn	Darcy	1975-77-81-87	4	11	1-8-2	1-3-0	0-1-1	0-4-1	2.0	0.18
Norman	Drew	1959	1	1	0-0-1	0-0-1	0-0-0	0-0-0	0.5	0.50
David	Feherty	1991	1	3	1-1-1	1-0-0	0-1-0	0-0-1	1.5	0.50
Padraig	Harrington	1999-2002-04	3	12	7-4-1	3-0-0	2-2-1	2-2-0	7.5	0.61
Jimmy	Martin	1965	1	1	0-1-0	0-0-0	0-1-0	0-0-0	0.0	0.00
Paul	McGinley	2002-04	2	6	2-1-3	1-0-1	1-1-0	0-0-2	3.5	0.58
Christy	O'Connor Jr	1975-89	2	4	1-3-0	1-0-0	0-2-0	0-1-0	1.0	0.25
Christy	O'Connor Sr	1955-57-59-61-63-65-67-69-71-73	10	36	11-21-4	2-10-2	6-6-1	3-5-1	13.0	0.36
John	O'Leary	1975	1	4	0-4-0	0-1-0	0-2-0	0-1-0	0.0	0.00
Eddie	Polland	1973	1	2	0-2-0	0-0-0	0-1-0	0-1-0	0.0	0.00
Ronan	Rafferty	1989	1	3	1-2-0	1-0-0	0-2-0	0-0-0	1.0	0.33
Des	Smyth	1979-81	2	7	2-5-0	0-2-0	1-2-0	1-1-0	2.0	0.27
Philip	Walton	1995	1	2	1-1-0	1-0-0	0-1-0	0-0-0	1.0	0.50

The Ryder Cup
US Players' Record

Player		Years played	Years	Matches played	Record W/L/H	Singles W/L/H	Foursomes W/L/H	Fourball W/L/H	Total Points won	Points %
Tommy	Aaron	1969-73	2	6	1-4-1	0-2-0	1-1-0	0-1-1	1.5	0.25
Skip	Alexander	1949-51	2	2	1-1-0	1-0-0	0-1-0	0-0-0	1.0	0.50
Paul	Azinger	1989-91-93-2002	4	15	5-7-3	2-0-2	2-2-0	1-5-1	6.5	0.43
Jerry	Barber	1955-61	2	5	1-4-0	0-3-0	1-1-0	0-0-0	1	0.20
Miller	Barber	1969-71	2	7	1-4-2	1-1-0	0-3-0	0-0-2	2	0.27
Herman	Barron	1947	1	1	1-0-0	0-0-0	1-0-0	0-0-0	1.0	1.00
Andy	Bean	1979-87	2	6	4-2-0	2-0-0	0-1-0	2-1-0	4.0	0.65
Frank	Beard	1969-71	2	8	2-3-3	0-1-1	0-2-1	2-0-1	3.5	0.42
Chip	Beck	1989-91-93	3	9	6-2-1	3-0-0	1-1-1	2-1-0	6.5	0.72
Homero	Blancas	1973	1	4	2-1-1	1-1-0	0-0-0	1-0-1	2.5	0.61
Tommy	Bolt	1955-57	2	4	3-1-0	1-1-0	2-0-0	0-0-0	3.0	0.75
Julius	Boros	1950-59-63-65-67	5	16	9-3-4	3-2-1	5-0-2	1-1-1	11.0	0.67
Gay	Brewer	1967-73	2	9	5-3-1	2-1-1	0-1-0	3-1-0	5.5	0.61
Billy	Burke	1931-33	2	3	3-0-0	1-0-0	2-0-0	0-0-0	3.0	1.00
Jack	Burke Jr.	1951-53-55-57-59	5	8	7-1-0	3-1-0	4-0-0	0-0-0	7.0	0.86
Walter	Burkemo	1953	1	1	0-1-0	0-0-0	0-1-0	0-0-0	0.0	0.00
Mark	Calcavecchia	1987-89-91-2002	4	14	6-7-1	1-2-1	4-1-0	1-4-0	6.5	0.46
Chad	Campbell	2004	1	3	1-2-0	1-0-0	0-0-0	0-2-0	1.0	0.33
Billy	Casper	1961-63-65-67-69-71-73-75	8	37	20-10-7	6-2-2	8-5-2	6-3-3	23.5	0.62
Stewart	Cink	2002-04	2	7	2-4-1	0-2-0	1-2-0	1-0-1	2.5	0.34
Bill	Collins	1961	1	3	1-2-0	0-1-0	1-1-0	0-0-0	1.0	0.33
Charles	Coody	1971	1	3	0-2-1	0-1-0	0-1-0	0-0-1	0.5	0.15
John	Cook	1993	1	2	1-1-0	0-1-0	0-0-0	1-0-0	1.0	0.50
Fred	Couples	1989-91-93-95-97	5	20	7-9-4	2-1-2	1-5-0	4-3-2	9.0	0.45
Wilfred	Cox	1931	1	2	2-0-0	1-0-0	1-0-0	0-0-0	2.0	1.00
Ben	Crenshaw	1981-83-87	4	12	3-8-1	2-2-0	1-2-0	0-4-1	3.5	0.29
Jimmy	Demaret	1947-49-51	3	6	6-0-0	3-0-0	3-0-0	0-0-0	6.0	1.00
Gardner	Dickinson	1967-71	2	10	9-1-0	2-1-0	4-0-0	3-0-0	9.0	0.90
Leo	Diegel	1927-29-31-33	4	6	3-3-0	2-1-0	1-2-0	0-0-0	3.0	0.50
Chris	DiMarco	2004	1	4	2-1-1	1-0-0	1-1-0	0-0-1	2.5	0.61
Dave	Douglas	1953	1	2	1-0-1	0-0-1	1-0-0	0-0-0	1.5	0.75
Dale	Douglass	1969	1	2	0-2-0	0-1-0	0-0-0	0-1-0	0.0	0.00
Ed	Dudley	1929-33-37	3	4	3-1-0	1-0-0	2-1-0	0-0-0	3.0	0.75
Olin	Dutra	1933-35	2	4	1-3-0	1-1-0	0-2-0	0-0-0	1.0	0.25
David	Duval	1999-2002	2	6	1-3-2	1-0-1	0-1-0	0-2-1	2.0	0.33
Lee	Elder	1979	1	4	1-3-0	0-1-0	0-1-0	1-1-0	1.0	0.25
Al	Espinosa	1927-29-31	3	4	2-1-1	1-0-1	1-1-0	0-0-0	2.5	0.61
Johnny	Farrell	1927-29-31	3	6	3-2-1	1-2-0	2-0-1	0-0-0	3.5	0.58
Brad	Faxon	1995-97	2	6	2-4-0	0-2-0	0-0-0	2-2-0	2.0	0.33
Dow	Finsterwald	1957-59-61-63	4	13	9-3-1	3-3-0	4-0-1	2-0-0	9.5	0.73
Raymond	Floyd	1969-75-77-81-83-85-91-93	8	31	12-16-3	4-4-0	4-8-0	4-4-3	13.5	0.42
Doug	Ford	1955-57-59-61	4	9	4-4-1	2-2-1	2-2-0	0-0-0	4.5	0.50
Fred	Funk	2004	1	3	0-3-0	0-1-0	0-2-0	0-0-0	0.0	0.00
Ed	Furgol	1957	1	1	0-1-0	0-1-0	0-0-0	0-0-0	0.0	0.00
Marty	Furgol	1955	1	1	0-1-0	0-1-0	0-0-0	0-0-0	0.0	0.00
Jim	Furyk	1997-99-2002-04	4	15	4-9-2	3-0-1	1-4-0	0-5-1	5.0	0.33
Jim	Gallagher Jr.	1993	1	3	2-1-0	1-0-0	0-0-0	1-1-0	2.0	0.65
Al	Geiberger	1967-75	2	9	5-1-3	2-0-1	2-1-0	1-0-2	6.5	0.72
Bob	Gilder	1983	1	4	2-2-0	1-0-0	0-2-0	1-0-0	2.0	0.50
Bob	Goalby	1963	1	5	3-1-1	2-0-0	1-0-0	0-1-1	3.5	0.70
Johnny	Golden	1927-29	2	3	3-0-0	1-0-0	2-0-0	0-0-0	3.0	1.00
Lou	Graham	1973-75-77	3	9	5-3-1	1-1-0	1-2-1	3-0-0	5.5	0.61
Hubert	Green	1977-79-85	3	7	4-3-0	3-0-0	0-1-0	1-2-0	4.0	0.57
Ken	Green	1989	1	4	2-2-0	0-1-0	2-0-0	0-1-0	2.0	0.50

The Ryder Cup
US Players' Record

Player		Years played	Years	Matches played	Record W/L/H	Singles W/L/H	Foursomes W/L/H	Fourball W/L/H	Total Points won	Points %
Ralph	Guldahl	1937	1	2	2-0-0	1-0-0	1-0-0	0-0-0	2.0	1.00
Jay	Haas	1983-95-2004	3	12	4-6-2	0-3-0	2-3-0	2-0-2	5.0	0.40
Fred	Haas Jr	1953	1	1	0-1-0	0-1-0	0-0-0	0-0-0	0.0	0.00
Walter	Hagen	1927-29-31-33-35	5	9	7-1-1	3-1-0	4-0-1	0-0-0	7.5	0.83
Bob	Hamilton	1949	1	2	0-2-0	0-1-0	0-1-0	0-0-0	0.0	0.00
Chick	Harbert	1949-55	2	2	2-0-0	2-0-0	0-0-0	0-0-0	2.0	1.00
Chandler	Harper	1955	1	1	0-1-0	0-0-0	0-1-0	0-0-0	0.0	0.00
Dutch	Harrison	1947-49-51	3	3	2-1-0	2-0-0	0-1-0	0-0-0	2.0	0.65
Fred	Hawkins	1957	1	2	1-1-0	1-0-0	0-1-0	0-0-0	1.0	0.50
Mark	Hayes	1979	1	3	1-2-0	1-0-0	0-1-0	0-1-0	1.0	0.33
Clayton	Heafner	1949-51	2	4	3-0-1	1-0-1	2-0-0	0-0-0	3.5	0.86
Jay	Hebert	1959-61	2	4	2-1-1	0-1-1	2-0-0	0-0-0	2.5	0.61
Lionel	Hebert	1957	1	1	0-1-0	0-1-0	0-0-0	0-0-0	0.0	0.00
Dave	Hill	1969-73-77	3	9	6-3-0	3-0-0	1-2-0	2-1-0	6.0	0.65
Scott	Hoch	1997-2002	2	7	2-3-2	0-1-1	2-1-0	0-1-1	3.0	0.41
Ben	Hogan	1947-51	2	3	3-0-0	1-0-0	2-0-0	0-0-0	3.0	1.00
Hale	Irwin	1975-77-79-81-91	5	20	13-5-2	3-1-2	6-1-0	4-3-0	14.0	0.70
Tommy	Jacobs	1965	1	4	3-1-0	1-1-0	0-0-0	2-0-0	3.0	0.75
Peter	Jacobsen	1985-95	2	6	2-4-0	0-2-0	2-0-0	0-2-0	2.0	0.33
Don	January	1965-77	2	7	2-3-2	0-1-1	0-2-1	2-0-0	3.0	0.41
Lee	Janzen	1993-97	2	5	2-3-0	1-1-0	1-1-0	0-1-0	2.0	0.40
Herman	Keiser	1947	1	1	0-1-0	0-1-0	0-0-0	0-0-0	0.0	0.00
Tom	Kite	1979-81-83-85-87-89-93	7	28	15-9-4	5-0-2	7-5-1	3-4-1	17.0	0.59
Ted	Kroll	1953-55-57	3	4	3-1-0	0-1-0	3-0-0	0-0-0	3.0	0.75
Ky	Laffon	1935	1	1	0-1-0	0-0-0	0-1-0	0-0-0	0.0	0.00
Tom	Lehman	1995-97-99	3	10	5-3-2	3-0-0	1-2-1	1-1-1	6.0	0.60
Tony	Lema	1963-65	2	11	8-1-2	3-0-1	3-0-1	2-1-0	9.0	0.80
Justin	Leonard	1997-99	2	8	0-3-5	0-0-2	0-2-1	0-1-2	2.5	0.31
Wayne	Levi	1991	1	2	0-2-0	0-1-0	0-0-0	0-1-0	0.0	0.00
Bruce	Lietzke	1981	1	3	0-2-1	0-0-1	0-1-0	0-1-0	0.5	0.15
Gene	Littler	1961-63-65-67-69-71-75	7	27	14-5-8	5-2-3	4-3-1	5-0-4	18.0	0.65
Davis	Love III	1993-95-97-99-2002-04	6	26	9-12-5	3-1-2	3-5-1	3-6-2	11.5	0.44
Jeff	Maggert	1995-97-99	3	11	6-5-0	1-2-0	4-2-0	1-1-0	6.0	0.53
John	Mahaffey	1979	1	3	1-2-0	1-0-0	0-1-0	0-1-0	1.0	0.33
Tony	Manero	1937	1	2	1-1-0	0-1-0	1-0-0	0-0-0	1.0	0.50
Lloyd	Mangrum	1947-49-51-53	4	8	6-2-0	3-1-0	3-1-0	0-0-0	6.0	0.75
Dave	Marr	1965	1	6	4-2-0	2-0-0	1-1-0	1-1-0	4.0	0.65
Billy	Maxwell	1963	1	4	4-0-0	1-0-0	1-0-0	2-0-0	4.0	1.00
Dick	Mayer	1957	1	2	1-0-1	0-0-1	1-0-0	0-0-0	1.5	0.75
Mark	McCumber	1989	1	3	2-1-0	1-0-0	0-0-0	1-1-0	2.0	0.65
Jerry	McGee	1977	1	2	1-1-0	0-1-0	1-0-0	0-0-0	1.0	0.50
Bill	Mehlhorn	1927	1	2	1-1-0	1-0-0	0-1-0	0-0-0	1.0	0.50
Phil	Mickelson	1995-97-99-2002-04	5	20	9-8-3	3-2-0	2-2-2	4-4-1	10.5	0.51
Cary	Middlecoff	1953-55-59	3	6	2-3-1	1-2-0	1-1-1	0-0-0	2.5	0.40
Johnny	Miller	1975-81	2	6	2-2-2	0-2-0	2-0-0	0-0-2	3.0	0.50
Larry	Mize	1987	1	4	1-1-2	0-0-1	0-1-1	1-0-0	2.0	0.50
Gil	Morgan	1979-83	2	6	1-2-3	0-1-1	1-0-1	0-1-1	2.5	0.40
Bob	Murphy	1975	1	4	2-1-1	2-0-0	0-1-0	0-0-1	2.5	0.61
Byron	Nelson	1937-47	2	4	3-1-0	1-1-0	2-0-0	0-0-0	3.0	0.75
Larry	Nelson	1979-81-87	3	13	9-3-1	2-0-1	4-2-0	3-1-0	9.5	0.73
Bobby	Nichols	1967	1	5	4-0-1	1-0-1	2-0-0	1-0-0	4.5	0.90
Jack	Nicklaus	1969-71-73-75-77-81	6	28	17-8-3	4-4-2	8-1-0	5-3-1	18.5	0.66
Andy	North	1985	1	3	0-3-0	0-1-0	0-0-0	0-2-0	0.0	0.00
Mark	O'Meara	1985-89-91-97-99	5	14	4-9-1	1-4-0	1-3-0	2-2-1	4.5	0.32

The Ryder Cup
US Players' Record

Player		Years played	Years	Matches played	Record W/L/H	Singles W/L/H	Foursomes W/L/H	Fourball W/L/H	Total Points won	Points %
Ed	Oliver	1947-51-53	3	5	3-2-0	1-1-0	2-1-0	0-0-0	3.0	0.60
Arnold	Palmer	1961-63-65-67-71-73	6	32	22-8-2	6-3-2	9-3-0	7-2-0	23.0	0.70
Johnny	Palmer	1949	1	2	0-2-0	0-1-0	0-1-0	0-0-0	0.0	0.00
Sam	Parks	1935	1	1	0-0-1	0-0-1	0-0-0	0-0-0	0.5	0.50
Jerry	Pate	1981	1	4	2-2-0	0-1-0	1-0-0	1-1-0	2.0	0.50
Steve	Pate	1991-99	2	5	2-2-1	1-0-1	1-0-0	0-2-0	2.5	0.50
Corey	Pavin	1991-93-95	3	13	8-5-0	2-1-0	2-2-0	4-2-0	8.0	0.60
Calvin	Peete	1983-85	2	7	4-2-1	2-0-0	2-1-0	0-1-1	4.5	0.64
Kevin	Perry	2004	1	2	0-2-0	0-1-0	0-1-0	0-0-0	0.0	0.00
Henry	Picard	1935-37	2	4	3-1-0	2-0-0	1-1-0	0-0-0	3.0	0.75
Dan	Pohl	1987	1	3	1-2-0	0-1-0	1-0-0	0-1-0	1.0	0.33
Johnny	Pott	1963-65-67	3	7	5-2-0	1-1-0	2-1-0	2-0-0	5.0	0.71
Dave	Ragan	1963	1	4	2-1-1	1-0-0	1-0-0	0-1-1	2.5	0.61
Henry	Ransom	1951	1	1	0-1-0	0-0-0	0-1-0	0-0-0	0.0	0.00
Johnny	Revolta	1935-37	2	3	2-1-0	1-0-0	1-1-0	0-0-0	2.0	0.65
Chris	Riley	2004	1	3	1-1-1	0-1-0	0-0-0	1-0-1	1.6	0.50
Chi Chi	Rodriguez	1973	1	2	0-1-1	0-0-0	0-1-1	0-0-0	0.5	0.25
Loren	Roberts	1995	1	4	3-1-0	0-1-0	1-0-0	2-0-0	3.0	0.75
Bill	Rogers	1981	1	4	1-2-1	0-0-1	1-1-0	0-1-0	1.5	0.36
Bob	Rosburg	1959	1	2	2-0-0	1-0-0	1-0-0	0-0-0	2.0	1.00
Mason	Rudolph	1971	1	3	1-1-1	0-1-0	0-0-1	1-0-0	1.5	0.50
Paul	Runyan	1933-35	2	4	2-2-0	1-1-0	1-1-0	0-0-0	2.0	0.50
Doug	Sanders	1967	1	5	2-3-0	0-2-0	0-1-0	2-0-0	2.0	0.40
Gene	Sarazen	1927-29-31-33-35-37	6	12	7-2-3	4-1-1	3-1-2	0-0-0	8.5	0.69
Denny	Shute	1931-33-37	3	6	2-2-2	1-1-1	1-1-1	0-0-0	3.0	0.50
Dan	Sikes	1969	1	3	2-1-0	1-0-0	1-0-0	0-1-0	2.0	0.65
Scott	Simpson	1987	1	2	1-1-0	1-0-0	0-0-0	0-1-0	1.0	0.50
Horton	Smith	1929-31-33-35-37	5	4	3-0-1	2-0-1	1-0-0	0-0-0	3.5	0.86
J.C.	Snead	1971-73-75	3	11	9-2-0	3-1-0	2-1-0	4-0-0	9.0	0.80
Sam	Snead	1937-47-49-51-53-55-59	7	13	10-2-1	6-1-0	4-1-1	0-0-0	10.5	0.79
Ed	Sneed	1977	1	2	1-0-1	0-0-0	0-0-1	1-0-0	1.5	0.75
Mike	Souchak	1959-61	2	6	5-1-0	3-0-0	2-1-0	0-0-0	5.0	0.83
Craig	Stadler	1983-85	2	8	4-2-2	2-0-0	1-2-0	1-0-2	5.0	0.61
Payne	Stewart	1987-89-91-93-99	5	19	8-9-2	2-3-0	4-5-1	2-1-1	9.0	0.47
Ken	Still	1969	1	3	1-2-0	0-1-0	0-1-0	1-0-0	1.0	0.33
Dave	Stockton	1971-77	2	5	3-1-1	1-0-1	1-1-0	1-0-0	3.5	0.70
Curtis	Strange	1983-85-87-89-95	5	20	6-12-2	2-3-0	4-4-1	0-5-1	7.0	0.35
Hal	Sutton	1985-87-99-2002	4	16	7-5-4	1-2-1	5-1-1	1-2-2	9.0	0.56
David	Toms	2002-04	2	8	4-3-1	1-1-0	2-0-1	1-2-0	4.5	0.56
Lee	Trevino	1969-71-73-75-79-81	6	30	17-7-6	6-2-2	5-3-2	6-2-2	20	0.65
Jim	Turnesa	1953	1	1	1-0-0	1-0-0	0-0-0	0-0-0	1	1.00
Joe	Turnesa	1927-29	2	4	1-2-1	0-2-0	1-0-1	0-0-0	1.5	0.36
Ken	Venturi	1965	1	4	1-3-0	0-1-0	0-2-0	1-0-0	1.0	0.25
Scott	Verplank	2002	1	3	2-1-0	1-0-0	1-1-0	0-0-0	2	0.65
Lanny	Wadkins	1977-79-83-85-87-89-91-93	8	34	20-11-3	4-2-2	9-6-0	7-3-1	21.5	0.63
Art	Wall	1957-59-61	3	6	4-2-0	2-0-0	2-2-0	0-0-0	4.0	0.65
Al	Watrous	1927-29	2	3	2-1-0	1-1-0	1-0-0	0-0-0	2.0	0.65
Tom	Watson	1977-81-83-89	4	15	10-4-1	2-2-0	4-1-1	4-1-0	10.5	0.70
Tom	Weiskopf	1973-75	2	10	7-2-1	2-0-1	3-1-0	2-1-0	7.5	0.75
Craig	Wood	1931-33-35	3	4	1-3-0	1-2-0	0-1-0	0-0-0	1.0	0.25
Tiger	Woods	1997-99-2002-04	4	20	7-11-2	2-1-1	2-5-1	3-5-0	8.0	0.40
Lew	Worsham	1947	1	2	2-0-0	1-0-0	1-0-0	0-0-0	2.0	1.00
Fuzzy	Zoeller	1979-83-85	3	10	1-8-1	0-2-1	0-2-0	1-4-0	1.5	0.15

35 Matches Spanning 77 Years

Britain/Europe 9 wins United States of America 24 wins
2 Ties

GREAT BRITAIN and IRELAND/EUROPE	UNITED STATES OF AMERICA
Highest Margin of Victory	
2004 at Oakland Hills 18 to 9	1967 in Houston, Texas 23 to 8
1985 at The Belfry, England 16 to 11	1947 in Portland, Oregon 11 to 1
Total Points Over 35 Matches	
Team points 338	Team points 450
Foursome points 96.5	Foursome points 128.5
Four-Ball points 77	Four-Ball points 88
Singles points 164.5	Singles points 233.5
Most times on a Ryder Cup team	
Nick Faldo 11 (1977-79-81-83-85-87-89-91-93-95-97)	Lanny Wadkins 8 (1977-79-83-85-87-89-91-93)
Christy O'Connor Sr 10 (1955-57-59-61-63-65-67-69-71-73)	Raymond Floyd 8 (1969-75-77-81-83-85-91-93)
Bernhard Langer 10 (1981-83-85-87-89-91-93-95-97-02)	Billy Casper 8 (1961-63-65-67-69-71-73-75)
Dai Rees 9 (1937-47-49-51-53-55-57-59-61)	Sam Snead 7 (1937-47-49-51-53-55-59)
Bernard Gallacher 8 (1969-71-73-75-77-79-81-83)	Tom Kite 7 (1979-81-83-85-87-89-93)
Bernard Hunt 8 (1953-57-59-61-63-65-67-69)	Gene Littler 7 (1961-63-65-67-69-71-75)
Ian Woosnam 8 (1983-85-87-89-91-93-95-97)	Arnold Palmer 6 (1961-63-65-67-71-73)
Neil Coles 8 (1961-63-65-67-69-71-73-77)	Gene Sarazen 6 (1927-29-31-33-35-37)
Peter Allis 8 (1953-57-59-61-63-65-67-69)	Jack Nicklaus 6 (1969-71-73-75-77-81)
Sam Torrance 8 (1981-83-85-87-89-91-93-95)	Lee Trevino 6 (1969-71-73-75-79-81)
Seve Ballesteros 8 (1979-83-85-87-89-91-93-95)	
Youngest Player	
Sergio Garcia in 1999 - age 19 years, 8 months, 15 days	Horton Smith in 1929 - age 21 years and 4 days
Nick Faldo in 1977 - age 20 years, 1 months, 28 days	Tiger Woods in 1997 - age 21 years, 8 months, 27 days
Paul Way in 1983 - age 20 years, 7 months, 3 days	Horton Smith in 1931 - age 23 years, 1 month, 5 days
Bernard Gallacher in 1969 - age 20 years, 7 months, 9 days	Tiger Woods in 1999 - age 23 years, 8 months, 25 days
Oldest Player	
Ted Ray in 1927 - age 50 years, 2 months, 5 days	Raymond Floyd in 1993 - age 51 years, 20 days
Christy O'Connor Sr in 1973 - age 48 years, 8 months, 30 days	Jay Haas in 2004 - age 50 years, 9 months, 15 days
	Raymond Floyd in 1991 - age 49 years, 20 days
Most Matches Played	
Nick Faldo 46	37 Billy Casper
Bernhard Langer 42	34 Lanny Wadkins
Neil Coles 40	32 Arnold Palmer
Seve Ballesteros 37	31 Raymond Floyd
Christy O'Connor Sr 36	30 Lee Trevino
Tony Jacklin 35	28 Tom Kite
Colin Montgomerie 32	28 Jack Nicklaus
Ian Woosnam, Bernard Gallacher 31	27 Gene Littler
Most Points Won	
Nick Faldo 25	23 Billy Casper
Bernard Langer 24	23 Arnold Palmer
Seve Ballesteros 22	21 Lanny Wadkins
Colin Montgomerie 21	20 Lee Trevino
Jose Maria Olazabal 17	18 Jack Nicklaus
Tony Jacklin 17	18 Gene Littler
Ian Woosnam 16	17 Tom Kite
Bernard Gallacher 15	14 Hale Irwin
Peter Oosterhuis 15	13 Raymond Floyd
Neil Coles 15	11 Julius Boros

GREAT BRITAIN and IRELAND/ EUROPE   UNITED STATES OF AMERICA

Best Point Percentage (Minimum of 3 Ryder Cup Matches)

GREAT BRITAIN and IRELAND/ EUROPE		UNITED STATES OF AMERICA
Sergio Garcia (10-3-2) 73%	100%	Jimmy Demaret (6-0-0)
Colin Montgomerie (16-7-5) 66%	86%	Jack Burke (7-1-0), Horton Smith (3-0-1)
Abe Mitchell (4-2-0) 65%	83%	Walter Hagen (7-1-1)
Jose Maria Olazabal (15-8-3) 61%	80%	J.C. Snead (9-2-0)
Seve Ballesteros (20-12-5) 59%	79%	Sam Snead (10-2-1)
Percy Alliss (3-2-1) 58%	75%	Lloyd Mangrum (6-2-0), Ed Dudley (3-1-0),
Bernhard Langer (21-15-6) 57%		Ted Kroll (3-1-0)75%
Lee Westwood (11-8-1) 56%		
Peter Oosteruis (14-11-3) 55%		
Nick Faldo (23-19-4) 54%		
Charles Whitcombe (3-2-4) 54%		

Most Singles Matches

Neil Coles	15	11	Arnold Palmer
Christy O'Connor Sr	14	10	Billy Casper
Peter Alliss	12	10	Gene Littler
Nick Faldo, Bernard Gallacher	11	10	Jack Nicklaus
Tony Jacklin	11	10	Lee Trevino
Brian Barnes, Bernard Hunt	10	8	Raymond Floyd
Bernard Langer	10	8	Lanny Wadkins

Most Foursome Matches

Nick Faldo	18	15	Billy Casper
Bernhard Langer	18	15	Lanny Wadkins
Seve Ballesteros	14	13	Tom Kite
Neil Cole	13	12	Raymond Floyd
Tony Jacklin	13	12	Arnold Palmer
Christy O' Connor Sr	13	10	Payne Stewart
Colin Montgomerie	12	10	Lee Trevino

Most Four-Ball Matches

Nick Faldo	17	12	Billy Casper
Seve Ballesteros	15	11	Raymond Floyd
Bernhard Langer	14	11	Lanny Wadkins
Ian Woosnam	14	10	Lee Trevino
Colin Montgomerie	13	9	Fred Couples
Neil Coles	12	9	Gene Littler
Jose Maria Olazabal	12	9	Davis Love III,
Sam Torrance	10	9	Jack Nicklaus
Tony Jacklin	11	9	Arnold Palmer

Most Matches Won

Nick Faldo	23	22	Arnold Palmer
Bernhard Langer	21	20	Billy Casper
Seve Ballesteros	20	20	Lanny Wadkins
Colin Montgomerie	19	17	Jack Nicklaus
Jose Maria Olazabal	15	17	Lee Trevino
Peter Oosterhuis	14	15	Tom Kite
Ian Woosnam	14	14	Gene Littler
Bernard Gallacher	13	13	Hale Irwin
Tony Jacklin	13	12	Raymond Floyd

The Ryder Cup
Player Records

Most Singles Matches Won

GB and Ireland/Europe		United States of America	
Nick Faldo	6	6	Billy Casper
Peter Oosterhuis	6	6	Arnold Palmer
Peter Alliss	5	6	Sam Snead
Brian Barnes	5	6	Lee Trevino
Neil Coles	5	5	Tom Kite
Colin Montgomerie	5	5	Gene Littler
Dai Rees	5		

Most Foursome Matches Won

GB and Ireland/Europe		United States of America	
Bernhard Langer	11	9	Arnold Palmer
Seve Ballesteros	10	9	Lanny Wadkins
Nick Faldo	10	8	Billy Casper
Tony Jacklin	8	8	Jack Nicklaus
Colin Montgomerie	8	7	Tom Kite
Jose Maria Olazabal	7	6	Hale Irwin
Sergio Garcia	6	5	Julius Boros
Christy O'Connor Sr	6	5	Hal Sutton
Lee Westwood	6	5	Lee Trevino

Most Four-Ball Matches Won

GB and Ireland/Europe		United States of America	
Ian Woosnam	10	7	Arnold Palmer
Seve Ballesteros	8	7	Lanny Wadkins
Nick Faldo	7	6	Billy Casper
Jose Maria Olazabal	7	6	Lee Trevino
Bernhard Langer	6	5	Gene Littler
Colin Montgomerie	6	5	Jack Nicklaus
Mark James	5	4	Fred Couples
Peter Oosterhuis	5	4	Raymond Floyd
Darren Clarke	4	4	Hale Irwin
Bernard Gallacher	4	4	Phil Mickelson
Lee Westwood	4	4	Corey Pavin
		4	J.C. Snead
		4	Tom Watson

Most Matches Lost

GB and Ireland/Europe		United States of America	
Christy O'Connor Sr	21	16	Raymond Floyd
Neil Coles	21	12	Davis Love III,
Nick Faldo	19	12	Curtis Strange
Bernard Hunt	16	11	Lanny Wadkins
Peter Alliss	15	11	Tiger Woods
Bernhard Langer	15	10	Billy Casper
Mark James	15	9	Fred Couples
Sam Torrance	15	9	Jim Furyk
Brian Barnes	14	9	Tom Kite
Tony Jacklin	14	9	Mark O'Meara
Bernard Gallacher	13	9	Payne Stewart
Seve Ballesteros	12	8	Paul Azinger
Ian Woosnam	12	8	Ben Crenshaw
Peter Oosterhuis	11	8	Phil Mickelson
Harry Weetman	11	8	Jack Nicklaus
George Will	11	8	Arnold Palmer
Brian Hugget	10	8	Fuzzy Zoeller
Dave Thomas	10		

Most Singles Matches Lost

GB and Ireland/Europe		United States of America	
Christy O'Connor Sr	10	4	Raymond Floyd
Tony Jacklin	8	4	Jack Nicklaus
Neil Coles	6	4	Mark O'Meara
Harry Weetman	6		
Ian Woosnam	6		

Most Foursome Matches Lost

GB and Ireland/Europe		United States of America	
Bernard Hunt	9	8	Raymond Floyd
Neil Coles	8	6	Lanny Wadkins
Mark James	7	5	Billy Casper
Sam Torrance	7	5	Fred Couples
Peter Alliss	6	5	Tom Kite
Nick Faldo	6	5	Davis Love III
Bernard Gallacher	6	5	Payne Stewart
Bernhard Langer	6	5	Tiger Woods
Christy O'Connor Sr	6		
Peter Oosterhuis	6		

Most Four-Ball Matches Lost

GB and Ireland/Europe		United States of America	
Nick Faldo	9	6	Davis Love III
Neil Coles	7	5	Paul Azinger
Bernhard Langer	6	5	Jim Furyk
Peter Alliss	5	5	Curtis Strange
Brian Barnes	5	5	Tiger Woods
Seve Ballesteros	5	4	Mark Calcavecchia
Tony Jacklin	5	4	Ben Crenshaw
Christy O'Connor Sr	5	4	Tom Kite
Colin Montgomerie	5	4	Raymond Floyd
Sam Torrance	5	4	Fuzzy Zoeller
George Will	5		

Most Matches Halved

GB and Ireland/Europe		United States of America	
Tony Jacklin	8	8	Gene Littler
Neil Coles	7	7	Billy Casper
Bernhard Langer	6	6	Lee Trevino
Sam Torrance	6	5	Justin Leonard
Brian Hugget	6	5	Davis Love III
Bernard Hunt	6	4	Julius Boros
		4	Fred Couples
		4	Tom Kite
		4	Hal Sutton

Most Singles Matches Halved

GB and Ireland/Europe		United States of America	
Neil Coles	4	3	Gene Littler
Bernard Gallacher	4	2	Paul Azinger
Peter Alliss	3	2	Tom Kite
Bernard Hunt	3	2	Billy Casper
Bernhard Langer	3	2	Fred Couples
Sam Torrance	3	2	Hale Irwin
Seve Ballesteros	2	2	Justin Leonard
Darren Clarke	2	2	Jack Nicklaus
Colin Montgomerie	2	2	Arnold Palmer
Christy O'Connor Sr.	2	2	Lee Trevino
Sam Torrance	2	2	Lanny Wadkins
Ian Woosnam	2	2	Billy Casper

GREAT BRITAIN and IRELAND/ EUROPE   UNITED STATES OF AMERICA

Most Foursome Matches Halved

Tony Jacklin	4	2	Julius Boros
Charles Whitcombe	3	2	Billy Casper
Nick Faldo	2	2	Phil Mickelson
Ignacio Garrido	2	2	Gene Sarazen
Brian Hugget	2	2	Lee Trevino
Jesper Parnevik	2		
Dave Thomas	2		
Harry Weetman	2		
Ian Woosnam	2		

Most Four-Ball Matches Halved

Brian Hugget	2	4	Gene Littler
Tony Jacklin	3	3	Billy Casper
Jose Maria Olazabal	3	3	Raymond Floyd
Sam Torrance	3	2	Miller Barber, Fred Couples, Al Geiberger, Jay Haas,
Seve Ballesteros, Maurice Bembridge, Peter Butler,	2		Justin Leonard, Davis Love III, Johnny Miller, Craig Stadler,
Neil Coles, Paul McGinley, Sergio Garcia, Bernard Hunt,			Hal Sutton, Lee Trevino
Bernhard Langer, Colin Montgomerie,			
Lionel Platts, Dave Thomas			

Players Selected, But Did Not Compete

George Gadd	1927	1927	Al Espinoza
Laurie Ayton	1949	1931, '37	Horton Smith
Abe Mitchell	1927	1951	Dutch Harrison
Jack Hargreaves	1951	1959	Jack Burke Jr
Percy Alliss	1929	1965	Johnny Pott
Ken Bousfield	1955	1979	Tom Watson
Stewart Burns	1929		
Peter Mills	1959		
Allan Dailey	1933		
John Garner	1973		
Eric Green	1947		
Jose Maria Olazabal	1995		
Reg Horne	1947		
Miguel Angel Martin	1997		

Teams Winning All Points in a Series

Foursomes

United States won all foursomes 4-0 in 1947

United States won second series foursomes 4-0 in 1963

United States won first series foursomes 4-0 in 1975

United States won second series foursomes 4-0 in 1981

Four-Ball

United States won first series four-ball 4-0 in 1967

United States won first series four-ball 4-0 in 1971

Europe won first series four-ball 4-0 in 1987

Europe won first series four-ball 4-0 in 1989

Singles

No side has ever had a clean sweep in the singles

MISCELLANEOUS
Relatives in Ryder Cup Matches
Father and Son
Percy Alliss (1929-33-35-37) and Peter Alliss (1953-57-59-61-63-65-67-69),
Antonio Garrido (1979) and Ignacio Garrido (1997)

Brothers
Charles Whitcombe (1927-29-3l-33-35-37), Reg Whitcombe (1935) and Ernest Whitcombe (1929-31-35)
Bernard Hunt (1953-57-59-61-63-65-67-69) and Geoffrey Hunt (1963)
Joe Turnesa (1927-29) and Jim Turnesa (1953)
Jay Hebert (1959-61) and Lionel Hebert (1957)

Uncles and Nephews
Christy O'Connor Sr (1955-57-59-61-63-65-67-69) and Christy O'Connor Jr (1975-89)
Sam Snead (1937-47-49-5l-53-55-59) and J.C. Snead (1971-73-75)
Bob Goalby (1963) and Jay Haas (1983-95, 2004)

Cousins
Jackie Burke Jr. (l951-53-55-57-59) and Dave Man (1965)

Brothers-in-law
Jerry Pate (1981) and Bruce Lietzke (1981)

Father and son-in-law
Max Faulkner (1947-49-51-53-57) and Brian Barnes (1969-71-73-75-77-79)

Pairings With Most Ryder Cup Wins
European Team
Seve Ballesteros and Jose Maria Olazabal 15 Matches: 11 Wins, 2 Losses, 2 Halves
Peter Alliss and Christy O'Connor Sr 12 Matches: 5 Wins, 6 Loss, 1 Halve
Nick Faldo and Ian Woosnam 10 Matches: 5 Wins, 3 Losses, 2 Halves
Bernard Gallacher and Brian Barnes 10 Matches: 5 Wins, 4 Losses, 1 Halve
Bernard Hunt and Neil Coles 8 Matches: 2 Wins, 5 Losses, 1 Halve
Colin Montgomerie and Nick Faldo 7 Matches: 3 Wins, 3 Losses, 1 Halve
Neil Coles and Christy O'Connor Sr 7 Matches: 3 Wins, 3 Losses, 1 Halve
Peter Oosterhuis and Tony Jacklin 7 Matches: 3 Wins, 2 Losses, 2 Halves

United States Team
Tom Kite and Curtis Strange 6 Matches: 2 Wins, 3 Losses, 1 Halve
Larry Nelson and Lanny Wadkins 6 Matches: 4 Wins, 2 Losses
David Toms and Phil Mickelson 5 Matches: 3 Wins, 1 Loss, I Halve
Arnold Palmer and Gardner Dickinson 5 Matches: 5 Wins, 0 Losses
Tony Lema and Julius Boros 5 Matches: 3 Wins, 1 Loss, 1 Halve
Jack Nicklaus and Tom Watson 4 Matches: 4 Wins, 0 Losses
Fred Couples and Raymond Floyd 4 Matches: 2 Wins, 2 Losses
Arnold Palmer and Dave Marr 4 Matches: 2 Wins, 2 Losses
Billy Casper and Gene Littler 4 Matches: 1 Win, 1 Loss, 2 Halves
Chip Beck and Paul Azinger 4 Matches: 2 Wins, 2 Losses
Lloyd Mangrum and Sam Snead 4 Matches: 3 Wins, 1 Loss

Highest Winning Margins, 36-Hole Team
10 and 9 (1931) Walter Hagen and Denny Shute beat George Duncan and Arthur Havers
10 and 9 (1947) Lew Worsham and Ed Oliver beat Henry Cotton and Arthur Lees
9 and 8 (1935) Paul Runyan and Horton Smith beat Bill Cox and Edward Jarman

Highest Winning Margins, 18-Hole Team
7 and 6 (1979) Hale Irwin and Tom Kite beat Ken Brown and Des Smyth
7 and 6 (1991) Paul Azinger and Mark O'Meara beat Nick Faldo and David Gilford
7 and 5 (1981) Lee Trevino and Jerry Pate beat Nick Faldo and Sam Torrance
7 and 5 (1983) Lanny Wadkins and Gil Morgan beat Sam Torrance and Jose Maria Canizares
7 and 5 (1985) Jose Maria Canizares and Jose Pinero beat Tom Kite and Calvin Peete
7 and 5 (1993) Bernhard Langer and Ian Woosnam beat Paul Azinger and Payne Stewart

MISCELLANEOUS
Highest Winning Margins, 36-Hole Singles
10 and 8 (1929) George Duncan beat Walter Hagen

9 and 8 (1929) Leo Diegel beat Abe Mitchell

9 and 8 (1933) Abe Mitchell beat Olin Dutra

9 and 7 (1953) Fred Daly beat Ted Kroll

Highest Winning Margins, 18-Hole Singles
8 and 7 (1997) Fred Couples beat Ian Woosnam

8 and 7 (1989) Tom Kite beat Howard Clark

7 and 6 (1969) Miller Barber beat Maurice Bembridge

7 and 6 (1971) Lee Trevino beat Brian Huggett

7 and 6 (1997) Tom Lehman beat Ignacio Garrido

6 and 5 (1963) Gene Littler beat Tom Haliburton

6 and 5 (1973) Gay Brewer beat Bernard Gallacher

6 and 5 (1973) Lee Trevino beat Neil Coles

6 and 5 (1999) Davis Love III beat Jean Van de Velde

6 and 4 (1965) Tony Lema beat Christy O'Connor Sr

6 and 4 (1981) Ben Crenshaw beat Des Smyth

6 and 4 (2004) Jim Furyk beat David Howell

Undefeated and Untied in Two or More Matches in Ryder Cup Play
EUROPE
Paul Broadhurst, John Jacobs - 2 wins

USA
Jimmy Demaret - 6 wins; Billy Maxwell - 4 wins; Ben Hogan, Billy Burke,

Johnny Golden - 3 wins; Chick Harbert, Wilfred Cox, Ralph Guldahl, Bob Rosburg, Lew Worsham – 2 wins

Captain's Selections: The format allowing the Europeans to choose "wild cards" began in 1979 and has operated since then except for 1983. The United States selection for "wild cards" began in 1989. Here is a look at the selections and how they have played:

2004 U.S.A: Stewart Cink: 1 win, 2 losses, 1 halve.

Jay Haas : 1 win, 2 losses, 1 halve

2004 Europe: Colin Montgomerie : 3 wins, 1 loss

Luke Donald : 2 wins, 1 loss, 1 halve

2002 U.S.A: Scott Verplank : 2 wins, 1 lost

Paul Azinger : 0 wins, 1 loss, 1 halve

2002 Europe: Sergio Garcia : 3 wins, 2 losses

Jesper Parnevik : 0 wins, 1 loss, 1 halve

1999 U.S.A: Tom Lehman : 2 wins, 1 loss

Steve Pate : 2 wins, 1 loss

1999 Europe: Jesper Parnevik : 3 wins, 1 loss, 1 halve

Andrew Coltart : 0 wins, 1 loss

1997 U.S.A: Fred Couples : 2 wins, 2 losses

Lee Janzen : 2 wins, 1 loss

1997 Europe: Nick Faldo : 2 wins, 3 losses

Jesper Parnevik : 1 win, 1 loss, 2 halves

1995 U.S.A: Fred Couples : 2 win, 1 loss, 1 halve

Curtis Strange : 0 wins, 3 losses

1995 Europe: Nick Faldo: 2 wins, 2 losses

Ian Woosnam : 1 win, 1 loss, 1 halve

Jose Maria Olazabal - was one of the captain's picks, but injury prevented him from playing, and he was replaced by Woosnam

1993 U.S.A: Lanny Wadkins : 2 win, 1 loss, 1 halve

Ray Floyd : 3 wins, 1 loss

1993 Europe: Joakim Haeggman: 1 win, 1 loss

Seve Ballesteros : 2 wins, 2 losses

Jose Maria Olazabal : 2 wins, 3 losses

1991 U.S.A: Chip Beck : 1 win, 2 losses

Ray Floyd : 2 wins, 2 losses

1991 Europe: Jose-Maria Olazabal : 3 wins, 1 loss, 1 halve

Nick Faldo : 1 win, 3 losses

Mark James : 2 wins, 3 losses

1989 U.S.A: Tom Watson : 1 win, I loss, 1 halve

Lanny Wadkins : 3 wins, 1 loss

1989 Europe: Bernhard Langer : 0 wins, 3 losses

Howard Clark : 2 wins, 2 losses

Christy O'Connor Jr. : 1 win, 1 loss

1987 Europe: Jose-Maria Olazabal : 3 wins, 2 losses

Sandy Lyle : 3 wins, 1 loss

Ken Brown : 0 wins, 2 losses

1985 Europe: Ken Brown : 1 win, 2 losses

Nick Faldo : 0 wins, 2 losses

Jose Rivero : 1 won, 1 loss

1983 Europe: Picked the team off the order of merit list and didn't have any captain picks

1981 Europe: Mark James : 2 wins, 3 losses

Peter Oosterhuis : 0 wins, 3 losses

1979 Europe: Peter Oosterhuis : 2 wins, 2 losses

Des Smyth : 0 wins, 2 losses

1927: WORCESTER COUNTRY CLUB, WORCESTER, MASSACHUSETTS, JUNE 3-4
Captains: E. Ray (GB), W. Hagen (USA)

GREAT BRITAIN			UNITED STATES OF AMERICA
Foursomes			
E. Ray & F. Robson	0	1	W. Hagen & J. Golden (2 and 1)
G. Duncan & A. Compston	0	1	J. Farrell & J. Turnesa (8 and 6)
A. G. Havers & H. C. Jolly	0	1	G. Sarazen & A. Watrous (3 and 2)
A. Boomer & C. A. Whitcombe (7 and 5)	1	0	L. Diegel & W. Mehlhorn
Singles			
A. Compston	0	1	W. Mehlhorn (1 hole)
A. Boomer	0	1	J. Farrell (5 and 4)
H. C. Jolly	0	1	J. Golden (8 and 7)
E. Ray	0	1	L. Diegel (7 and 5)
C. A. Whitcombe (halved)	½	½	G. Sarazen (halved)
A. G. Havers	0	1	W. Hagen (2 and 1)
F. Robson	0	1	A. Watrous (3 and 2)
G. Duncan (1 hole)	1	0	J. Turnesa
GREAT BRITAIN	2½	9½	**UNITED STATES OF AMERICA**

1929: MOORTOWN, LEEDS, MAY 26-27
Captains: G. Duncan (GB), W. Hagen (USA)

GREAT BRITAIN			UNITED STATES OF AMERICA
Foursomes			
C. A. Whitcombe & A. Compston (halved)	½	½	J. Farrell & J. Turnesa (halved)
A. Boomer & G. Duncan	0	1	L. Diegel & A. Espinosa (7 and 5)
A. Mitchell & F. Robson (2 and 1)	1	0	G. Sarazen & E. Dudley
E. R. Whitcombe & T. H. Cotton	0	1	J. Golden & W. Hagen (2 holes)
Singles			
C. A. Whitcombe (8 and 6)	1	0	J. Farrell
G. Duncan (10 and 8)	1	0	W. Hagen
A. Mitchell	0	1	L. Diegel (9 and 8)
A. Compston (6 and 4)	1	0	G. Sarazen
A. Boomer (4 and 3)	1	0	J. Turnesa
F. Robson	0	1	H. Smith (4 and 2)
T. H. Cotton (4 and 3)	1	0	A. Watrous
E. R. Whitcombe (halved)	½	½	A. Espinosa (halved)
GREAT BRITAIN	7	5	**UNITED STATES OF AMERICA**

1931: SCIOTO COUNTRY CLUB, COLUMBUS, OHIO, JUNE 26-27
Captains: C. A. Whitcombe (GB), W. Hagen (USA)

GREAT BRITAIN			UNITED STATES OF AMERICA
Foursomes			
A. Compston & W. H. Davies	0	1	G. Sarazen & J. Farrell (8 and 7)
G. Duncan & A. G. Havers	0	1	W. Hagen & D. Shute (10 and 9)
A. Mitchell & F. Robson (3 and 1)	1	0	L. Diegel & A. Espinosa
S. Easterbrook & E. R. Whitcombe	0	1	W. Burke & W. Cox (3 and 2)
Singles			
A. Compston	0	1	W. Burke (7 and 6)
F. Robson	0	1	G. Sarazen (7 and 6)
W. H. Davies (4 and 3)	1	0	J. Farrell
A. Mitchell	0	1	W. Cox (3 and 1)
C. A. Whitcombe	0	1	W. Hagen (4 and 3)
B. Hodson	0	1	D. Shute (8 and 6)
E. R. Whitcombe	0	1	A. Espinosa (2 and 1)
A. G. Havers (4 and 3)	1	0	C. Wood
GREAT BRITAIN	3	9	**UNITED STATES OF AMERICA**

1933: SOUTHPORT AND AINSDALE, SOUTHPORT, JUNE 26-27
Captains: J. H. Taylor (GB), W. Hagen (USA)

GREAT BRITAIN			UNITED STATES OF AMERICA
Foursomes			
P. Alliss & C. A. Whitcombe (halved)	½	½	G. Sarazen & W. Hagen (halved)
A. Mitchell & A. G. Havers (3 and 2)	1	0	O. Dutra & D. Shute
W. H. Davies & S. Easterbrook (1 hole)	1	0	C. Wood & P. Runyan
A. H. Padgham & A. Perry	0	1	E. Dudley & W. Burke (1 hole)
Singles			
A. H. Padgham	0	1	G. Sarazen (6 and 4)
A. Mitchell (9 and 8)	1	0	O. Dutra
A. J. Lacey	0	1	W. Hagen (2 and 1)
W. H. Davies	0	1	C. Wood (4 and 3)
P. Alliss (2 and 1)	1	0	P. Runyan
A. G. Havers (4 and 3)	1	0	L. Diegel
S. Easterbrook (1 hole)	1	0	D. Shute
C. A. Whitcombe	0	1	H. Smith (2 and 1)
GREAT BRITAIN	6½	5½	**UNITED STATES OF AMERICA**

1935: RIDGEWOOD COUNTRY CLUB, NEW JERSEY, SEPTEMBER 28-29
Captains: C.A. Whitcombe (GB), W. Hagen (USA)

GREAT BRITAIN			UNITED STATES OF AMERICA
Foursomes			
A. Perry & J. J. Busson	0	1	G. Sarazen & W. Hagen (7 and 6)
A. H. Padgham & P. Alliss	0	1	H. Picard & J. Revolta (6 and 5)
W. J. Cox & E. W. Jarman	0	1	P. Runyan & H. Smith (9 and 8)
C. A. & E. R. Whitcombe (1 hole)	1	0	O. Dutra & K. Laffoon
Singles			
J. J. Busson	0	1	G. Sarazen (3 and 2)
R. Burton	0	1	P. Runyan (5 and 3)
R. A. Whitcombe	0	1	J. Revolta (2 and 1)
A. H. Padgham	0	1	O. Dutra (4 and 2)
P. Alliss (1 hole)	1	0	C. Wood
W. J. Cox (halved)	½	½	H. Smith (halved)
E. R. Whitcombe	0	1	H. Picard (3 and 2)
A. Perry (halved)	½	½	S. Parks (halved)
GREAT BRITAIN	3	9	**UNITED STATES OF AMERICA**

1937: SOUTHPORT AND AINSDALE, SOUTHPORT, JUNE 29-30
Captains: C. A. Whitcombe (GB), W. Hagen (USA)

GREAT BRITAIN			UNITED STATES OF AMERICA
Foursomes			
A. H. Padgham & T. H. Cotton	0	1	E. Dudley & B. Nelson (4 and 2)
A. J. Lacey & W. J. Cox	0	1	R. Guldahl & T. Manero (2 and 1)
C. A. Whitcombe & D. J. Rees (halved)	½	½	G. Sarazen & D. Shute (halved)
P. Alliss & R. Burton (2 and 1)	1	0	H. Picard & J. Revolta
Singles			
A. H. Padgham	0	1	R. Guldahl (8 and 7)
S. L. King (halved)	½	½	D. Shute (halved)
D. J. Rees (3 and 1)	1	0	B. Nelson
T. H. Cotton (5 and 3)	1	0	T. Manero
P. Alliss	0	1	G. Sarazen (1 hole)
R. Burton	0	1	S. Snead (5 and 4)
A. Perry	0	1	E. Dudley (2 and 1)
A. J. Lacey	0	1	H. Picard (2 and 1)
GREAT BRITAIN	4	8	**UNITED STATES OF AMERICA**

1947: PORTLAND GOLF CLUB, PORTLAND, OREGON, NOVEMBER 1-2
Captains: T. H. Cotton (GB), B. Hogan (USA)

GREAT BRITAIN			UNITED STATES OF AMERICA
Foursomes			
T. H. Cotton & A. Lees	0	1	E. Oliver & L. Worsham (10 and 9)
F. Daly & C. H. Ward	0	1	S. Snead & L. Mangrum (6 and 5)
J. Adams & M. Faulkner	0	1	B. Hogan & J. Demaret (2 holes)
D. J. Rees & S. L. King	0	1	B. Nelson & H. Barron (2 and 1)
Singles			
F. Daly	0	1	E. J. Harrison (5 and 4)
J. Adams	0	1	L. Worsham (3 and 2)
M. Faulkner	0	1	L. Mangrum (6 and 5)
C. H. Ward	0	1	E. Oliver (4 and 3)
A. Lees	0	1	B. Nelson (2 and 1)
T. H. Cotton	0	1	S. Snead (5 and 4)
D. J. Rees	0	1	J. Demaret (3 and 2)
S. L. King (4 and 3)	1	0	H. Keiser
GREAT BRITAIN	1	11	**UNITED STATES OF AMERICA**

1949: GANTON, SCARBOROUGH, SEPTEMBER 16-17
Captains: C.A. Whitcombe (GB), B. Hogan (USA)

GREAT BRITAIN			UNITED STATES OF AMERICA
Foursomes			
M. Faulkner & J. Adams (2 and 1)	1	0	E. J. Harrison & J. Palmer
F. Daly & K. Bousfield (4 and 2)	1	0	R. Hamilton & S. Alexander
C. H. Ward & S. L. King	0	1	J. Demaret & C. Heafner (4 and 3)
R. Burton & A. Lees (1 hole)	1	0	S. Snead & L. Mangrum
Singles			
M. Faulkner	0	1	E. J. Harrison (8 and 7)
J. Adams (2 and 1)	1	0	J. Palmer
C. H. Ward	0	1	S. Snead (6 and 5)
D. J. Rees (6 and 4)	1	0	R. Hamilton
R. Burton	0	1	C. Heafner (3 and 2)
S. L. King	0	1	C. Harbert (4 and 3)
A. Lees	0	1	J. Demaret (7 and 6)
F. Daly	0	1	L. Mangrum (4 and 3)
GREAT BRITAIN	5	7	**UNITED STATES OF AMERICA**

1951: PINEHURST COUNTRY CLUB, NORTH CAROLINA, NOVEMBER 2 and 4
Captains: A. J. Lacey (GB), S. Snead (USA)
GREAT BRITAIN   UNITED STATES OF AMERICA

Foursomes
M. Faulkner & D. J. Rees	0	1	C. Heafner & J. Burke (5 and 3)
C. H. Ward & A. Lees (2 and 1)	1	0	E. Oliver & H. Ransom
J. Adams & J. Panton	0	1	S. Snead & L. Mangrum (5 and 4)
F. Daly & K. Bousfield	0	1	B. Hogan & J. Demaret (5 and 4)

Singles
J. Adams	0	1	J. Burke (4 and 3)
D. J. Rees	0	1	J. Demaret (2 holes)
F. Daly (halved)	½	½	C. Heafner (halved)
H. Weetman	0	1	L. Mangrum (6 and 5)
A. Lees (2 and 1)	1	0	E. Oliver
C. H. Ward	0	1	B. Hogan (3 and 2)
J. Panton	0	1	S. Alexander (8 and 7)
M. Faulkner	0	1	S. Snead (4 and 3)

GREAT BRITAIN 2½ 9½ UNITED STATES OF AMERICA

1955: THUNDERBIRD GOLF & COUNTRY CLUB, CALIFORNIA, NOVEMBER 5-6
Captains: D. J. Rees (GB), C. Harbert (USA)
GREAT BRITAIN & IRELAND   UNITED STATES OF AMERICA

Foursomes
J. Fallon & J. R. M. Jacobs (1 hole)	1	0	C. Harper & J. Barber
E. C. Brown & S. S. Scott	0	1	D. Ford & T. Kroll (5 and 4)
A. Lees & H. Weetman	0	1	J. Burke & T. Bolt (1 hole)
H. Bradshaw & D. J. Rees	0	1	S. Snead & C. Middlecoff (3 and 2)

Singles
C. O'Connor	0	1	T. Bolt (4 and 2)
S. S. Scott	0	1	C. Harbert (3 and 2)
J. R. M. Jacobs (1 hole)	1	0	C. Middlecoff
D. J. Rees	0	1	S. Snead (3 and 1)
A. Lees (3 and 2)	1	0	M. Furgol
E. C. Brown (3 and 2)	1	0	J. Barber
H. Bradshaw	0	1	J. Burke (3 and 2)
H. Weetman	0	1	D. Ford (3 and 2)

GREAT BRITAIN & IRELAND 4 8 UNITED STATES OF AMERICA

1959: ELDORADO COUNTRY CLUB, CALIFORNIA, NOVEMBER 6-7
Captains: D. J. Rees (GB), S. Snead (USA)
GREAT BRITAIN & IRELAND   UNITED STATES OF AMERICA

Foursomes
B. J. Hunt & E. C. Brown	0	1	R. Rosburg & M. Souchak (5 and 4)
D. J. Rees & K. Bousfield	0	1	J. Boros & D. Finsterwald (2 holes)
C. O'Connor & P. Alliss (3 and 2)	1	0	A. Wall & D. Ford
H. Weetman & D. C. Thomas (halved)	½	½	S. Snead & C. Middlecoff (halved)

Singles
N. V. Drew (halved)	½	½	D. Ford (halved)
K. Bousfield	0	1	M. Souchak (3 and 2)
H. Weetman	0	1	R. Rosburg (6 and 5)
D. C. Thomas	0	1	S. Snead (6 and 5)
C. O'Connor	0	1	A. Wall (7 and 6)
D. J. Rees	0	1	D. Finsterwald (1 hole)
P. Alliss (halved)	½	½	J. Hebert (halved)
E. C. Brown (4 and 3)	1	0	C. Middlecoff

GREAT BRITAIN & IRELAND 3½ 8½ UNITED STATES OF AMERICA

1953: WENTWORTH CLUB, VIRGINIA WATER, OCTOBER 2-3
Captains: T. H. Cotton (GB), L. Mangrum (USA)
GREAT BRITAIN & IRELAND   UNITED STATES OF AMERICA

Foursomes
H. Weetman & P. Alliss	0	1	D. Douglas & E. Oliver (2 and 1)
E. C. Brown & J. Panton	0	1	L. Mangrum & S. Snead (8 and 7)
J. Adams & B. J. Hunt	0	1	T. Kroll & J. Burke (7 and 5)
F. Daly & H. Bradshaw (1 hole)	1	0	W. Burkemo & C. Middlecoff

Singles
D. J. Rees	0	1	J. Burke (2 and 1)
F. Daly (9 and 7)	1	0	T. Kroll
E. C. Brown (2 holes)	1	0	L. Mangrum
H. Weetman (1 hole)	1	0	S. Snead
M. Faulkner	0	1	C. Middlecoff (3 and 1)
P. Alliss	0	1	J. Turnesa (1 hole)
B. J. Hunt (halved)	½	½	D. Douglas (halved)
H. Bradshaw (3 and 2)	1	0	F. Haas

GREAT BRITAIN & IRELAND 5½ 6½ UNITED STATES OF AMERICA

1957: LINDRICK GOLF CLUB, SHEFFIELD, OCTOBER 4-5
Captains: D. J. Rees (GB), J. Burke (USA)
GREAT BRITAIN & IRELAND   UNITED STATES OF AMERICA

Foursomes
P. Alliss & B. J. Hunt	0	1	D. Ford & D. Finsterwald (2 and 1)
K. Bousfield & D. J. Rees (3 and 2)	1	0	A. Wall & F. Hawkins
M. Faulkner & H. Weetman	0	1	T. Kroll & J. Burke (4 and 3)
C. O'Connor & E. C. Brown	0	1	R. Mayer & T. Bolt (7 and 5)

Singles
E. C. Brown (4 and 3)	1	0	T. Bolt
R. P. Mills (5 and 3)	1	0	J. Burke
P. Alliss	0	1	F. Hawkins (2 and 1)
K. Bousfield (4 and 3)	1	0	L. Hebert
D. J. Rees (7 and 6)	1	0	E. Furgol
B. J. Hunt (6 and 5)	1	0	D. Ford
C. O'Connor (7 and 6)	1	0	D. Finsterwald
H. Bradshaw (halved)	½	½	R. Mayer (halved)

GREAT BRITAIN & IRELAND 7½ 4½ UNITED STATES OF AMERICA

1961: ROYAL LYTHAM & ST. ANNES, ST. ANNES, OCTOBER 13-14
Captains: D. J. Rees (GB), J. Barber (USA)
GREAT BRITAIN & IRELAND   UNITED STATES OF AMERICA

Foursomes (morning)
C. O'Connor & P. Alliss (4 and 3)	1	0	D. Ford & G. Littler
J. Panton & B. J. Hunt	0	1	A. Wall & J. Hebert (4 and 3)
D. J. Rees & K. Bousfield	0	1	W. Casper & A. Palmer (2 and 1)
T. B. Haliburton & N. C. Coles	0	1	W. Collins & M. Souchak (1hole)

Foursomes (afternoon)
C. O'Connor & P. Alliss	0	1	A. Wall & J. Hebert (1 hole)
J. Panton & B. J. Hunt	0	1	W. Casper & A. Palmer (5 and 4)
D. J. Rees & K. Bousfield (4 and 2)	1	0	W. Collins & M. Souchak
T. B. Haliburton & N. C. Coles	0	1	J. Barber & D. Finsterwald (1 hole)

Singles (morning)
H. Weetman	0	1	D. Ford (1 hole)
R. L. Moffitt	0	1	M. Souchak (5 and 4)
P. Alliss (halved)	½	½	A. Palmer (halved)
K. Bousfield	0	1	W. Casper (5 and 3)
D. J. Rees (2 and 1)	1	0	J. Hebert
N. C. Coles (halved)	½	½	G. Littler (halved)
B. J. Hunt (5 and 4)	1	0	J. Barber
C. O'Connor	0	1	D. Finsterwald (2 and 1)

Singles (afternoon)
H. Weetman	0	1	A. Wall (1 hole)
P. Alliss (3 and 2)	1	0	W. Collins
B. J. Hunt	0	1	M. Souchak (2 and 1)
T. B. Haliburton	0	1	A. Palmer (2 and 1)
D. J. Rees (4 and 3)	1	0	D. Ford
K. Bousfield (1 hole)	1	0	J. Barber
N. C. Coles (1 hole)	1	0	D. Finsterwald
C. O'Connor (halved)	½	½	G. Littler (halved)

GREAT BRITAIN & IRELAND 9½ 14½ UNITED STATES OF AMERICA

The Ryder Cup
1963-1969

1963: EAST LAKE COUNTRY CLUB, ATLANTA, GEORGIA, OCTOBER 11-13
Captains: J. Fallon (GB), A. Palmer (USA)

GREAT BRITAIN & IRELAND   **UNITED STATES OF AMERICA**

Foursomes (morning)
B. Huggett & G. Will (3 and 2)	1	0	A. Palmer & J. Pott
P. Alliss & C. O.Connor	0	1	W. Casper & D. Ragan (1 hole)
D. Thomas & H. Weetman (halved)	½	½	G. Littler & D. Finsterwald (halved)
N. C. Coles & B. J. Hunt (halved)	½	½	J. Boros & A. Lema (halved)

Foursomes (afternoon)
D. Thomas & H. Weetman	0	1	W. Maxwell & R. Goalby (4 and 3)
B. Huggett & G. Will	0	1	A. Palmer & W. Casper (5 and 4)
N. C. Coles & G. M. Hunt	0	1	G. Littler & D. Finsterwald (2 and 1)
T. B. Haliburton & B. J. Hunt	0	1	J. Boros & A. Lema (1 hole)

Four-Balls (morning)
B. Huggett & D. Thomas	0	1	A. Palmer & D. Finsterwald (5 and 4)
P. Alliss & B. J. Hunt (halved)	½	½	G. Littler & J. Boros (halved)
H. Weetman & G. Wil	0	1	W. Casper & W. Maxwell (3 and 2)
N. C. Coles & C. O'Connor (1 hole)	1	0	R. Goalby & D. Ragan

Four-Balls (afternoon)
N. C. Coles & C. O'Connor	0	1	A. Palmer & D. Finsterwald (3 and 2)
P. Alliss & B. J. Hunt	0	1	A. Lema & J. Pott (1 hole)
T. B. Haliburton & G. M. Hunt	0	1	W. Casper & W. Maxwell (2 and 1)
B. Huggett & D. Thomas (halved)	½	½	R. Goalby & D. Ragan (halved)

Singles (morning)
G. M. Hunt	0	1	A. Lema (5 and 3)
B. Huggett (3 and 1)	1	0	J. Pott
P. Alliss (1 hole)	1	0	A. Palmer
N. C. Coles (halved)	½	½	W. Casper (halved)
D. Thomas	0	1	R. Goalby (3 and 2)
C. O'Connor	0	1	G. Littler (1 hole)
H. Weetman (1 hole)	1	0	J. Boros
B. J. Hunt (2 holes)	1	0	D. Finsterwald

Singles (afternoon)
G. Wil	0	1	A. Palmer (3 and 2)
N. C. Coles	0	1	D. Ragan (2 and 1)
P. Alliss (halved)	½	½	A. Lema (halved)
T. B. Haliburton	0	1	G. Littler (6 and 5)
H. Weetman	0	1	J. Boros (2 and 1)
C. O'Connor	0	1	W. Maxwell (2 and 1)
D. Thomas	0	1	D. Finsterwald (4 and 3)
B. J. Hunt	0	1	R. Goalby (2 and 1)

GREAT BRITAIN & IRELAND 9   23 **UNITED STATES OF AMERICA**

1965: ROYAL BIRKDALE, SOUTHPORT, OCTOBER 7-9
Captains: H. Weetman (GB), B. Nelson (USA)

GREAT BRITAIN & IRELAND   **UNITED STATES OF AMERICA**

Foursomes (morning)
L. Platts & P. J. Butler	0	1	J. & A. Lema (1 hole)
D. C. Thomas & G. Will (6 and 5)	1	0	A. Palmer & D. Marr
B. J. Hunt & N. C. Coles	0	1	W. Casper & G. Littler (2 and 1)
P. Alliss & C. O'Connor (5 and 4)	1	0	K. Venturi & D. January

Foursomes (afternoon)
D. C. Thomas & G. Wil	0	1	A. Palmer & D. Marr (6 and 5)
P. Alliss & C. O'Connor (2 and 1)	1	0	W. Casper & G. Littler
J. Martin & J. Hitchcock	0	1	J. Boros & A. Lema (5 and 4)
B. J. Hunt & N. C. Coles (3 and 2)	1	0	K. Venturi & D. January

Four-Balls (morning)
D. C. Thomas & G. Wil	0	1	D. January & T. Jacobs (1 hole)
L. Platts & P. J. Butler (halved)	½	½	W. Casper & G. Littler (halved)
P. Alliss & C. O'Connor	0	1	A. Palmer & D. Marr (6 and 4)
B. J. Hunt & N. C. Coles (1 hole)	1	0	J. Boros & A. Lema

Four-Ballsl (afternoon)
P. Alliss & C. O'Connor (1 hole)	1	0	A. Palmer & D. Marr
D. C. Thomas & G. Wil	0	1	D. January & T. Jacobs (1 hole)
L. Platts & P. J. Butler (halved)	½	½	W. Casper & G. Littler (halved)
B. J. Hunt & N. C. Coles	0	1	K. Venturi & A. Lema (1 hole)

Singles (morning)
J. Hitchcock	0	1	A. Palmer (3 and 2)
L. Platts	0	1	J. Boros (4 and 2)
P. J. Butler	0	1	A. Lema (1 hole)
N. C. Coles	0	1	D. Marr (2 holes)
B. J. Hunt (2 holes)	1	0	G. Littler
D. C. Thomas	0	1	T. Jacobs (2 and 1)
P. Alliss (1 hole)	1	0	W. Casper
G. Will (halved)	½	½	D. January (halved)

Singles (afternoon)
C. O'Connor	0	1	A. Lema (6 and 4)
J. Hitchcock	0	1	J. Boros (2 and 1)
P. J. Butler	0	1	A. Palmer (2 holes)
P. Alliss (3 and 1)	1	0	K. Venturi
N. C. Coles (3 and 2)	1	0	W. Casper
G. Wil	0	1	G. Littler (2 and 1)
B. J. Hunt	0	1	D. Marr (1 hole)
L. Platts (1 hole)	1	0	T. Jacobs

GREAT BRITAIN & IRELAND 12½   19½ **UNITED STATES OF AMERICA**

1967: CHAMPIONS GOLF CLUB, HOUSTON, TEXAS, OCTOBER 20-22
Captains: D. J. Rees (GB), B. Hogan (USA)

GREAT BRITAIN & IRELAND   **UNITED STATES OF AMERICA**

Foursomes (morning)
B. G. C. Huggett & G. Wil (halved)	½	½	W. Casper & J. Boros (halved)
P. Alliss & C. O'Connor	0	1	A. Palmer & G. Dickinson (2 and1)
A. Jacklin & D. C. Thomas (4 and 3)	1	0	D. Sanders & G. Brewer
B. J. Hunt N. C. Coles	0	1	R. Nichols & J. Pott (6 and 5)

Foursomes (afternoon)
B. G. C. Huggett & G. Wil	0	1	W. Casper & J. Boros (1 hole)
M. Gregson & H. Boyle	0	1	G. Dickinson & A. Palmer (5 and 4)
A. Jacklin & D. C. Thomas (3 and 2)	1	0	G. Littler & A. Geiberger
P. Alliss & C. O'Connor	0	1	R. Nichols & J. Pott (2 and1)

Four-Balls (morning)
P. Alliss & C.O'Connor	0	1	W. Casper & G. Brewer (3 and 2)
B. J. Hunt & N. C. Coles	0	1	R. Nichols & J. Pott (1 hole)
A. Jacklin & D. C. Thomas	0	1	G. Littler & A. Geiberger (1 hole)
B. G. C. Huggett & G. Wil	0	1	G. Dickinson & D. Sanders (3 and 2)

Four-Balls (afternoon)
B. J. Hunt & N. C. Coles	0	1	W. Casper & G. Brewer (5 and 3)
P. Alliss & M. Gregson	0	1	G. Dickinson & D. Sanders (3 and 2)
G. Will & H. Boyle	0	1	A. Palmer & J. Boros (1 hole)
A. Jacklin & D. C. Thomas (halved)	½	½	G. Littler & A. Gelberger (halved)

Singles (morning)
H. Boyle	0	1	G. Brewer (4 and 3)
P. Alliss	0	1	W. Casper (2 and 1)
A. Jacklin	0	1	A. Palmer (3 and 2)
B. G. C. Huggett (1 hole)	1	0	J. Boros
N. C. Coles (2 and 1)	1	0	D. Sanders
M. Gregson	0	1	A. Geiberger (4 and 2)
D. C. Thomas (halved)	½	½	G. Littler (halved)
B. J. Hunt (halved)	½	½	R. Nichols (halved)

Singles (afternoon)
B. G. C. Huggett	0	1	A. Palmer (5 and 3)
P. Alliss (2 and 1)	1	0	G. Brewer
A. Jacklin	0	1	G. Dickinson (3 and 2)
C. O'Connor	0	1	R. Nichols (3 and 2)
G. Wil	0	1	J. Pott (3 and 1)
M. Gregson	0	1	A.Geiberger (2 and1)
B. J. Hunt (halved)	½	½	J. Boros (halved)
N. C. Coles (2 and 1)	1	0	D. Sanders

GREAT BRITAIN & IRELAND 8½   23½ **UNITED STATES OF AMERICA**

1969: ROYAL BIRKDALE, SOUTHPORT, SEPTEMBER 18-20
Captains: E. C. Brown (GB), S. Snead (USA)

GREAT BRITAIN & IRELAND   **UNITED STATES OF AMERICA**

Foursomes (morning)
N. C. Coles & B. G. C. Huggett (3 and 2)	1	0	M. Barber & R. Floyd
B. Gallacher & M. Bembridge (2 and1)	1	0	L. Trevino & K. Still
A. Jacklin & P. Townsend (3 and1)	1	0	D. Hill & T. Aaron
C. O'Connor & P. Alliss (halved)	½	½	W. Casper & F. Beard (halved)

Foursomes (afternoon)
N. C. Coles & B.G.C. Huggett	0	1	D. Hill & T. Aaron (1 hole)
B. Gallacher & M. Bembridge	0	1	L. Trevino & G. Littler (2 holes)
A. Jacklin & P. Townsend (1 hole)	1	0	W. Casper & F. Beard
P. J. Butler & B. J. Hunt	0	1	J. Nicklaus & D. Sikes (1 hole)

Four-Balls (morning)
C . O'Connor & P. Townsend (1 hole)	1	0	D. Hill & D. Douglass
B. G. C. Huggett & G. A. Caygill (halved)	½	½	R. Floyd & M. Barber (halved)
B. Barnes & P. Alliss	0	1	L. Trevino & G. Littler (1 hole)
A. Jacklin & N. C. Coles (1 hole)	1	0	J. Nicklaus & D. Sikes

Four-Balls (afternoon)
P. J. Butler & P. Townsend	0	1	W. Casper & F. Beard (2 holes)
B. G. C. Huggett & B. Gallacher	0	1	D. Hill & K. Still (2 and 1)
M. Bembridge & B. J. Hunt (halved)	½	½	T. Aaron & R. Floyd (halved)
A. Jacklin & N. C. Coles (halved)	½	½	L. Trevino & M. Barber (halved)

Singles (morning)
P. Alliss	0	1	L. Trevino (2 and 1)
P. Townsend	0	1	D. Hill (5 and 4)
N. C. Coles (1 hole)	1	0	T. Aaron
B. Barnes	0	1	W. Casper (1 hole)
C. O'Connor (5 and 4)	1	0	F. Beard
M. Bembridge (1 hole)	1	0	K. Still
P. J. Butler (1 hole)	1	0	R. Floyd
A.Jacklin (4 and 3)	1	0	J. Nicklaus

Singles (afternoon)
B. Barnes	0	1	D. Hill (4 and 2)
B. Gallacher (4 and 3)	1	0	L. Trevino
M. Bembridge	0	1	M. Barber (7 and 6)
P. J. Butler (3 and 2)	1	0	D. Douglass
N. C. Coles	0	1	D. Sikes (4 and 3)
C. O'Connor	0	1	G. Littler (2 and 1)
B. G. C. Huggett (halved)	½	½	W. Casper (halved)
A. Jacklin (halved)	½	½	J. Nicklaus (halved)

GREAT BRITAIN & IRELAND 16   16 **UNITED STATES OF AMERICA**

1971: OLD WARSON COUNTRY CLUB, ST. LOUIS, MISSOURI, SEPTEMBER 16-18

Captains: E. C. Brown (GB), J. Hebert (USA)

GREAT BRITAIN & IRELAND			UNITED STATES OF AMERICA

Foursomes (morning)

N. C. Coles & C. O'Connor (2 and 1)	1	0	W. Casper & M. Barber
P. Townsend & P. Oosterhuis	0	1	A. Palmer & G. Dickinson (2 holes)
B.G.C. Huggett & A. Jacklin (3 and 2)	1	0	J. Nicklaus & D. Stockton
M. Bembridge & P. J. Butler (1 hole)	1	0	C. Coody & F. Beard

Foursomes (afternoon)

H. Bannerman & B. Gallacher (2 and 1)	1	0	W. Casper & M. Barber
P. Townsend & P. Oosterhuis	0	1	A. Palmer & G. Dickinson (1 hole)
B. G. C. Huggett & A. Jacklin (halved)	½	½	L. Trevino & M. Rudolph (halved)
M. Bembridge & P. J. Butler	0	1	J. Nicklaus & J. C. Snead (5 and 3)

Four-Balls (morning)

C. O'Connor & B. Barnes	0	1	L. Trevino & M. Rudolph (2 and 1)
N. C. Coles & J. Garner	0	1	F. Beard & J. C. Snead (2 and 1)
P. Oosterhuis & B. Gallacher	0	1	A. Palmer & G. Dickinson (5 and 4)
P. Townsend & H. Bannerman	0	1	J. Nicklaus & G. Littler (2 and 1)

Four-Balls (afternoon)

B.Gallacher & P. Oosterhuis (1 hole)	1	0	L. Trevino & W. Casper
A. Jacklin & B. G. C. Huggett	0	1	G. Littler & J. C. Snead (2 and 1)
P. Townsend & H. Bannerman	0	1	A. Palmer & J. Nicklaus (1 hole)
N. C. Coles & C. O'Connor (halved)	½	½	C. Coody & F. Beard (halved)

Singles (morning)

A. Jacklin	0	1	L. Trevino (1 hole)
B. Gallacher (halved)	½	½	D. Stockton (halved)
B. Barnes (1 hole)	1	0	M. Rudolph
P. Oosterhuis (4 and 3)	1	0	G. Littler
P. Townsend	0	1	J. Nicklaus (3 and 2)
C. O'Connor	0	1	G. Dickinson (5 and 4)
H. Bannerman (halved)	½	½	A. Palmer (halved)
N. C. Coles (halved)	½	½	F. Beard (halved)

Singles (afternoon)

B. G. C. Huggett	0	1	L. Trevino (7 and 6)
A. Jacklin	0	1	J. C. Snead (1 hole)
B. Barnes (2 and 1)	1	0	M. Barber
P. Townsend	0	1	D. Stockton (1 hole)
B. Gallacher (2 and 1)	1	0	C. Coody
N. C. Coles	0	1	J. Nicklaus (5 and 3)
P. Oosterhuis (3 and 2)	1	0	A. Palmer
H. Bannerman (2 and 1)	1	0	G. Dickinson

GREAT BRITAIN & IRELAND 13½ 18½ UNITED STATES OF AMERICA

1973: MUIRFIELD, SCOTLAND, SEPTEMBER 20-22

Captains: B. J. Hunt (GB), J. Burke (USA)

GREAT BRITAIN & IRELAND			UNITED STATES OF AMERICA

Foursomes (morning)

B. W. Barnes & B. J. Gallacher (1 hole)	1	0	L. Trevino & W. J. Casper
C. O'Connor & N. C. Coles (3 and 2)	1	0	T. Weiskopf & J. C. Snead
A. Jacklin & P. A. Oosterhuis (halved)	½	½	J. Rodriguez & L. Graham (halved)
M. E. Bembridge & E. Polland	0	1	J. W. Nicklaus & A. Palmer (6 and 5)

Four-Balls (afternoon)

B. W. Barnes & B. J. Gallacher (5 and 4)	1	0	T Aaron & G Brewer
M.Bembridge &B.G.C. Huggett (3 and 1)	1	0	A. Palmer & J. W. Nicklaus
A. Jacklin & P. A. Oosterhuis (3 and 1)	1	0	T. Weiskopf & W. J. Casper
C. O'Connor & N. C. Coles	0	1	L. Trevino & H. Blancas (2 and 1)

Foursomes (morning)

B. W. Barnes & P. J. Butler	0	1	J. W. Nicklaus & T. Weiskopf (1 hole)
P. A. Oosterhuis & A. Jacklin (2 holes)	1	0	A. Palmer & D. Hill
M.Bembridge &B.G.C. Huggett (5 and 4)	1	0	J. Rodriguez & L. Graham
N. C. Coles & C. O'Connor	0	1	L. Trevino & W. Casper (2 and1)

Four-Balls (afternoon)

B. W. Barnes & P. J. Butler	0	1	J. C. Snead & A. Palmer (2 holes)
A. Jacklin & P. A. Oosterhuis	0	1	G. Brewer & W. J. Casper (3 and 2)
C. Clark & E. Polland	0	1	J. W. Nicklaus & T. Weiskopf (3 and 2)
M.E.Bembridge & B.G.C. Huggett (halved)	½	½	L. Trevino & H. Blancas (halved)

Singles (morning)

B. W. Barnes	0	1	W. J. Casper (2 and 1)
B. J. Gallacher	0	1	T. Weiskopf (3 and 1)
P. J. Butler	0	1	H. Blancas (5 and 4)
A. Jacklin (2 and 1)	1	0	T. Aaron
N. C. Coles (halved)	½	½	G. Brewer (halved)
C. O'Connor	0	1	J. C. Snead (1 hole)
M. E. Bembridge (halved)	½	½	J. W. Nicklaus (halved)
P. A. Oosterhuis (halved)	½	½	L. Trevino (halved)

Singles (afternoon)

B. G. C. Huggett (4 and 2)	1	0	H. Blancas
B. W. Barnes	0	1	J. C. Snead (3 and 1)
B. J. Gallacher	0	1	G. Brewer (6 and 5)
A. Jacklin	0	1	W. J. Casper (2 and 1)
N. C. Coles	0	1	L. Trevino (6 and 5)
C. O'Connor (halved)	½	½	T. Weiskopf (halved)
M. E. Bembridge	0	1	J. W. Nicklaus (2 holes)
P. A. Oosterhuis (4 and 2)	1	0	A. Palmer

GREAT BRITAIN & IRELAND 13 19 UNITED STATES OF AMERICA

1975: LAUREL VALLEY GOLF CLUB, LIGONIER, PENNSYLVANIA, SEPTEMBER 19-21

Captains: B.J. Hunt (GB), A. Palmer (USA)

GREAT BRITAIN & IRELAND			UNITED STATES OF AMERICA

Foursomes (morning)

B. W. Barnes & B. J. Gallacher	0	1	J. W. Nicklaus & T. Weiskopf (5 and 4)
N. Wood & M. Bembridge	0	1	G. Littler & H. Irwin (4 and 3)
A. Jacklin & P. Oosterhuis	0	1	A. Geiberger & J. Miller (3 and 1)
T. Horton & J. O'Leary	0	1	L. Trevino & J. C. Snead (2 and 1)

Four-Balls (afternoon)

P. Oosterhuis & A. Jacklin (2 and 1)	1	0	W. J. Casper & R. Floyd
E. Darcy & C. O'Connor, Jnr	0	1	T. Weiskopf & L. Graham (3 and 2)
B.W.Barnes & B.J.Gallacher (halved)	½	½	J. W. Nicklaus & R. Murphy (halved)
T. Horton & J. O'Leary	0	1	L. Trevino & H. Irwin (2 and 1)

Four-Balls (morning)

P. Oosterhuis & A. Jacklin (halved)	½	½	W.J. Casper & J. Miller (halved)
T. Horton & N. Wood	0	1	J. W. Nicklaus & J. C. Snead (4 and 2)
B. W. Barnes & B. J. Gallacher	0	1	G. Littler & L. Graham (5 and 3)
E. Darcy & G. L. Hunt (halved)	½	½	A. Geiberger & R. Floyd (halved)

Foursomes (afternoon)

A. Jacklin & B. G. C. Huggett (3 and 2)	1	0	L. Trevino & R. Murphy
C. O'Connor, Jnr & J. O'Leary	0	1	T. Weiskopf & J. Miller (5 and 3)
P. Oosterhuis & M. Bembridge	0	1	H. Irwin & W. J. Casper (3 and 2)
E. Darcy & G. L. Hunt	0	1	A. Geiberger & L. Graham (3 and 2)

Singles (morning)

A. Jacklin	0	1	R. Murphy (2 and 1)
P. Oosterhuis (2 holes)	1	0	J. Miller
B. J. Gallacher (halved)	½	½	L. Trevino (halved)
T. Horton (halved)	½	½	H. Irwin (halved)
B. G. C. Huggett	0	1	G. Littler (4 and 2)
E. Darcy	0	1	W. J. Casper (3 and 2)
G. L. Hunt	0	1	T. Weiskopf (5 and 3)
B. W. Barnes (4 and 2)	1	0	J. W. Nicklaus

Singles (afternoon)

A. Jacklin	0	1	R. Floyd (1 hole)
P. Oosterhuis (3 and 2)	1	0	J. C. Snead
B. J. Gallacher (halved)	½	½	A. Geiberger (halved)
T. Horton (2 and 1)	1	0	L. Graham
J. O'Leary	0	1	H. Irwin (2 and 1)
M. Bembridge	0	1	R. Murphy (2 and 1)
N. Wood (2 and 1)	1	0	L. Trevino
B. W. Barnes (2 and 1)	1	0	J. W. Nicklaus

GREAT BRITAIN & IRELAND 11 21 UNITED STATES OF AMERICA

1977: ROYAL LYTHAM & ST ANNES, ST ANNES, SEPTEMBER 15-17

Captains: B. Huggett (GB), D. Finsterwald (USA)

GREAT BRITAIN & IRELAND			UNITED STATES OF AMERICA

Foursomes

B. J. Gallacher & B. W. Barnes	0	1	L. Wadkins & H. Irwin (3 and 1)
N. C. Coles & P. Dawson	0	1	D. Stockton & J. McGee (1 hole)
N. Faldo & P. Oosterhuis (2 and 1)	1	0	R. Floyd & L. Graham
E. Darcy & A. Jacklin (halved)	½	½	E. Sneed & D. January (halved)
T. Horton & M. James	0	1	J. W. Nicklaus & T. Watson (5 and 4)

Four-Balls

B. W. Barnes & T. Horton	0	1	T. Watson & H. Green (5 and 4)
N. C. Coles & P. Dawson	0	1	E. Sneed & L. Wadkins (5 and 3)
N. Faldo & P. Oosterhuis (3 and 1)	1	0	J. W. Nicklaus & R. Floyd
A. Jacklin & E. Darcy	0	1	D. Hill & D. Stockton (5 and 3)
M. James & K. Brown	0	1	H. Irwin & L. Graham (1 hole)

Singles

H. Clark	0	1	L. Wadkins (4 and 3)
N. C. Coles	0	1	L. Graham (5 and 3)
P. Dawson (5 and 4)	1	0	D. January
B. W. Barnes (1 hole)	1	0	H. Irwin
T. Horton	0	1	D. Hill 5 and 4)
B. J. Gallacher (1 hole)	1	0	J. W. Nicklaus
E. Darcy	0	1	H. Green (1 hole)
M. James	0	1	R. Floyd (2 and 1)
N. Faldo (1 hole)	1	0	T. Watson
P. Oosterhuis (2 holes)	1	0	J. McGee

GREAT BRITAIN & IRELAND 7½ 12½ UNITED STATES OF AMERICA

The Ryder Cup
1979-1985

1979: THE GREENBRIER, WEST VIRGINIA, SEPTEMBER 14-16
Captains: J. Jacobs (EUROPE), W. Casper (USA)

EUROPE   **UNITED STATES OF AMERICA**

Four-Balls (morning)
A. Garrido & S. Ballesteros   0   1   L. Wadkins & L. Nelson (2 and 1)
K. Brown & M. James   0   1   L. Trevino & F. Zoeller (3 and 2)
P. Oosterhuis & N. Faldo   0   1   A. Bean & L. Elder (2 and 1)
B. Gallacher & B. Barnes (2 and 1)   1   0   H. Irwin & J. Mahaffey

Foursomes (afternoon)
K. Brown & D. Smyth   0   1   H. Irwin & T. Kite (7 and 6)
S. Ballesteros & A. Garrido (3 and 2)   1   0   F. Zoeller & H. Green
A. Lyle & A. Jacklin (halved)   ½   ½   L. Trevino & G. Morgan (halved)
B. Gallacher & B. Barnes   0   1   L. Wadkins & L. Nelson (4 and 3)

Foursomes (morning)
A. Jacklin & A. Lyle (5 and 4)   1   0   L. Elder & J. Mahaffey
N. Faldo & P. Oosterhuis (6 and 5)   1   0   A. Bean & T. Kite
B. Gallacher & B. Barnes (2 and 1)   1   0   F. Zoeller & M. Hayes
S. Ballesteros & A. Garrido   0   1   L. Wadkins & L. Nelson (3 and 2)

Four-Balls (afternoon)
S. Ballesteros & A. Garrido   0   1   L. Wadkins & L. Nelson (5 and 4)
A. Jacklin & A. Lyle   0   1   H. Irwin & T. Kite (1 hole)
B. Gallacher & B. Barnes (3 and 2)   1   0   L. Trevino & F. Zoeller
N. Faldo & P. Oosterhuis (1 hole)   1   0   L. Elder & M. Hayes

Singles (morning)
B. Gallacher (3 and 2)   1   0   L. Wadkins
S. Ballesteros   0   1   L. Nelson (3 and 2)
A. Jacklin   0   1   T. Kite (1 hole)
A Garrido   0   1   M. Hayes (1 hole)
M. King   0   1   A. Bean (4 and 3)
B. Barnes   0   1   J. Mahaffey (1 hole)

Singles (afternoon)
N. Faldo (3 and 2)   1   0   L. Elder
D. Smyth   0   1   H. Irwin (5 and 3)
P. Oosterhuis   0   1   H. Green (2 holes)
K. Brown (1 hole)   1   0   F. Zoeller
A. Lyle   0   1   L. Trevino (2 and 1)
*M. James   ½   ½   G. Morgan

EUROPE 11   17 **UNITED STATES OF AMERICA**

James injured, match not played

1981: WALTON HEATH, SURREY, SEPTEMBER 18-20
Captains: J. Jacobs (EUROPE), D. Marr (USA)

EUROPE   **UNITED STATES OF AMERICA**

Foursomes (morning)
B. Langer & M. Piñero   0   1   L. Trevino & L. Nelson (1 hole)
A. Lyle & M. James (2 and 1)   1   0   B. Rogers & B. Lietzke
B. Gallacher & D. Smyth (3 and 2)   1   0   H. Irwin & R. Floyd
P. Oosterhuis & N. Faldo   0   1   T. Watson & J. Nicklaus (4 and 3)

Four-Balls (afternoon)
S. Torrance & H. Clark (halved)   ½   ½   T. Kite & J. Miller (halved)
A. Lyle & M. James (3 and 2)   1   0   B. Crenshaw & J. Pate
D. Smyth & J. M. Cañizares (6 and 5)   1   0   B. Rogers & B. Lietzke
B. Gallacher & E. Darcy   0   1   H. Irwin & R. Floyd (2 and 1)

Four-Balls (morning)
N. Faldo & S. Torrance   0   1   L. Trevino & J. Pate (7 and 5)
A. Lyle & M. James   0   1   L. Nelson & T. Kite (1 hole)
B. Langer & M. Piñero (2 and 1)   1   0   R. Floyd & H. Irwin
J. M. Cañizares & D. Smyth   0   1   J. Nicklaus & T. Watson (3 and 2)

Foursomes (afternoon)
P. Oosterhuis & S. Torrance   0   1   L. Trevino & J. Pate (2 and 1)
B. Langer & M. Piñero   0   1   J. Nicklaus & T. Watson (3 and 2)
A. Lyle & M. James   0   1   B. Rogers & R. Floyd (3 and 2)
D. Smyth & B. Gallacher   0   1   T. Kite & L. Nelson (3 and 2)

Singles
S. Torrance   0   1   L. Trevino (5 and 3)
A. Lyle   0   1   T. Kite (3 and 2)
B. Gallacher (halved)   ½   ½   B. Rogers (halved)
M. James   0   1   L. Nelson (2 holes)
D. Smyth   0   1   B. Crenshaw (6 and 4)
B. Langer (halved)   ½   ½   B. Lietzke (halved)
M. Piñero (4 and 2)   1   0   J. Pate
J. M. Cañizares   0   1   H. Irwin (1 hole)
N. Faldo (2 and 1)   1   0   J. Miller
H. Clark (4 and 3)   1   0   T. Watson
P. Oosterhuis   0   1   R. Floyd (1 hole)
E. Darcy   0   1   J. Nicklaus (5 and 3)

EUROPE 9½   18½ **UNITED STATES OF AMERICA**

1983: PGA NATIONAL GOLF CLUB, FLORIDA, OCTOBER 14-16
Captains: A. Jacklin (Europe), J. Nicklaus (USA)

EUROPE   **UNITED STATES OF AMERICA**

Foursomes (morning)
B. Gallacher & A. Lyle   0   1   T. Watson & B. Crenshaw (5 and 4)
N. Faldo & B. Langer (4 and 2)   1   0   L. Wadkins & C. Stadler
J. M. Cañizares & S. Torrance (4 and 3)   1   0   R. Floyd & B. Gilder
S. Ballesteros & P. Way   0   1   T. Kite & C. Peete (2 and 1)

Four-Balls (afternoon)
B. Waites & K. Brown (2 and 1)   1   0   G. Morgan & F. Zoeller
N. Faldo & B. Langer   0   1   T. Watson & J. Haas (2 and 1)
S. Ballesteros & P. Way (1 hole)   1   0   R. Floyd & C. Strange
S. Torrance & I. Woosnam (halved)   ½   ½   B. Crenshaw & C. Peete (halved)

Four-Balls (morning)
B. Waites & K. Brown   0   1   L. Wadkins & C. Stadler (1 hole)
N. Faldo & B. Langer (4 and 2)   1   0   B. Crenshaw & C. Peete
S. Ballesteros & P. Way (halved)   ½   ½   G. Morgan & J. Haas (halved)
S. Torrance & I. Woosnam   0   1   T. Watson & B. Gilder (5 and 4)

Foursomes (afternoon)
N. Faldo & B. Langer (3 and 2)   1   0   T. Kite & R. Floyd
S. Torrance & J. M. Cañizares   0   1   G. Morgan & L. Wadkins (7 and 5)
S. Ballesteros & P. Way (2 and 1)   1   0   T. Watson & B. Gilder
B. Waites & K. Brown   0   1   J. Haas & C. Strange (3 and 2)

Singles
S. Ballesteros (halved)   ½   ½   F. Zoeller (halved)
N. Faldo (2 and 1)   1   0   J. Haas
B. Langer (2 holes)   1   0   G. Morgan
G. J. Brand   0   1   B. Gilder (2 holes)
A. Lyle   0   1   B. Crenshaw (3 and 1)
B. Waites   0   1   C. Peete (1 hole)
P. Way (2 and 1)   1   0   C. Strange
S. Torrance (halved)   ½   ½   T. Kite (halved)
I. Woosnam   0   1   C. Stadler (3 and 2)
J. M. Cañizares (halved)   ½   ½   L. Wadkins (halved)
K. Brown (4 and 3)   1   0   R. Floyd
B. Gallacher   0   1   T. Watson (2 and 1)

EUROPE 13½   14½ **UNITED STATES OF AMERICA**

1985: THE DE VERE BELFRY, W. MIDLANDS, SEPTEMBER 13-15
Captains: A. Jacklin (Europe), L. Trevino (USA)

EUROPE   **UNITED STATES OF AMERICA**

Foursomes (morning)
S. Ballesteros & M. Piñero (2 and 1)   1   0   C. Strange & M. O'Meara
B. Langer & N. Faldo   0   1   C. Peete & T.Kite (3 and 2)
A. Lyle & K. Brown   0   1   L. Wadkins & R. Floyd (4 and 3)
H. Clark & S. Torrance   0   1   C. Stadler & H. Sutton (3 and 2)

Four-Balls (afternoon)
P. Way & I. Woosnam (1 hole)   1   0   F. Zoeller & H. Green
S. Ballesteros & M. Piñero (2 and 1)   1   0   A. North & P. Jacobsen
B. Langer & J. M. Cañizares (halved)   ½   ½   C. Stadler & H. Sutton (halved)
S. Torrance & H. Clark   0   1   R. Floyd & L. Wadkins (1 hole)

Four-Balls (morning)
S. Torrance & H. Clark (2 and 1)   1   0   T. Kite & A. North
P. Way & I. Woosnam (4 and 3)   1   0   H. Green & F. Zoeller
S. Ballesteros & M. Piñero   0   1   M. O'Meara & L. Wadkins (3 and 2)
B. Langer & A. Lyle (halved)   ½   ½   C. Stadler & C. Strange (halved)

Foursomes (afternoon)
J. M. Cañizares & J. Rivero (7 and 5)   1   0   T. Kite & C. Peete
S. Ballesteros & M. Piñero (5 and 4)   1   0   C. Stadler & H. Sutton
P. Way & I. Woosnam   0   1   C. Strange & P. Jacobsen (4 and 2)
B. Langer & K. Brown (3 and 2)   1   0   R. Floyd & L. Wadkins

Singles
M. Piñero (3 and 1)   1   0   L. Wadkins
I. Woosnam   0   1   C. Stadler (2 and 1)
P. Way (2 holes)   1   0   R. Floyd
S. Ballesteros (halved)   ½   ½   T. Kite (halved)
A. Lyle (3 and 2)   1   0   P. Jacobsen
B. Langer (5 and 4)   1   0   H. Sutton
S. Torrance (1 hole)   1   0   A. North
H. Clark (1 hole)   1   0   M. O'Meara
N. Faldo   0   1   H. Green (3 and 1)
J. Rivero   0   1   C. Peete (1 hole)
J. M. Cañizares (2 holes)   1   0   F. Zoeller
K. Brown   0   1   C. Strange (4 and 2)

EUROPE 16½   11½ **UNITED STATES OF AMERICA**

1987: MUIRFIELD VILLAGE, COLUMBUS, OHIO, SEPTEMBER 25-27
Captains: A. Jacklin (Europe), J.W. Nicklaus (USA)

EUROPE UNITED STATES OF AMERICA

Foursomes (morning)
S. Torrance & H. Clark 0 1 C. Strange & T. Kite (4 and 2)
K. Brown & B. Langer 0 1 H. Sutton & D. Pohl (2 and 1)
N. Faldo & I. Woosnam (2 holes) 1 0 L. Wadkins & L. Mize
S. Ballesteros & J. M. Olazábal (1 hole) 1 0 L. Nelson & P. Stewart

Four-Balls (afternoon)
G. Brand Jnr. & J. Rivero (3 and 2) 1 0 B. Crenshaw & S. Simpson
A. Lyle & B. Langer (1 hole) 1 0 A. Bean & M. Calcavecchia
N. Faldo & I. Woosnam (2 and 1) 1 0 H. Sutton & D. Pohl
S. Ballesteros & J. M. Olazábal (2 and 1) 1 0 C. Strange & T. Kite

Foursomes (morning)
J. Rivero & G. Brand Jnr 0 1 C. Strange & T. Kite (3 and 1)
N. Faldo & I. Woosnam (halved) ½ ½ H. Sutton & L. Mize (halved)
A. Lyle & B. Langer (2 and 1) 1 0 L. Wadkins & L. Nelson
S. Ballesteros & J. M. Olazábal (1 hole) 1 0 B. Crenshaw & P. Stewart

Four-Balls (afternoon)
N. Faldo & I. Woosnam (5 and 4) 1 0 C. Strange & T. Kite
E. Darcy & G. Brand Jnr 0 1 A. Bean & P. Stewart (3 and 2)
S. Ballesteros & J. M. Olazábal 0 1 H. Sutton & L. Mize (2 and 1)
A. Lyle & B. Langer (1 hole) 1 0 L. Wadkins & L. Nelson

Singles
I. Woosnam 0 1 A. Bean (1 hole)
H. Clark (1 hole) 1 0 D. Pohl
S. Torrance (halved) ½ ½ L. Mize (halved)
N. Faldo 0 1 M. Calcavecchia (1 hole)
J. M. Olazábal 0 1 P. Stewart (2 holes)
E. Darcy (1 hole) 1 0 B. Crenshaw
J. Rivero 0 1 S. Simpson (2 and 1)
B. Langer (halved) ½ ½ L. Nelson (halved)
A. Lyle 0 1 T. Kite (3 and 2)
S. Ballesteros (2 and 1) 1 0 C. Strange
G. Brand Jnr (halved) ½ ½ H. Sutton (halved)
K. Brown 0 1 L. Wadkins (3 and 2)

EUROPE 15 13 UNITED STATES OF AMERICA

1989: THE DE VERE BELFRY, W. MIDLANDS, SEPTEMBER 27-29
Captains: A. Jacklin (Europe), R. Floyd (USA)

EUROPE UNITED STATES OF AMERICA

Foursomes (morning)
N. Faldo & I. Woosnam (halved) ½ ½ T. Kite & C. Strange (halved)
H. Clark & M. James 0 1 L. Wadkins & P. Stewart (1 hole)
S. Ballesteros & J. M.Olazábal (halved) ½ ½ T. Watson & C. Beck (halved)
B. Langer & R. Rafferty 0 1 M. Calcavecchia & K. Green (2 and 1)

Four-Balls (afternoon)
S. Torrance & G. Brand Jnr. (1 hole) 1 0 C. Strange & P. Azinger
H. Clark & M. James (3 and 2) 1 0 F. Couples & L. Wadkins
N. Faldo & I. Woosnam (2 holes) 1 0 M. Calcavecchia & M. McCumber
S. Ballesteros & J. M. Olazábal (6 and 5) 1 0 T. Watson & M. O'Meara

Foursomes (morning)
I. Woosnam & N. Faldo (3 and 2) 1 0 L. Wadkins & P. Stewart
G. Brand Jnr. & S. Torrance 0 1 C. Beck & P. Azinger (4 and 3)
C. OConnor Jnr. & R. Rafferty 0 1 M. Calcavecchia & K. Green (3 and 2)
S. Ballesteros & J. M. Olazábal 0 1 T. Kite & C. Strange

Four-Balls (afternoon)
N. Faldo & I. Woosnam 0 1 C. Beck & P. Azinger (2 and 1)
B. Langer & J. M. Cañizares 0 1 T. Kite & M. McCumber (2 and 1)
H. Clark & M. James (1 hole) 1 0 P. Stewart & C. Strange
S. Ballesteros & J. M. Olazábal (4 and 2) 1 0 M. Calcavecchia & K. Green

Singles
S. Ballesteros 0 1 P. Azinger (1 hole)
B. Langer 0 1 C. Beck (3 & 1)
J. M. Olazábal (1 hole) 1 0 P. Stewart
R. Rafferty (1 hole) 1 0 M. Calcavecchia
H. Clark 0 1 T. Kite (8 and 7)
M. James (3 and 2) 1 0 M. O'Meara
C. OConnor Jnr. (1 hole) 1 0 F. Couples
J. M. Cañizares (1 hole) 1 0 K. Green
G. Brand Jnr 0 1 M. McCumber (1 hole)
S. Torrance 0 1 T. Watson (3 and 1)
N. Faldo 0 1 L. Wadkins (1 hole)
I. Woosnam 0 1 C. Strange (2 holes)

EUROPE 14 14 UNITED STATES OF AMERICA

1991: KIAWAH ISLAND, SOUTH CAROLINA, SEPTEMBER 27-29
Captains: B. Gallacher (Europe), D. Stockton (USA)

EUROPE UNITED STATES OF AMERICA

Foursomes (morning)
S. Ballesteros & J. M. Olazábal (2 and 1) 1 0 P. Azinger & C. Beck
B. Langer & M. James 0 1 R. Floyd & F. Couples (2 and 1)
D. Gilford & C. Montgomerie 0 1 L. Wadkins & H. Irwin (4 and 2)
N Faldo & I. Woosnam 0 1 P. Stewart & M. Calcavecchia (1 hole)

Four-Balls (afternoon)
S. Torrance & D. Feherty (halved) ½ ½ L. Wadkins & M. O'Meara (halved)
S. Ballesteros & J. M. Olazábal (2 and 1) 1 0 P. Azinger & C. Beck
S. Richardson & M. James (5 and 4) 1 0 C. Pavin & M. Calcavecchia
N. Faldo & I. Woosnam 0 1 R. Floyd & F. Couples (5 and 3)

Foursomes (morning)
S. Torrance & D. Feherty 0 1 H. Irwin & L. Wadkins (4 and 2)
M. James & S. Richardson 0 1 M. Calcavecchia & P. Stewart (1 hole)
N. Faldo & D. Gilford 0 1 P. Azinger & M. O'Meara (7 and 6)
S. Ballesteros & J. M. Olazábal (3 and 2) 1 0 F. Couples & R. Floyd

Four-Balls (afternoon)
I. Woosnam & P. Broadhurst (2 and 1) 1 0 P. Azinger & H. Irwin
B. Langer & C. Montgomerie (2 and 1) 1 0 S. Pate & C. Pavin
M. James & S. Richardson (3 and 1) 1 0 L. Wadkins & W. Levi
S. Ballesteros & J. M. Olazábal (halved) ½ ½ F. Couples & P. Stewart (halved)

Singles
N. Faldo (2 holes) 1 0 R. Floyd
D. Feherty (2 and 1) 1 0 P. Stewart
C. Montgomerie (halved) ½ ½ M. Calcavecchia (halved)
J. M. Olazábal 0 1 P. Azinger (2 holes)
S. Richardson 0 1 C. Pavin (2 and 1)
S. Ballesteros (3 and 2) 1 0 W. Levi
I. Woosnam 0 1 C. Beck (3 and 1)
P. Broadhurst (3 and 1) 1 0 M. O'Meara
S. Torrance 0 1 F. Couples (3 and 2)
M. James 0 1 L. Wadkins (3 and 2)
B. Langer (halved) ½ ½ H. Irwin (halved)
D. Gilford (halved) ½ ½ S. Pate* (halved)

EUROPE 13½ 14½ UNITED STATES OF AMERICA

Pate withdrawn at start of day

1993: THE DE VERE BELFRY, W. MIDLANDS, SEPTEMBER 24-26
Captains: B. Gallacher (Europe), T. Watson (USA)

EUROPE UNITED STATES OF AMERICA

Foursomes (morning)
S. Torrance & M. James 0 1 L. Wadkins & C. Pavin (4 & 3)
I. Woosnam & B. Langer (7 & 5) 1 0 P. Azinger & P. Stewart
S. Ballesteros & J. M. Olazábal 0 1 T. Kite & D. Love III (2 & 1)
N. Faldo & C. Montgomerie (4 & 3) 1 0 R. Floyd & F. Couples

Four-Balls (afternoon)
I. Woosnam & P. Baker (1 hole) 1 0 J. Gallagher Jnr & L. Janzen
B. Langer & B. Lane 0 1 L. Wadkins & C. Pavin (4 & 2)
N. Faldo & C. Montgomerie (halved) ½ ½ P. Azinger & F. Couples (halved)
S. Ballesteros & J. M. Olazábal (4 & 3) 1 0 D. Love III & T. Kite

Foursomes (morning)
N. Faldo & C. Montgomerie (3 & 2) 1 0 L. Wadkins & C. Pavin
B. Langer & I. Woosnam (2 & 1) 1 0 F. Couples & P. Azinger
P. Baker & B. Lane 0 1 R .Floyd & P. Stewart (3 & 2)
S. Ballesteros & J. M. Olazábal (2 & 1) 1 0 D. Love III & T. Kite

Four-Balls (afternoon)
N. Faldo & C. Montgomerie 0 1 J. Cook & C. Beck (2 holes)
M. James & C. Rocca 0 1 C. Pavin & J. Gallagher Jnr (5 & 4)
I. Woosnam & P. Baker (6 & 5) 1 0 F. Couples & P. Azinger
J. M. Olazábal & J. Haeggman 0 1 R. Floyd & P. Stewart (2 & 1)

Singles
I. Woosnam (halved) ½ ½ F. Couples (halved)
B. Lane 0 1 C. Beck (1 hole)
C. Montgomerie (1 hole) 1 0 L. Janzen
P. Baker (2 holes) 1 0 C. Pavin
J. Haeggman (1 hole) 1 0 J. Cook
M. James 0 1 P. Stewart (3 & 2)
C. Rocca 0 1 D. Love III (1 hole)
S. Ballesteros 0 1 J. Gallagher Jnr (3 & 2)
J. M. Olazábal 0 1 R. Floyd (2 holes)
B. Langer 0 1 T. Kite (5 & 3)
N. Faldo (halved) ½ ½ P. Azinger (halved)
S. Torrance (halved)* ½ ½ L. Wadkins (halved)

EUROPE 13 15 UNITED STATES OF AMERICA

Torrance withdrawn at start of day

The Ryder Cup
1995-2002

1995: OAK HILL COUNTRY CLUB, ROCHESTER, NEW YORK, SEPTEMBER 22-24
Captains: B. Gallacher (EUROPE), L. Wadkins (USA)

EUROPE   **UNITED STATES OF AMERICA**

Foursomes (morning)
EUROPE			UNITED STATES OF AMERICA
N. Faldo & C. Montgomerie	0	1	C. Pavin & T. Lehman (1hole)
S. Torrance & C. Rocca (3 & 2)	1	0	J. Haas & F. Couples
H. Clark & M. James	0	1	D. Love III & J. Maggert (4 & 3)
B. Langer & P.-U. Johansson (1 hole)	1	0	B. Crenshaw & C. Strange

Four-Balls (afternoon)
D. Gilford & S. Ballesteros (4 & 3)	1	0	B. Faxon & P. Jacobsen
S. Torrance & C. Rocca	0	1	J. Maggert & L. Roberts (6 & 5)
N. Faldo & C. Montgomerie	0	1	F. Couples & D. Love III (3 & 2)
B. Langer & P.-U. Johansson	0	1	C. Pavin & P. Mickelson (6 & 4)

Foursomes (morning)
N. Faldo & C. Montgomerie (4 & 2)	1	0	C. Strange & J. Haas
S. Torrance & C. Rocca (6 & 5)	1	0	D. Love III & J. Maggert
I. Woosnam & P. Walton	0	1	L. Roberts & .P Jacobsen (1 hole)
B. Langer & D. Gilford (4 & 3)	1	0	C. Pavin & T. Lehman

Four-Balls (afternoon)
S. Torrance & C. Montgomerie	0	1	B. Faxon & F. Couples (4 & 2)
I. Woosnam & C. Rocca (3 & 2)	1	0	D. Love III & B. Crenshaw
S. Ballesteros & D. Gilford	0	1	J. Haas & P. Mickelson (3 & 2)
N. Faldo & B. Langer	0	1	C. Pavin & L. Roberts (1 hole)

Singles
S. Ballesteros	0	1	T. Lehman (4 & 3)
H. Clark (1 hole)	1	0	P. Jacobsen
M. James (4 & 3)	1	0	J. Maggert
I. Woosnam (halved)	½	½	F. Couples (halved)
C. Rocca	0	1	D. Love III (3 & 2)
D. Gilford (1 hole)	1	0	B. Faxon
C. Montgomerie (3 & 1)	1	0	B. Crenshaw
N. Faldo (1 hole)	1	0	C. Strange
S. Torrance (2 & 1)	1	0	L. Roberts
B. Langer	0	1	C. Pavin (3 & 2)
P. Walton (1 hole)	1	0	J. Haas
P.-U. Johansson	0	1	P. Mickelson (2 & 1)

EUROPE 14½ 13½ **UNITED STATES OF AMERICA**

1997: CLUB DE GOLF VALDERRAMA, SOTOGRANDE, SPAIN, SEPTEMBER 26-28
Captains: S. Ballesteros (EUROPE), T.Kite (USA)

EUROPE   **UNITED STATES OF AMERICA**

Four-Balls (morning)
EUROPE			UNITED STATES OF AMERICA
J. M. Olazábal & C. Rocca (1 hole)	1	0	D. Love III & P. Mickelson
N. Faldo & L. Westwood	0	1	F. Couples & B. Faxon (1 hole)
J. Parnevik & P-U. Johansson (1 hole)	1	0	T. Lehman & J. Furyk
B. Langer & C. Montgomerie	0	1	T. Woods & M. O'Meara (3&2)

Foursomes (afternoon)
J. M. Olazábal & C. Rocca	0	1	S. Hoch & L. Janzen (1 hole)
B. Langer & C. Montgomerie (5&3)	1	0	T. Woods & M. O'Meara
N. Faldo & L. Westwood (3&2)	1	0	J. Leonard & J. Maggert
I. Garrido & J. Parnevik (halved)	½	½	P. Mickelson & T. Lehman (halved)

Four-Balls (morning)
C. Montgomerie & D. Clarke (1 hole)	1	0	F. Couples & D. Love III
I. Woosnam & T. Björn (2&1)	1	0	J. Leonard & B. Faxon
N. Faldo & L. Westwood (2&1)	1	0	T. Woods & M. O'Meara
J. M. Olazábal & I. Garrido (halved)	½	½	P. Mickleson & T. Lehman (halved)

Foursomes (afternoon)
C. Montgomerie & B. Langer (1 hole)	1	0	L. Janzen & J. Furyk
N. Faldo & L. Westwood	0	1	S. Hoch & J. Maggert (2&1)
J. Parnevik & I. Garrido (halved)	½	½	T. Woods & J. Leonard (halved)
J. M. Olazábal & C. Rocca (5&4)	1	0	F. Couples & D. Love III

Singles
I. Woosnam	0	1	F. Couples (8&7)
P-U. Johansson (3&2)	1	0	D. Love III
C. Rocca (4&2)	1	0	T. Woods
T. Björn (halved)	½	½	J. Leonard (halved)
D. Clarke	0	1	P. Mickelson (2&1)
J. Parnevik	0	1	M. O'Meara (5&4)
J. M. Olazábal	0	1	L. Janzen (1 hole)
B. Langer (2&1)	1	0	B. Faxon
L. Westwood	0	1	J. Maggert (3&2)
C. Montgomerie (halved)	½	½	S. Hoch (halved)
N. Faldo	0	1	J. Furyk (3&2)
I. Garrido	0	1	T. Lehman (7&6)

EUROPE 14½ 13½ **UNITED STATES OF AMERICA**

1999: THE COUNTRY CLUB, BROOKLINE, MASSACHUSETTS, SEPTEMBER 24-26
Captains: M. James (EUROPE), B.Crenshaw (USA)

EUROPE   **UNITED STATES OF AMERICA**

Foursomes (morning)
EUROPE			UNITED STATES OF AMERICA
C. Montgomerie & P. Lawrie (3&2)	1	0	D. Duval & P. Mickelson
J. Parnevik & S. Garcia (2&1)	1	0	T. Lehman & T. Woods
M. A. Jiménez & P. Harrington (halved)	½	½	D. Love III & P. Stewart (halved)
D. Clarke & L. Westwood	0	1	H. Sutton & J. Maggert (3&2)

Four-Balls (afternoon)
C. Montgomerie & P. Lawrie (halved)	½	½	D. Love III & J. Leonard (halved)
J. Parnevik & S. Garcia (1 hole)	1	0	P. Mickelson & J. Furyk
M. A. Jiménez & J. M. Olazábal (2&1)	1	0	H. Sutton & J. Maggert
D. Clarke & L. Westwood (1 hole)	1	0	D. Duval & T. Woods

Foursomes (morning)
C. Montgomerie & P. Lawrie	0	1	H. Sutton & J. Maggert (1 hole)
D. Clarke & L. Westwood (3&2)	1	0	J. Furyk & M. O'Meara
M. A. Jiménez & P. Harrington	0	1	S. Pate & T. Woods (1 hole)
J. Parnevik & S. Garcia (3&2)	1	0	P. Stewart & J. Leonard

Four-Balls (afternoon)
D. Clarke & L. Westwood	0	1	P. Mickelson & T. Lehman (2&1)
J. Parnevik & S. Garcia (halved)	½	½	D. Love III & D. Duval (halved)
M. A. Jiménez & J. M. Olazábal (halved)	½	½	J. Leonard & H. Sutton (halved)
C. Montgomerie & P. Lawrie (2&1)	1	0	S. Pate & T. Woods

Singles
L. Westwood	0	1	T. Lehman (3&2)
D. Clarke	0	1	H. Sutton (4&2)
J. Sandelin	0	1	P. Mickelson (4&3)
J. Van de Velde	0	1	D. Love III (6&5)
A. Coltart	0	1	T. Woods (3&2)
J. Parnevik	0	1	D. Duval (5&4)
P. Harrington (1 hole)	1	0	M. O'Meara
M. A. Jiménez	0	1	S. Pate (2&1)
J. M. Olazábal (halved).	½	½	J. Leonard (halved)
C. Montgomerie (1 hole)	1	0	P. Stewart
S. Garcia	0	1	J. Furyk (4&3)
P. Lawrie (4&3)	1	0	J. Maggert

EUROPE 13½ 14½ **UNITED STATES OF AMERICA**

2002: THE DE VERE BELFRY, SUTTON COLDFIELD, W. MIDLANDS, SEPTEMBER 27-29
Matches postponed from 2001
Captains: S. Torrance (EUROPE), C. Strange (USA)

EUROPE   **UNITED STATES OF AMERICA**

Four-Balls (morning)
EUROPE			UNITED STATES OF AMERICA
D. Clarke & T. Björn	0	1	T. Woods & P. Azinger
S. Garcia & L. Westwood (4&3)	1	0	D. Duval & D. Love III
C. Montgomerie & B. Langer (4&3)	1	0	S. Hoch & J. Furyk
P. Harrington & N. Fasth	0	1	P. Mickelson & D. Toms (1 hole)

Foursomes (afternoon)
D. Clarke & T. Björn	0	1	H. Sutton & S. Verplank (2&1)
S. Garcia & L. Westwood (2&1)	1	0	T. Woods & M. Calcavecchia
C. Montgomerie & B. Langer (halved)	½	½	P. Mickelson & D. Toms (halved)
P. Harrington & P. McGinley	0	1	S. Cink & J. Furyk (3&2)

Foursomes (morning)
P. Fulke & P. Price	0	1	P. Mickelson & D. Toms (2&1)
L. Westwood & S. Garcia (2&1)	1	0	S. Cink & J. Furyk
C. Montgomerie & B. Langer (1 hole)	1	0	S. Verplank & S. Hoch
D. Clarke & T. Björn	0	1	T. Woods & D. Love III (4&3)

Four-Balls (afternoon)
N. Fasth & J. Parnevik	0	1	M. Calcavecchia & D. Duval (1 hole)
C. Montgomerie & P. Harrington (2&1)	1	0	P. Mickelson & D. Toms
S. Garcia & L. Westwood	0	1	T. Woods & D. Love III (1 hole)
D. Clarke & P. McGinley (halved)	½	½	S. Hoch & J. Furyk (halved)

Singles
C. Montgomerie (5&4)	1	0	S. Hoch
S. Garcia	0	1	D. Toms (1 hole)
D. Clarke (halved)	½	½	D. Duval (halved)
B. Langer (4&3)	1	0	H. Sutton
P. Harrington (5&4)	1	0	M. Calcavecchia
T. Björn (2&1)	1	0	S. Cink
L. Westwood	0	1	S. Verplank (2&1)
N. Fasth (halved)	½	½	P. Azinger (halved)
P. McGinley (halved)	½	½	J. Furyk (halved)
P. Fulke (halved)	½	½	D. Love III (halved)
P. Price (3&2)	1	0	P. Mickelson
J. Parnevik (halved)	½	½	T. Woods (halved)

EUROPE 15½ 12½ **UNITED STATES OF AMERICA**

2004: OAKLAND HILLS CC, MICHIGAN, USA SEPTEMBER 17-19

Captains: Bernhard Langer (EUROPE)   Hal Sutton (USA)

EUROPE			UNITED STATES OF AMERICA

Four-Balls (Day 1)

C. Montgomerie & P. Harrington (2&1)	1	0	P. Mickelson & T. Woods
D. Clarke & M. A. Jiménez (5&4)	1	0	D. Love III & C. Campbell
P. McGinley & L. Donald (halved)	½	½	C. Riley & S. Cink (halved)
S. Garcia & L. Westwood (5&3)	1	0	D. Toms & J. Furyk

Foursomes (Day 1)

M. A. Jiménez & T. Levet	0	1	C. DiMarco & J. Haas (3&2)
C. Montgomerie & P. Harrington (4&2)	1	0	D. Love III & F. Funk
D. Clarke & L. Westwood (1 hole)	1	0	P. Mickelson & T. Woods
S. Garcia & L. Donald (2&1)	1	0	K. Perry & S. Cink

Four-Balls (Day 2)

S. Garcia & L. Westwood (halved)	½	½	J. Haas & C. DiMarco (halved)
D. Clarke & I. Poulter	0	1	T. Woods & C. Riley (4&3)
P. Casey & D. Howell (1 hole)	1	0	J. Furyk & C. Campbell
C. Montgomerie & P. Harrington	0	1	S. Cink & D. Love III (3&2)

Foursomes (Day 2)

D. Clarke & L. Westwood (5&4)	1	0	J Haas & C DiMarco
M. A. Jiménez & T. Levet	0	1	P Mickelson & D Toms (4&3)
S. Garcia & L. Donald (1 hole)	1	0	J Furyk & F Funk
P. Harrington & P. McGinley (4&3)	1	0	D Love III & T Woods

Singles

P. Casey	0	1	T. Woods (3&2)
S. Garcia (3&2)	1	0	P. Mickelson
D. Clarke (halved)	½	½	D. Love III (halved)
D. Howell	0	1	J. Furyk (6&4)
L. Westwood (1 hole)	1	0	K. Perry
C. Montgomerie (1 hole)	1	0	D. Toms
L. Donald	0	1	C. Campbell (5&3)
M. A. Jiménez	0	1	C. DiMarco (1 hole)
T. Levet (1 hole)	1	0	F. Funk
I. Poulter (3&2)	1	0	C. Riley
P. Harrington (1 hole)	1	0	J. Haas
P. McGinley (3&2)	1	0	S. Cink

EUROPE 18½ 9½ **UNITED STATES OF AMERICA**

2004 Final European Ryder Cup Team Standings

Player	Ryder Cup Pts.	World Pts. (Rank)
1. Miguel Angel Jimenez (Spain)	1,895,225.18	174.24(4)
2. Lee Westwood (England)	1,685,128.72	153.60(5)
3. Darren Clarke (No. Ireland)	1,573,284.18	191.80(3)
4. Thomas Levet (France)	1,552,371.35	136.60(7)
5. Padraig Harrington (Ireland)	1,339,938.25	234.94(1)
6. Paul Casey (England)	1,302,912.67	124.30(8)
7. David Howell (England)	1,153,682.19	105.57(13)
8. Paul McGinley (Ireland)	1,149,576.96	109.05(11)
9. Ian Poulter (England)	1,136,184.33	110.80(10)
10. Fredrik Jacobson (Sweden)	1,085,510.37	106.95(12)
23.Sergio Garcia (Spain)	660,060.27	225.56(2)

Captain's Selections

16. Colin Montgomerie (Scotland)	799,072.15	77.62(19)
36 Luke Donald (England)	415,290.76	116.09(9)

The leading five players qualified through the World Points List (see right column), and the next five team members through the European Ryder Cup Points list. Captain selections completed the 12-member team.

2004 Final U.S. Ryder Cup Team Standings

Player	Points
1. Tiger Woods	1,856.67
2. Phil Mickelson	1,835.25
3. Davis Love III	1,114.11
4. Jim Furyk	859.479
5. Kenny Perry	780.107
6. David Toms	695.125
7. Chad Campbell	680.00
8. Chris DiMarco	653.048
9. Fred Funk	596.959
10. Chris Riley	576.786
Captain's Selections	
12. Jay Haas	525.917
14. Stewart Cink	506.846

2004 Ryder Cup Individual Player Totals

UNITED STATES OF AMERICA Hal Sutton, Captain

Player	Overall Fourballs	Foursomes	Singles	Wins	Losses	Halves	Points
Chris DiMarco	0-0-1	1-1-0	1-0-0	2	1	1	2.5
Tiger Woods	1-1-0	0-2-0	1-0-0	2	3	0	2.0
Stewart Cink (c)	1-0-1	0-1-0	0-1-0	1	2	1	1.5
Jay Haas (c)	0-0-1	1-1-0	0-1-0	1	2	1	1.5
Davis Love III	1-1-0	0-2-0	0-0-1	1	3	1	1.5
Cods Riley (r)	1-0-1	0-0-0	0-1-0	1	1	1	1.5
Chad Campbell (r)	0-2-0	0-0-0	0-1-0	1	2	0	1.0
Jim Furyk	0-2-0	0-1-0	1-0-0	1	3	0	1.0
Phil Mickelson	0-1-0	1-1-0	0-1-0	1	3	0	1.0
David Toms	0-1-0	1-0-0	0-1-0	1	2	0	1.0
Fred Funk (r)	0-0-0	0-2-0	0-1-0	0	3	0	0
Kenny Perry (r)	0-0-0	0-1-0	0-1-0	0	2	0	0

EUROPE Bernhard Langer, Captain

Player	Overall Fourballs	Foursomes	Singles	Wins	Losses	Halves	Points
Sergio Garcia	1-0-1	2-0-0	1-0-0	4	0	1	4.5
Lee Westwood	1-0-1	2-0-0	1-0-0	4	0	0	4.5
Padraig Harrington	1-1-0	2-0-0	1-0-0	4	1	0	4.0
Darren Clarke	1-1-0	2-0-0	0-0-1	3	1	1	3.5
Colin Montgomerie (c)	1-1-0	1-0-0	1-0-0	3	1	0	3.0
Luke Donald (r) & (c)	0-0-1	2-0-0	0-1-0	2	1	1	2.5
Paul McGinley	0-0-1	1-0-0	1-0-0	2	0	1	2.5
Paul Casey (r)	1-0-0	0-0-0	0-1-0	1	1	0	1.0
David Howel l(r)	1-0-0	0-0-0	0-1-0	1	1	0	1.0
Miguel Angel Jimenez	1-0-0	0-2-0	0-1-0	1	3	0	1.0
Thomas Levet (r)	0-0-0	0-2-0	1-0-0	1	2	0	1.0
Ian Poulter -r	0-1-0	0-0-0	1-0-0	1	1	0	1.0

r = Ryder Cup rookies (c) = Captain choice

The author acknowledges the generosity of the PGA of America and the PGA European Tour in permitting the reproduction of these statistics

Index

199